RAILWAY LIFE AT ASHFORD

The Railway Works
in Peace and War

GORDON TURNER

Published by
BETTY H. J. TURNER
Ashford, Kent
2007
1st Edition Cloth

RAILWAY LIFE
AT ASHFORD

The Railway Works
in Peace and War

by
GORDON TURNER

Printed by
Headley Brothers Ltd
Lower Queens Road, Ashford, Kent

CONTENTS

Introduction	Dawning of the Railway Age	1
Chapter One	Pioneers	6
Chapter Two	Cudworth is King	24
Chapter Three	Stirling Era	49
Chapter Four	Wainwright Elegance	65
Chapter Five	Maunsell Arrives	79
Chapter Six	Difficult Times	120
Chapter Seven	Ashford at War	142
Chapter Eight	A Forlorn Hope	195

DEDICATION

This book is dedicated to those Ashford railwaymen whose skill and devotion from the times of the early pioneers to the present day has brought credit and recognition to their own town. Also, to the dedicated group of volunteers working to keep the Klondyke Works as a "Railway Heritage Centre Museum". A fitting tribute to the Ashford railway workers past and present.

Chart Leacon Depot. Left-to-right: Brian Gavin, Brian "Biffo" Sharp, Steve Epps, Paul Crockford, Frank Roberts, Colin Bunn, Richard Woodrow.

ACKNOWLEDGEMENTS

Libraries throughout the land are fully endowed with books describing railway lines constructed and locomotives, carriages and wagons built. Within this vast collection very little is recorded about railway works and the lives of the people who worked in them. So far as Ashford is concerned this book is a modest attempt to remedy that. The achievements of these railwaymen from the early days to modern times deserves greater recognition. Their courage during World War II was exemplary when production never faltered despite the constant threats of air raids.

This history is not confined to activities within the Works but covers a broader sweep of those national and local events that impinged upon the workforce. Included are glimpses of the home and social life of families providing an intimate picture of the railway community. Within parts of this volume I have drawn upon research carried out for my previous book 'Ashford – The Coming of the Railway' but for purposes of historical completeness this has been unavoidable.

I am greatly indebted to those many people who have helped with the compilation of this history.

The story of the transactions surrounding the acquisition of land for the Railway Works during 1846 and 1847 is entirely due to the careful research of Ashford historian Arthur Ruderman. His kindness in allowing me to disclose the result of his studies is greatly appreciated.

The American gentleman who was very kind in making available the diary of his great-great uncle, George Hollands, which provided an eye-witness account of New Town and the works during the period 1848-1856. Details of the railway connection of Ashford's Mather family, as provided by James Mather were of great interest. Thanks are due to Jack Archer, formally of South Willesborough for providing a truly harrowing account of life during the depression years.

I must extend a particular word of gratitude to Frederick Imms. He most generously allowed me to quote from his reminiscences about life at Ashford during the nineteen-thirties, which offer a detailed portrayal of life in the Works.

Contributions were received from a number of sources concerning the experiences of railwaymen during the war and these are named in the narrative but particular mention must be made of the contribution of Robert Barham for his striking description of the air attack of March 1943.

Victor Packman's assistance with the war period was most helpful, as was that of Ronald Hover whose duties took him to every nook and cranny of the Locomotive Works.

The nostalgic reminiscences of Richard Bourne, which so truly take us back to the days of steam, were a treasured writing.

The interest of Clive Young was invaluable and the details of his family history together with his great knowledge of the Works during its final thirty years were essential in providing a record of the period.

Mrs Dorothy Hymers kindly allowed me to peruse records left by her late husband, Douglas, which provided a rare source of information concerning the wagon export programme of the nineteen seventies, an achievement insufficiently acknowledged hitherto.

I must also acknowledge my debt of gratitude to Mrs Mary Harmer for her great kindness in allowing me access to a collection of photographs taken by her late husband Derek during the nineteen sixties, pre-dating the modernisation programme.

Throughout the period of writing I have had regular discussions with Tony Addey and his guidance has been greatly appreciated.

My thanks also to staff at Ashford Library who are always so helpful and in particular to Mrs Shirley Sheridan and Bob Payne who always showed great patience with my many enquiries.

Finally to Gary Wright, Ivor Warne and John Blackford, who most kindly agreed to proof read my original manuscript and offered a number of helpful suggestions.

FURTHER ACKNOWLEDGEMENTS FROM BETTY TURNER

Fourteen years after his first book, 'The Coming of the Railway' was published Gordon began sketching notes for another book taking the Works from 1910 to the end of the Second World War.

Sadly in 1998 he was diagnosed with cancer. After treatment when he began to feel better he retired to his sunny little office overlooking the garden, put his best typing-finger forward and began, 'Railway Life at Ashford.'

On completion of the manuscript the printer required it to be transferred to a disc, but Gordon was not going to get involved in computers no matter how hard we all tried. But not to worry, we were all rescued by a young university graduate by the name of William Mort, soon to be known as 'Young Will' who took the burden from his shoulders and got the book ready for the printer.

Publishing this book has been an enormous task for me, to have 'Young Will' at the end of the phone has been a great support. My other big Thank

You goes to Bernie Epps, employed by the Railway at Ashford in the accounts department since a young lad and now retired. For his patience and time in going through endless photographs trying to select from such a collection.

Grateful thanks to you both from me in helping me get Gordon's book onto the shelves in the bookshops.

Finally, a big thank you to all the people at Headley Brothers printing works involved with the production of this book, from Mrs Ann Hills (Reception), Graham Ellender (Production) and Craig Carter (Sales) your help and patience was much appreciated.

Betty Turner

OTHER BATTLES FOUGHT BY GORDON:

The fire-risk houses in Aylesford Place built with fire-risk material proven with a report from a local builder. This ended in the explosion and fire of one of the houses, causing the death of the elderly tenant. All recorded in the Tuesday Express with support of the brave editor and reporter.

The tremendous battle with the dedicated residents to stop a giant power station next to Victoria Park. Two chimneys twice the height of the church and belching out 2 1/2 tons of sulphur dioxide per hour — well documented in the local press.

The certain threat of destruction of the architecturally unique houses in Elwick Road and the Victorian town houses in Queen Street (just behind Elwick Road) then restored to its Victorian beauty. The triumphant group photographed in the local press and somewhere in that area a time capsule was buried.

B.T.

FOREWORD

I was going to write the foreword about Gordon and his 27 years as Councillor for Newtown and South Willesborough, and then I found this farewell letter written to all the residents when he retired, what more can I say!

B.T.

Dear Friends,

It is with great sadness that I have to retire as your Councillor. My link with South Willesborough and Newtown goes back to 1972 and ever since I have been privileged to receive your friendship and support.

Much water has flowed under the bridge since then. Literally in fact, since the week that I was first elected, South Willesborough suffered flooding. Not for the first time, nor the last, but thankfully that problem now lies in the past.

Times have changed greatly since then. The Railway Works had been a major influence for so long and there were strong bonds of family relationships and friendships. Twenty-seven years is a long time and sadly so many of the grand old folk of those years are no longer with us. However, they left behind a lasting tradition — a strong community spirit which still prevails.

We have been involved together in many struggles. Firstly, the battle to save Newtown from demolition and its replacement with an industrial estate. There was solid support from the Newtown Action Group and thankfully the community was preserved. The Wainwright wheels on the Green mark the victory. The Council wanted to build on the Green — that was stopped. They also wanted to pull down the old Railway School and replace it with a block of flats. As always they had to be opposed and the building is now pleasantly converted.

It took thirteen years to persuade the Council that a new hall was needed to replace Gladstone Road's leaking 'tin hut'. Land belonging to Mr. Currah and British Rail was bought and the Swan Centre and Mallards were built. Fine developments. The former potato/cabbage fields stretching across to the railway are now public open space. The remainder of the land alongside the Aylesford Stream is now to be cleansed of contamination. The Cudworth Road frontage could be suitable for old folks' bungalows, but the 'wilderness area' and its wildlife should be left undisturbed.

The Railway wanted to close the Willesborough level crossing. We all worked together on that. Your support when I had to go twice to Parliament and later get the support of the House of Lords was vital. Sufficient to say that we won. There will now be a short and well-lit underpass, suitable in particular for the elderly, the disabled and mothers with prams.

Twenty-seven years ago every road on the 'island' needed reconstruction. Some had been a result from horse and buggy days. It was found that they had only a tarred surface with no real foundation.

There have been disappointments, not for the want of our trying. There ought to have been a green field buffer between Canterbury Road and the new commercial development. The planners and other Councillors thought otherwise. There was no excuse for the Council allowing future building on Gilbert's Field. A Planning Inspector has said that South Willesborough has lost too much of its green space. I'll say amen to that!

I have always sought to see that Council taxpayers received value for money. Moneywise the Council really have done some daft things. The trouble is, you pay! There has always been a need to help folk in various ways. Sometimes one has needed to have a quiet word, sometimes something more vigorous has been needed. Anyway, thank you for your thanks.

If I have one regret it is the time and effort to stop the wrong things happening. One always has to fight against authority instead of their offering co-operation. It seems to be the way of life.

Although I am standing down as your Councillor I shall not be deserting the ship. One cannot just walk off and turn one's back on a community that has been the heart of attention for over a quarter of a century. I have been asked if I will continue to help the South Willesborough and Newtown Residents' Association, and I shall be very pleased to do so.

Thank you for all your many kindnesses and giving me memories which will stay with me for the rest of my life.

We all share a secret — South Willesborough and Newtown are special.

Yours truly,

Introduction

DAWNING OF THE RAILWAY AGES

Wake, England, Wake! 'tis now the hour
To sweep away this black disgrace –
The want of locomotive power
In so enjoyable a place.

J. K. Stephen

With the coming of turnpikes in the latter part of the eighteenth century Ashford acquired a better means of communication with the outside world. The coach, which passed through from Folkestone to London, was a daily excitement. Royal Mail services had improved with a daily mail cart from Canterbury. Supplies of goods were more easily received from the port of Faversham and the town's agricultural connection was strengthened with better roads to Tenterden and the Romney Marsh. Nevertheless, road travel was hazardous and Ashford remained one of the quietest and most rural of all Kentish towns.

Even with the heralded coming of railways, Ashford may have continued to slumber. Early routes were projected to follow a northern coastal line shadowing the old Dover Road. Fierce opposition was met from the landed gentry and the steam navigation interests, whilst the Guardians of Rochester Bridge blocked a Medway crossing. All hope of progress here was barred.

In 1835 South Eastern railway promoters turned their attention to the prospect of a mid-Kent route. The line would have connected the metropolis with Dover via Maidstone and Ashford. The most fierce opposition emerged. Ridicule and contempt were poured upon the scheme from all sides. Landowners combined to oppose it, as did the leading townsmen of Maidstone. Nor were the vested interests silent. Hoymen feared for their long established river connection with London, and turnpike operators, coachmen, horse-keepers and innkeepers could see their businesses threatened.

Mere ignorance did not prevent many from expressing the wildest fears about the effect of steam locomotives. 'Engine smoke will poison the birds', 'Animals grazing the fields through which the line passes will die of fright', 'Sparks from the engine will set fields alight burning the crops to cinders and famine will follow plague'. In the event the proposal eventually floundered when the promoters also found themselves faced with substantial engineering problems.

Determined to pursue their objective, the South Eastern enlisted the help of Captain Pringle of the Royal Engineers. He proposed commencing the line at Wandsworth Common and proceeding by way of Croydon through the Weald of Kent to Dover. The line was extremely circuitous but presented little in the way of engineering difficulties. It was well away from the centres of population in the North Kent towns but also away from the main areas of opposition. The South Eastern claimed that the line would open up the Wealden areas, which were served by appallingly bad roads and they promised branch lines to Maidstone, Canterbury and Hastings.

Opposition appeared in the form of two rival lines, one running through Central Kent via Ashford and the other through North Kent which would have by-passed the town. Meetings at Cranbrook, Folkestone and Dover were not unnaturally greatly in favour of the South Eastern. The reverse was true at Maidstone. Realising at last the inevitability of a railway through Kent the townspeople became alarmed at the prospect of being out on a limb. In a dramatic change of feeling they called for a direct line to be built through the town. The Burghers of Canterbury were not enchanted with either the South Eastern or the Central Kent proposals. They also feared being left out on a branch and supported the plans of the Kent Railway with a direct line through the City.

Throughout the winter and spring of 1836 the battle between the protagonists raged. Uproar attended the many meetings, which were held across the County. Resolutions for or against the three competing companies were passed. Signatures were eagerly canvassed for the many petitions. Traders and merchants lined up behind whoever they thought would most benefit their personal interests. Landowners vehemently protested, some genuinely, others with an eye to increased compensation if the company won. The coaching trade was united in its fear of the consequences of railway development. The labouring population looked on in the hope of a new and regular source of work.

Two meetings were held in Ashford, both on the same day, 10th March 1836, and both advertised as being held at the Saracens Head Hotel. So great was the support for the pro-railway meeting they had to adjourn to the much larger Assembly Rooms. This 'highly respectable and influential meeting' was presided over by local banker William Jemmett. Those present declared for the South Eastern and believing that the railway would be of great advantage to the town and agricultural communities as well as the coastal and fishery interests, agreed to sign a requisition for support and present it to the county Members of Parliament.

Meanwhile the anti-rail meeting of landowners proceeded in the Saracens Head with Sir Edward Dering in the chair. They were unanimous in their resolve to deny the railway passage. They viewed all plans 'with distrust and apprehension' believing that the majority were 'founded on fallacious calculations' which would lead their promoters to ruin. They declared their view 'that no Bill for a railway through Kent should pass during the present session of Parliament'. Petitions were signed by all those present, one to the House of Lords and one to the Commons.

The parliamentary battle began on 18th February 1836 when proceedings upon the South Eastern Railway Bill formally commenced. Sir Edward Knatchbull (East Kent) and Mr Bernal (Rochester) declared their opposition. They were supported by a series of petitions from Maidstone and the North Kent towns. The trustees of the Ashford to Maidstone Turnpike also protested. William Deedes expressed the hostility of landowners along the route.

Supporters of the two rival lines – the Central Kent and the Kent Railway – pressed the claimed advantages of their plans.

The evidence provided by the South Eastern's supporters gives a fascinating insight into living conditions at the time. William Hinds, hop farmer of Smarden, decried the state of the roads, likewise Samuel Steddy, timber merchant of Ashford. John Neve, a Biddenden farmer, spoke of loss of stock on the drive to Smithfield Market, while George Hayward, a butcher, described the difficulties of trading with London. William Jeffrey, High Street grocer complained of the high costs of transport. The fishermen's representative complained about the slowness of road travel and said that during summer months 'fish would often go bad before it could be got to the London market'. And so the procession of witnesses continued. Trades from ironmongery to hop and corn dealers travelled to London to plead the case for better transportation.

All manner of trades and interests had been represented from all parts of the county but at the conclusion of the examination of witnesses, Ashford had clearly provided a larger number than any other town. Much technical verification was submitted by all three competing companies, the most lengthy evidence being introduced by Henry Robinson Palmer, the designer of the South Eastern line.

Finally the day of decision arrived. On 16th May 1836 after eight long weeks, the parliamentary committee made known its report, which favoured the South Eastern. The report passed to the House of Commons on 31st May and although the majority of Kentish members voted against they were unable to influence the final result – victory for the South Eastern, those in favour numbering 175 and those against 24. There were great lamentations in the county press, which had vehemently opposed the scheme, but the church bells rang out at Ashford in celebration.

There followed a period of agonising delay. A new engineer-in-chief had to be found when Palmer fell sick. The crown fell to William Cubitt who immediately set about revising Palmer's plans by proposing five major deviations. Parliament also intervened by deciding that in order to keep rail outlets from London to a minimum the South Eastern Railway had to share successive lines with the Greenwich, Croydon and Brighton companies as far out as Redhill. Sir John Rennie tried to persuade the Board to accept an entirely new and more direct route but without success. Meanwhile the Company was faced with financial problems and had to make further calls upon their shareholders.

In 1839 parliamentary intervention in the form of a Royal Commission concerned itself with the congestion caused by four companies using the London Bridge terminus. There was more financial trouble with defaulting shareholders, the contractor on the Dover tunnel walked off the job and a few months later another went bankrupt. By 1841 however things were going more smoothly. Construction of the line was moving on apace, contracts had been awarded for the Ashford section and new locomotives ordered.

At the commencement of 1842, works were underway along the entire route of the railway between Tonbridge and Ashford. To a large extent tales of debauchery involving the Cornish and Irish navvies were absent from the South Eastern line. The contractor was the Baptist, Samuel Morton Peto, whose Christian virtues were shared by teachers who had been specially engaged to care for and educate his men. The district became a great work camp as smithies, carpenter shops and stables were built. Tons of clay was excavated for brick making – in early March alone an order was placed for one and a half million bricks. The flat land through the Vale of Kent enabled the contractor to make speedy progress, but the cuttings and embankments in the vicinity of Ashford called for more and more muscle power from a constantly expanding workforce.

By September work on the Ashford station was well advanced. It was South Eastern practice at main stations to provide two through lines with a slip line to each platform. The single-story building was built with traditional clapboard and lit by oil, facilities being provided for booking offices, waiting and refreshment rooms. To pass from one platform to another, passengers had to cross the line by means of a level crossing. The railway paraphernalia adjoining the station was extensive with carriage sheds, coke sheds and water tanks for each platform. In addition there was an engine shed capable of housing sixteen locomotives. On the south side were loading docks for horses and their carriages and a very large cattle dock. On the north side were situated the goods warehouse and coal wharf. In addition there were six hand-operated turntables with a number of sidings sprouting from them. The Superintendent's house and four pairs of cottages for staff completed the complex.

The contract was for Ashford to be reached by 31st December 1842 but an urgent request by the Directors resulted in the line opening one month earlier. For some months there had been a mounting tide of excitement in Ashford as rumour and curiosity joined forces. By the morning of 28th November when the first train was due to arrive, excitement was at fever pitch. Even the continuing rain failed to dampen the high spirits. The town was awake at an early hour and as dawn broke villagers from the surrounding countryside poured in. Many walked; others arrived on horseback or in wagons, gigs and carriages. The streets of the little town soon became choked with a jostling mass of people and horse-drawn conveyances. There were joyful meetings as friends and relatives met together. On all sides there was a noise and commotion rarely seen in the town. The inns and taverns were full, a band played national and patriotic airs from the roof of the Royal Oak and the church bells rang out.

Towards noon the weather cleared and hundreds of highly excited people began to gather around the newly completed station. The new railway bridge was profusely decorated, flags were flying, the church chimes played a concert of tunes and the local band played with gusto. Everything quietened as a cry went up that the special train had been sighted. Then the scene exploded with exultant and joyous elation. In a cloud of steam and smoke, the green locomotive, with sun glinting on its highly-polished brass work and its whistle shrieking its triumph, swept beneath the arch of the bridge to the accompaniment of singing, clapping and cheer upon cheer from the enraptured spectators.

The railway Directors and their party were welcomed by a group of the district's influential gentlemen and they all adjourned for a celebration dinner in the station waiting room, which had been especially embellished for the occasion. Dinner was served, toasts were proposed and seconded and the speech from Joseph Baxendale, Chairman of the Company was followed by many others. However, the discipline of railway time intruded, the train had to depart by 3.30 p.m. So to more cheers, the ringing of the bells and the accompaniment of the town band, the train steamed out of the station, arriving back in London at seven o'clock. In Ashford the celebrations continued with all those employed on the works being liberally provided with all manner of refreshments.

Five lines would eventually sweep into the town from London, Dover, Margate, Hastings and Maidstone. That alone would have been enough to put the town firmly on the map and bring about those changes associated with an important railway junction. But overshadowing all this would be the decision to situate the locomotive, carriage and wagon works of the South Eastern Railway in Ashford.

Chapter One

PIONEERS

*They come' the shrieking steam ascends,
Slow moves the banner'd train,
They rush! The towering vapour bends -
The kindled wave again.*

Ebenezer Elliott

By the mid eighteen-forties the South Eastern Railway boasted a rapidly expanding network of services to many of Kent's largest towns in addition to the running of continental expresses. In a period of rapid expansion their Bricklayers Arms depot at New Cross, held on temporary lease and shared with the Croydon and Brighton companies, was proving to be quite inadequate. In those early years the South Eastern brought in stock designs from locomotive and carriage manufacturers but with the growing scale of their activities, it became evident greater control needed to be exercised over the construction, repair and maintenance of rolling stock.

In the autumn of 1845 the Directors decided to follow the lead set by other companies and build a completely new works to more fully provide for their needs, the only question being where it should be built. Their requirements were land, labour, a plentiful water supply and an ease of access to the network. Tonbridge, Maidstone and Ashford were all considered suitable for consideration but upon investigation competing demands for water extraction posed difficulties in the first two towns. Coke ovens were already established at Ashford producing over 600 tons of coke each week to fuel the Company's locomotives, the town's central situation on the main line added to its attractions and the ready availability of both land and labour helped swing the final decision in its favour.

Parliamentary approval of the venture was secured together with authority to spend up to £500,000. The new enterprise was planned for land to the south-east of the town where lay the East Stour river and its tributaries, forming what were known as the Ashford Marshes. The decision would not have been heard by some of the local populace without a pang of regret since the area had provided them with an opportunity for wild duck shooting since time immemorial.

Negotiations began with a number of the district's leading landowners and the most important of these was the Earl of Thanet on whose land the main structure of the Works would be erected. Also of significance was land belonging to the Whitfield family on which would be built much of the railway village of New Town and later Works extensions. The purchase of these lands, all south of the London to Dover railway line was completed in the spring of 1846. For whatever reason, that in the ownership of James Wall which lay to the east in the parish of Willesborough was not acquired until May 1847 after he had been pressed by the local Improvement Commissioners to sell.

The land purchases south of the railway were extensive. Much of that purchased from George Maud, a member of the local Jemmett family, was later sold for the construction of workmen's cottages. In addition land which stretched towards the hamlet of Beaver in the ownership of Thomas Kirkbank was secured. In all, the railway company took possession of 185 acres of countryside for what was considered the reasonable price of £21,000.

The Works site comprised fields known as 'Goose Pits', 'Upper Oasted' and 'Gifford Mill'. Also included in the purchases were a number of cottages situated to the north of the main line. These were located in the little hamlet of Aylesford Green and their removal would result in the spot losing its identity as an inhabited place of any significance. A further stretch of land comprising 'Further Post Field', 'Footway Mead', 'Storth House Mead' and 'Three Corner Field' was held against future development.

Leading figures involved in the erection of the Works were the nationally acclaimed Robert Stephenson who contributed his planning skill, Samuel Peto, renowned for building the Houses of Parliament and Thomas Grissell, famed for railway building, who supervised construction.

Buildings were on a scale never before seen in Ashford with the main workshop 396 feet long, 90 feet wide and 28 feet high. This block contained the machine shop (or turnery), tender shop, smith's shop (with twenty fires), wheel hooping and boiler shop (with furnaces for bending) and a hydraulic press for stretching tyres. The engine repair shop boasted a large crane capable of lifting twenty tons. Adjacent was a large 280-foot long engine shed above which was located a 56,700 gallon water tank. The 200-foot storeroom, described as a model of neatness, was able to supply every article that could possibly be required from the most huge and unwieldy to the smallest screw.

The primary figure to emerge at this time was a man whose destiny it was to become 'Kingpin' at Ashford for the next thirty years – James l'Anson Cudworth. Born at Darlington and a lifelong Quaker, Cudworth was a pupil at Robert Stephenson & Company in Newcastle and later had charge of the Great North of England Railway works at Darlington. On 22nd May 1845 he was appointed Locomotive Superintendent of the South Eastern Railway at a salary of £350 per annum, later increased to £500. Although only twenty-eight years of age he had already shown great promise as a most able engineer. Following his appointment at the South Eastern Railway Bricklayers Arms depot he was made responsible for the selection of most of the new Works machinery and given control of its locomotive department. There was some delay in obtaining all the required machinery for the erecting and boiler shops but the problem was overcome by importing the needed apparatus from the Continent.

The Locomotive Works became operational in October 1847 and its opening was followed four years later by the transfer of the carriage and wagon department from Bricklayers Arms, necessitating a 645 foot building capable of holding fifty carriages and eighty wagons. Other additions included a cupola for smelting iron, six extra forges and a complete foundry.

These original carriage and wagon buildings have been demolished but most of the other buildings presently survive, including twenty-five bays of the locomotive workshops, which formed the core of the range. This core is of considerable interest as one of the earliest surviving layouts of locomotive workshops anywhere in the country.

The new Works transformed the town. There was a plentiful supply of unskilled labour and the factory acted like a magnet upon the district's low-paid agricultural workers. Soon too, the accents of craftsmen and engineers from other counties could be heard mingling with those of Kentish folk. Key men were needed and these were to be found in the North Country where steam engineers had been employed for a number of years, particularly in the collieries.

To begin with the Locomotive Works limited itself to repair and maintenance although one curious little engine was a stock job until its completion in 1850. Nicknamed 'The Coffee Pot' it had been partially constructed at Bricklayers Arms and was used for line inspections by the Company Directors and Chief Engineer. Its intended use had been for use on parcels services in the London area, a purpose for which it was found to be unsuitable.

The New Town

In addition to the building of a works the Directors decided to build a village to house its workpeople. Experience in other parts of the country had shown the necessity of providing housing close to the workplace. The large number of men who had to be brought in from outside the immediate locality and the demands of shift working, both for the locomotive force and the mechanics, quickly convinced management of the need for railway villages.

Ashford's new town was unique in Victorian south-east England being a company-owned town based upon a single industry. The land on which it was built comprised fields known locally as 'Lower Oasted', 'Fuller's Field' and 'Little Hook'. It was blessed with a notable architect in Samuel Beazley who had already received a number of commissions from the South Eastern including that of the Lord Warden Hotel at Dover.

A report in May 1847 gave news of houses under construction with a number already slated and inside walls cemented over. The first forty were ready for occupation by October and a further thirty-two soon followed. The builders Golder and Lucas had successfully tendered an average charge of £560 for each block of four cottages to be erected in long terraces.

Of Italianate design they comprised ground and first floor flats and were reputed to be the only cottages of their type in southern England. The accommodation was basic with oil lighting, no piped fresh water supply and an ash pit in a very small garden area for sewage disposal, although a compensating feature was the adjoining open countryside. Fresh drinking water was supplied by pumps, which were erected at each of the three corners of the green.

With 200 carriage and wagon makers moving down from the Bricklayers Arms depot, sixty more cottages were built together with shops and a tavern. These cottages were dwellings of a superior design and known, because of their appearance, as Dutch gable houses. Clustered around the large open green, the village set standards that were regarded as advanced for its day.

A gas works, sited on the South Willesborough side of the Aylesford Stream was erected to supply both the Works and the village. Coal supplies were effected by a line of rail, which crossed the New Town road near the Willesborough Gate. A gas supply was a boon to those tenants who could afford it but the Company required them to pay for the pipes to connect a supply into their homes.

Street lamps were introduced providing one old timer with the time-honoured occupation of lamplighter. The lamps also lit the way for 'call boys' whose task it was to rouse any engine driver whose duties commenced between the hours of midnight and six in the morning. To assist the 'boys' to the right door all houses occupied by drivers had white painted gateposts.

At this time the Maidstone Journal reported: 'New Ashford and the extensive works adjoining it are built upon a piece of land which was little better than waste a few years since. The situation is most eligible and healthy and altogether this little community of industrious artisans and their families gives promise to become very flourishing, at once comfortable and cleanly in all their internal arrangements and highly picturesque in outward appearance.'

The truth was less romantic. A number of deaths occurred in New Town during the diphtheria epidemic of 1858-1860 with the closeness of the houses contributing to the spread of the disease. The sewer from New Town discharged into open ditches, which were an all too regular feature of life at the time.

An inhabitant complained: 'A few weeks since I saw that our Local Board took credit for having removed the nuisance arising from our ditch in Beaver Fields. I therefore beg to inform them that the sewerage is all back again in the ditch and looks more disgusting and stinks worse than ever this hot season. I can never understand why this filthy ditch is suffered across and alongside a public and much-frequented walk and so close to the town. Why is the ditch not kept cleaned out and the sewerage put on the land at a distance from the footpath? It would be invaluable as manure and the odour would be absorbed and destroyed by the earth.'

The sanitary authority in the form of the Ashford Local Board instructed the Railway Company to pipe in the sewerage outlets but by 1864 there were complaints that the river was still being polluted. The Commissioners of Sewerage, being the river authority, waged a long campaign against the pollution of the Stour by raw sewage but although the river was Ashford's source for drinking water it was not until 1889 that trunk sewerage treatment for the town was provided.

In 1850 a chaplain, in the person of the Reverend John Pughe was appointed as a result of the direct intervention of the Archbishop of Canterbury, his salary being met entirely by the company. Quickly emerging as a champion of the workpeople he defended their interests, challenging the company when necessary, particularly where accident benefits were concerned. He made a strong plea to the railway board for a school building and after a great deal of discussion the company agreed to provide one.

Erected by builder Albert Smith in 1852 it owes its design to William Tress, an enthusiast for 'gothic' styling. During the same year his work included the railway station at Battle and the two buildings show a remarkable similarity. The architectural importance of the school has since been demonstrated by its having been given a Grade II heritage listing.

The good Reverend also tried to persuade the South Eastern to provide a church and a fund was started but finally it was agreed that one of the large schoolrooms should be used on Sundays as a chapel-at-ease. Perhaps because of the Reverend Pughe's forcefulness, his appointment was terminated in 1855 and the spiritual welfare of the railwaymen became the responsibility of the Vicar of St Mary's Ashford. His departure was not allowed to go unmarked. It was said the 'he endeared himself to everyone with his unobtrusive kindness and generosity' and the inhabitants of Ashford joined with the New Town in a joint testimonial.

Despite the company's use of the title 'Alfred' for their new town, the name failed to pass into common usage. The reasons behind this rather strange title are a mystery. No documentary evidence remains to explain the unusual choice of name although an Ashford railwayman wrote a piece of poetry at the end of the 19th century in which he clearly believed that the village has been named after Alfred the Great. This would be in keeping with Victorian tradition and also reflects the activities of the Saxon King in the Ninth Century when his army was positioned in the district and succeeded in rebuffing a Danish invasion.

Bagshot's 'Kent' remarks in 1847: 'Here many houses have been built since the completion of the railway, which are called the "New Town". Both the 1851 census and the Post Office Directory for that year refer to Alfred New Town but by 1861 the Post Office Directory speaks of "New Town" as generally known, or "Alfred" as originally named by its proprietors the South Eastern Railway Company.'

A local newspaper was launched in 1855 with the title The Ashford and Alfred News and this contains references to 'the twin towns of Ashford and Alfred'. The railwaymen themselves launched their own bakery company known as the Alfred Joint Stock Company. The tavern on the green, known as the Mechanics Arms was renamed the Alfred Arms, but all this failed to dislodge the name by which the village has become known and remains to this day – New Town. By 1859 'Alfred' had disappeared from the title of the local newspaper which became the Kentish Express and Ashford News.

The new inhabitants were largely 'foreigners' to the district. One fifth came from Kent but another fifth came from Northumberland and Durham with the remainder from all parts of Great Britain. From its very inception the New Town, with its common work interest was a close-knit community. Added to this, most of the 'migrants' were young families and their earnings gave them a better than average lifestyle. They paid rent of 3s. 6d. which was deducted from their wages. A feature of life in the New Town was the presence of a large number of railwaymen who were taken into many of the homes as lodgers. Ample evidence of this is contained in the 1851 census. This also showed a large number of railwaymen living in the old town of Ashford with 98 living in and around the High Street of whom 38 were lodgers. It was convenient for single country people and their payments were a welcome addition to the family purse of their hosts.

The new mobility of working people at this time was demonstrated by the record of coach painter James Campbell and his wife Jane who came to live at 104 New Town. They had four children who were each born in a different town: Manchester, Liverpool, Camberwell and Birmingham.

The tale is told of a young couple who, desperate for work, walked with a babe in arms from Bristol to Ashford. Their courage evidently impressed the railway management because a job was offered in the works together with a house.

A paternal attitude on the part of the company was shown in the appointment of a 'monthly nurse' in the person of Diana Beeching who was given a cottage at 100 New Town.

George Holland's Diary

Life in those times was recorded in a diary written by George Hollands who came to Ashford from Sutton Valance in 1848 whilst still a boy. The family first lived at 13 Barrow Hill Terrace but a move was made to 49 New Town, his father having obtained a position at the Locomotive Works as an assistant storekeeper. George Hollands wrote:

'These houses were so arranged that the downstair part fronted toward a crescent-shaped Green and the upstairs part fronted towards the Railway Works. We had a double house and a communication was cut through from one to the other. Father was employed as storekeeper and mother tried to keep a small grocery shop for a little while but found it did not pay, the cheese dried quickly.'

'Mr Headley, a Quaker and friend of Mr Cudworth, the Superintendent of the Locomotive department of the Railway Works opened a large grocery shop and took the trade away. Our stock of grocery and all the things were sold off and then for a time we had only the upstairs part of the house until we moved to 95 New Town. The houses around the Crescent were built while we were there. The end houses of each block were a little larger than the others. I think there were four small ones and one larger at each end. The end ones were ornamented with several small points, the walls were of brick and covered with a composition of sand and cement in imitation of stone slabs. Stucco or compo fronts they were called. During the building of these houses some Irish labourers got into a quarrel and fought desperately with shovels. One threw another headfirst into a vat of nearly slaked lime that was being prepared for plastering the interior. I was greatly alarmed.'

'I went to Sutton Valance to see Grandfather Hollands, they gave me a young magpie and a wicker cage and going home to Ashford from Headcorn, the nearest station, we rode in a 'open to the sky' third-class carriage and it was raining. The poor magpie got drenched and only lived a day or two after I got home with it.'

'A neighbour kept several rabbits in the bank where the ground had been excavated level for the workshops of the Carriage department. The ground had been dug out to quite a depth leaving a steep bank.'

'One fifth of November I acted as a Guy Fawkes, had on a mask and was padded with hay to make me appear very stout and with a number of boys went round to all the houses – many gave us pennies for fireworks. In the evening we built a large bonfire on the Green, shot off our fireworks and burned another Guy Fawkes in the fire. On the first day of May Chimney Sweeps dress up in fantastic dresses and colours. Sometimes they have a pole, dance round it and expect people to give them money. Little girls carry around garlands covered over with perhaps a doll in the centre.'

'I used to play with the children of Mr William Williams, the Head Storekeeper, and often took meals with them. A favourite place to play was in the 'Store' on the immense bags of cotton waste piled up almost to the very girders of the roof and jump from one to the other. There was little danger of being hurt. The store always had a peculiar smell from the numerous things it contained. There were large black tarpaulins marked with white letters S.E.R. hanging from the rafters. Bolts and nuts of every conceivable size and other things too numerous to mention. Files in large quantities, brass filings or borings, speltre, oils, turpentine, varnish, soap, tallow, American cloth (an imitation leather), India runner and leather belting, whole skins of leather, screws of innumerable sizes and upholstering materials.'

'I and my sister Jennie were sent to the Misses Wardell's school at the New Town. Reverend Pughe often came in and exercised a sort of supervision. The youngest, Miss Louise Wardell was my favourite. She was afterwards married to Mr Keener the head bookkeeper in the Locomotive department.'

'We went hop picking at Beaver, out Kingsnorth way, from where the milkman came twice every day with two large pails full of milk which he carried with a yoke. He had a small square piece of wood floating on the milk in each pail to prevent it from spilling over.'

'The water supply was derived from a small brook that ran near in which we used to catch minnows and gudgeon. It was pumped into a large tank over the centre block, the building between two long rows of houses. This tank was generally covered with a green weed like scum. It would be turned on periodically and originated a saying "is the water turned off?" when any of us had a face that was not quite presentable or our hands were not overclean. In the flannel bag that was usually tied over the tap at the sink we would often find minnows and a green scummy weed.'

A fire occurred at the Store, which completely destroyed it. We watched the flames in great fear from the bedroom windows of No. 95. After the fire, father was made head bookkeeper at a store in the Carriage department, Richard Christopher Mansell was then the Superintendent.'

'I was sent to school at Mrs Burvell's near Barrow Hill and would walk to and 'fro morning and afternoon. After I left school I was given a position in father's office. My principal duty was to keep the invoice book, do a little journalizing and bookkeeping and having considerable time on my hands studied writing by imitating Mr Morris alias "Tiddlewick and Heartshorn". He wrote a beautiful free hand and did a little Latin and mechanical drawing. I think I gained as much education or more than I would have done at school. I copied some receipts and tables from a book of Beecroft Butler & Co. At the dinner hour and often during working hours I would walk through the Works, both the Locomotive and the Carriage. It was very interesting to me to see the men working – the fitters, turners, smiths, strikers and boilermakers also Naismith's steam hammer, the upright and circular saws and the drilling and iron planing machines. The upright saws were worked several together and cut a complete ball of timber into thin boards for panels and other purposes. They used a large quantity of teak.'

'In the carriage department there was a hydraulic press used to force the tyres of the carriage wheels on to centres composed of solid wood, a patent process of Mr R C Mansell with which all the wheels of the carriages on the whole line were equipped. The royalty on this must have produced him a large income.'

'I liked to watch the process of faggotting scrap iron and the long iron shavings turn from engine driving wheels into large lumps of solid iron under the steam hammer and ultimately converted into heavy crankshafts. The noise of the steam hammer and the vibration in the ground could be heard and felt for a long distance. They sometimes worked at night and the jarring would awaken you out of your sleep.'

'There were pattern makers, moulders, brass and iron founders, coach builders, carriage trimmers and painters, in fact all the different occupations there are in the manufacture of complete locomotive engines and carriages. Mr Isaac Hendy was foreman under Mr Mansell. He had a peculiar walk leaning a little to one side and forward carrying his left arm as if it were useless to him, though it was not.'

'The Royal Carriages kept there were of interest to me as well as to all visitors to the Works. I have sat in the Queen's seat many times. Joe Gimber was the storekeeper and an old lame man named Bernard his assistant. There was also Ashenden (he had very red hair) who attended a circular saw, father was the means of getting him work there, also a Mr Moore of Ashford who made and covered a large Ash easy chair for father. Mr William Blackburn was an old gentleman that had been well-to-do - a "Yeoman of Kent" and had met with reverses of fortune. He was in father's office a little while – he gave me three small books "Ovids Metamorphosis", "Herdibeas" and "Telemachus". He was employed to sweep out the shops, his son, quite a stripling, was office boy. The old gentleman had married a young lady and had a large family. I pitied him greatly.'

'The men going in and out of the Works looked like bees going in and out of a hive, Mr Rose being the timekeeper. Each workman as he passed in took a brass ticket or check with his number on it and delivered it up as he passed out.'

'The Carriage department was built some time after we went to live at the New Town. There was only the Locomotive department at first. They had a Mechanics Institute in connection with the Railway Works where they often had lectures, readings and concerts. Charles Dickens came and read his "Christmas Carol". We went to hear him – there was a very large audience, they cleared out a large part of the Carriage Trimming department for the occasion. The concerts in the schoolroom were generally under my father's leadership while Mr Mansell wielded the baton.'

'At the back of our house, No 95, was a tract of land divided into allotments and rented out for gardens to many of the workmen employed in the Works. There was a marked difference between what one man or another would produce on this ground with equal opportunities, showing that a great deal depended upon the man as to the results. At the foot of the gardens, ran the clear little brook, the water from which was pumped up into the tank to supply the inhabitants and the workshops. In this brook on one particular evening I remember laying some lines and leaving them all night. In the night came up a severe thunder storm and heavy rain. In the morning I went to take up my line and found to my great astonishment a very large eel which I pulled out, took home and mother made into a pudding. Having caught it myself I enjoyed the eating.'

'Near the main line of the South Eastern Railway and nearer to Willesborough were a great number of the old iron and wooden trucks that had been used in the construction of the railroad. They had remained there since about 1840 or perhaps earlier simply rusting and decaying. In and around these trucks we boys and sometimes the girls played many games.'

'The road around the crescent at the New Town had been repaired with broken stone and the drivers of vehicles had used one side more than the other so the authorities hit upon a plan to make them drive so as to wear the road evenly. This was by placing old railway sleepers across the worn part. Mother had gone out before it was dark but was returning later and not remembering the sleepers in crossing the road fell across one on to the broken stones and broke the bridge of her nose. I went to the door to let her in and was greatly frightened to see her bleeding profusely but she assured us she was not much hurt and dressed her injuries with brown paper and vinegar. She carries the scars yet. The paths all around the New Town were made of cinders and very unpleasant to walk on, on account of the crunching noise they made.'

'The lead water pipes at No 95 were brought up out of the ground at the back of the house just outside the wall and then carved through the wall into the kitchen. Almost every winter there was just sufficient frost to burst this pipe and then there was a little flood and we were much annoyed by having to fetch water from a neighbour until a man was sent to repair it. Sometimes our neighbours would call upon us in similar circumstances.'

'Our neighbours were a Mr and Mrs Pearce and daughter Jane, North Country people. Mrs Pearce usually wore a white cap; Mr Pearce was a smith and welded the large tyres of the driving wheels of the engines. Another neighbour was Mrs Boyce whose husband had been killed between the buffers of two carriages. After he died she was employed in the Carriage Trimming department.'

'Mr Harris, a red haired man, foreman of the trimmers, was able to make his own shoes. He showed father how to make a pair of leather slippers but it was dirty work for the hands, having to use shoemaker's wax. I wore heavy shoes with nails, heel and toe plates, and leather leggings that came up over the knees and fastened with a strap to the suspender buttons. They were buttoned all the way up with round-headed leather buttons.'

'On the road to Willesborough where we went quite often, we had to cross over the South Eastern Railway on a level with the road. There are few such crossings, nearly all the roads are raised on each side with a brick arch over the railroad. At this crossing there was a gatekeeper named Bumpstead who lived with his family in a little brick house built for his accommodation. He had a wooden leg and opened the gates when anyone wanted to cross over if there was no danger of a train passing at that time. On the banks at the side of this road we could gather primroses in abundance as well as scented violets, both blue and white, and sometimes wild strawberries. This was a delightful walk to the Church whose spire is covered with small split oak shingles and leans over a little out of perpendicular. The walk across the field to Willesborough was even more delightful than by the road especially when the wheat, oats, barley, tares and beans were ripe and the sky lark would rise up gradually from the field in a perpendicular line until nearly out of sight and descend in the same line to where he started and sing continually all the time he was rising and falling.'

'The travelling clothes-peg makers (the same class of people that used to make Lucifer matches) often came to the Green at the New Town and fixed tin around the ends of willow clothes pegs that they made. They used cast iron tacks and very thin "tagging tin".'

'September 9th 1855. Fall of Sebstapol. About two weeks prior to this what was supposed to be the news of the victory reached England. There was great rejoicing. The bells in Ashford were "fired", that is all rung at the same instant and it made the tower sway to and fro with the vibration. In the High Street they burned barrels of tar and shot off fireworks. All was excitement but as soon as the false news was contradicted there was much depression of spirits. However, they did not have to wait much longer but the second rejoicing did not have as much life in it as the first. It was a tame affair perhaps on account of the fear that this might prove to be untrue.'

'At East Stour Farm between Ashford and Willesborough I saw some ploughing by steam engine, the same farm where we bought the pig. Our pigsty was paved with brick and it was my work to keep it cleaned out and put in fresh straw for him. I also kept some rabbits.'

'Owing to some changes at the Works, father's office was no longer required, he and I therefore had to look for some other employment.'

The Holland family left Ashford in 1856, Mr Holland senior having obtained a post in the Relieving Officership at Cranbrook. Some years later George Holland married a local girl, emigrated to the United States and was connected with the building of the North Western railroad.

Institute and School

The facilities of the railway village gave it a measure of independence but there was obviously much commercial and social interchange between the old town and the new. 1857 saw the opening of the great Bath House on the New Town Green, the luxury of this benefit being welcomed by everyone, rail folk and townspeople alike. The hot baths were advertised in the local newspaper, opening hours being 9 a.m. until 1 p.m. for ladies and 1 p.m. until 9 p.m. for men, Thursday, Friday and Saturday only.

Two gates were erected on the roads leading into the New Town, one near the railway station and the other by the Aylesford Crossing. Foot travellers passed freely but traders' vans and wagons were required to be in possession of a company pass in order to gain access.

The Mechanics Institute first opened on the ground floor of one of the New Town cottages but later a purpose built building was erected on a corner of the Green near the clock tower. With the Company chairman James MacGregor as President, James Cudworth as Treasurer, John Leener as Secretary and a sixteen-man committee the Institute flourished from its very beginning. The Company were persuaded to supply the furnishings which consisted of three dozen chairs, two round and two oblong tables, four champhine lamps, two fenders, two sets of fire irons, a candlestick and two brushes.

Newspapers made available included The Times, Daily News, Liverpool Albion and Gateshead Observer, the latter two in response to requests from railwaymen who had arrived from the North Country. Technical and leisure journals covered a range of subjects and consisted of the Railway Times, Railway Gazette, Mechanics Magazine, Builder Magazine, Teetotal Times, Gardeners Chronicle and Punch.

Lectures were arranged on the electric telegraph and classes set up to teach reading, writing and arithmetic with members acting as teachers. Local teachers were later hired to give lessons in English grammar, French language, mechanical drawing and mathematics. A library was instituted with over 200 books, most being donated, including twelve volumes of Shakespeare. Readings were given of passages from celebrated authors. The Institute committee also concerned itself with social events, setting up a chess club and inaugurating a glee choir under conductor J. Firth. The cost of membership was very low at eight pence per month for those whose weekly wages exceeded twenty-four shillings and four pence per month for those who earned less.

After much consideration the committee respectfully asked the Directors to consider providing an excursion train to take employees on a day trip to Dover and from there on to Calais by steamboat. The Company agreed and so it came about that August 1848 saw the first Works excursion. 1,818 people, including wives, enjoyed the day, starting out at 6.45 a.m. at a cost of either one shilling or sixpence, depending upon the level of wages received.

Perhaps the idea had been triggered off by the Company's generosity in providing a free trip to Dover in late July for 220 boys and girls from the Ashford National School and the neighbouring villages.

The following year a soiree was held in the Works Tender shop. With no local hall available for entertainment purposes it was not unusual for a workshop to be cleared and made available to the men and their families for social gatherings.

In April 1852 a start was made on creating an adjoining community to the New Town following an agreement between the landowners Curteis Norwood and Mordaunt Monro and the National Freehold Land Society, making over a large area of land subsequently known as South Willesborough. Plans were drawn up for public highways, the area divided into building lots and then advertised as the Ashford Estate. The new roads were named Mead Road, Cudworth Road, East Lane and Back Lane. Canterbury Lane, as it was then called, was to be widened. The Deed of Covenant also mentions a Water Lane. One of the many stipulations of the Covenant read 'On no lot shall any house be erected of less value than £80'.

The completion of New Town School initiated an event, which became a regular custom. In July 1853 pupils set out on a railway excursion to Dover with all costs borne by the Company. The day was so successful that a seaside treat became a regular highlight of the scholar's year. With open carriages still in vogue, it was sometimes the practice to send out a special train containing the Ashford Town Band to meet the returning excursion and play the children home.

From the outset the school received a Government grant and was therefore required to conform to approved standards and appoint "proper staff".

Upon opening, these were Frederick Nelman as Principal Teacher with Francis Garraway as his assistant and they arranged their scholars into three groups, boys, girls and infants. Because of the district's agricultural connections, the hop-picking season affected attendance and so flexible summer holidays were arranged, a three-week break normally being taken in August with a further three weeks in September.

Samuel Smiles as Secretary of the Company influenced the form of teaching and gave copies of his books as prizes. The Vicar and James Cudworth visited regularly and when boys reached the age of fourteen, Cudworth selected some for such as boilermakers, pattern makers, smiths, turners and office staff. Richard Mansell also selected boys although he sometimes complained that they often were not strong enough for his needs. It was not unusual for boys to stay on at school beyond the normal leaving age in the hope of filling a later vacancy.

Francis Garraway was later appointed Principal Teacher and faithfully recorded the schools' activities in a special register. Some of the notes for 1863 read:

June 19th	Admitted 30 boys from the Infants Schools, 12 of them were placed in the sixth class and the remainder formed a new class.
July 5th	William Wood aged 11 years 10 months played the truant yesterday afternoon.
July 6th	Cautioned the boys who go past the pumping engine on their way home, about throwing over the palings and breaking the windows of the engine house.
July 15th	Dissenters School treat for children, several boys absent in afternoon.
July 23rd	Cautioned the boys about entering the wood place and throwing the wood about and breaking the windows in it.
July 24th	Examined 3rd class homework, found several had not done their work and the rest very badly, only two sums right among the whole.
July 27th	Mistress Mansell married. Children went out in front of the school to cheer while the carriages were passing in going to church, allowed them to leave at four o'clock in the afternoon.
August 26th	Punished W. Rawling rather severely for his audacity and sent Joshua Hollands home for insubordination.
August 27th	J. Hollands brought to school and made to submit.
December 20th	Stove smoked and obliged to put the fire out.
December 23rd	Morning attendance 168. Children assembled at half past three o'clock to receive prizes and see a Magic Lantern exhibition arranged by Mr Mansell.

In the years that followed the school continued to progress, offering scholars a wide range of subjects and subjecting them to regular examinations. Prize day was always an important and much anticipated day in the school and as was usual that in 1865 was attended by the Vicar together with James Cudworth and his wife. It was observed that 'the general appearance of the scholars was as intelligent and cleanly as could be possibly seen in an institution for the education of the working classes'. Nevertheless the Vicar clearly felt there was a need for a few words of kindly counsel. Urging attendance at Church he said young lads went into the Works and soon earned enough to be independent of their parents but too many of them were to be seen sauntering about on Sundays. However, he looked upon the school with a great deal of satisfaction because he saw before him a large number of the rising generation – children of toil – who must be brought up to fill stations in life more or less connected with toil and who if blessed with health might look forward to support themselves. Their parents were not like many parents who could not say what they might have to do tomorrow. They were in receipt of regular wages and they had the means of doing by their children what 30 or 40 years ago could not have been done by parents in the same station of life.

By 1868 French was being taught from Cassell's instruction books and the following year boys were learning phonography by taking a course of 15 lessons from Mr. Pitman's well known book. Books on shorthand were awarded as prizes and presented by the Company Secretary. Ashford's open-air swimming baths were visited every summer and school treats were arranged to places such as Folkestone and Dover for pupils who had attended school 200 times during the year.

Early Days

The effect of the railway upon Ashford is clearly shown in the census figures. By 1852 the town's population had risen from 3,000 to 5,000 and within ten years would grow to nearly 7,000. With five lines radiating from its junction and the presence of a railway works there had been an enormous impact upon the town's way of life.

For ten years Ashford had been a hive of constructional activity creating tremendous demands for bricks, iron, coal and labour. Unemployment problems that had pressed so heavily upon the surrounding villages were greatly eased. In normal circumstances a railway company was a major employer with opportunities to become engine drivers, stokers, signalmen, linesmen, stationmasters, booking clerks, ticket collectors and porters. At Ashford those involved in such tasks were almost minor compared with the five-hundred strong labour force of engineers, fitters, turners, smiths, drillers, lamp makers, carpenters, painters and labourers that were needed at the new Works.

Working conditions in 19th century factories were severe and Ashford was no exception. The Works clock would strike at 6 a.m. to signal the commencement of another working day. Men and boys from the country districts rose early. Soon after four o'clock they were astir and after a light breakfast began the long walk into Ashford. Those that lived in villages only a short distance from the town first attended to their kitchen gardens, chickens and pigs. Some even gave a hand to the local farmer, helping with milking or fieldwork.

Regardless of weather, men made their daily journey. In the event of flooding or heavy snowfall they either had to stay at home or if caught at the Works, take a lodging in the town until the weather cleared. Railwaymen living in the town were up and about by five o'clock and as is usually the case, those that lived nearest the Works arrived last.

The Alfred Arms on New Town Green was open for those who needed to start the day with a mug of ale or porter. Outside the main gate alongside the clock tower stood a coffee stall, which charged a halfpenny for a cup and the same for a bun. The men arrived in a trickle at first but as the hour of six approached this swelled to a flood. Hundreds of men, some looking fit and healthy, others drawn, white faced, yet others still partly grimed with yesterday's black soot, poured toward the entrance gate.

Five minutes after the clock tower bell had clanged its six strokes everyone had to be at his shop. Each man was issued with a brass "coin", referred to as his "chit". Similar to a penny piece, it had his personal number stamped on it, which related to his name in the register. This was handed out upon arrival at the Works and returned at the end of the working day and was the only accepted proof of attendance. If a man was five minutes late he was docked fifteen minutes pay or thirty minutes pay for lateness of ten minutes. After that time no man was admitted until after breakfast. This was taken between 8.30 a.m. and 9 a.m. Men from the New Town ran home for theirs whilst others brought a packed meal and ate in the mess room of their shop.

Clerks arrived a little later and left earlier whilst the principal office staff worked from 9 a.m. until 5.30 p.m. Although working conditions were onerous the men had the advantage of permanent work and wages higher than local farm workers. There was also the annual excursion, which was highly prized and looked forward to with great anticipation. However, if for any reason men were stood off, they received but one day's notice.

It was the lot of many to work continually in an inferno of noise, smoke, fumes and thick black dust. There was the heat, blast and glare of the furnaces, as the forgers set to work, roaring belching steam from gigantic boilers and the noise of belts, pulleys, presses, rattling wheels and hydraulic punches. Accidents were frequent and many a highly-skilled man finished up labouring in the yard with a broom and barrow. By contrast the joinery men and painters had a much easier occupation.

The men delighted in demonstrating their expertise with the great steam hammer. They could place a watch on the plinth and bring the hammer crashing down so that it touched the watch but without harming it. Likewise they could crack the shell of a nut, leaving the kernel unharmed. The rolling mill was situated near the Willesborough gate.

Despite all the hardships, every morning when work was available, unemployed men and boys crowded around the Works main entrance in their cloth jackets, corduroy trousers and coloured mufflers, hoping to catch the eye of the foreman when he returned from breakfast and thus join the ranks of the railwaymen.

The highest paid were usually the smiths who received from 24 shillings to 36 shillings, depending upon their experience and skill. They were closely followed by the turners earning between 21 shillings and 34 shillings. Fitters received 24 shillings and 30 shillings and carriage painters earned a similar amount, between 21 shillings and 30 shillings. There was a great variation in rates for the lamp-makers, who would start as low as 16 shillings but could rise to a top rate of 36 shillings. Drillers rates varied from 16 shillings to 22 whilst the lowly labourer had to be content with 15 shillings to 18 shillings. Apart from payment, hours worked were part of the conditions of occupation with the skilled workman devoting three hours less per week than the unskilled.

Rates of pay remained stable for the remainder of the century although the length of the working week was reduced. The Company exercised a strong discipline, reasons for dismissal including insolence, carelessness, drunkenness, dishonesty, bad timekeeping, disobedience, neglect of duty and stealing brass. One 21 year old wagon maker was sacked for throwing an empty nail bag about the shop. There appears to have been a large turnover in men during the early years although this might be attributed to the unacceptably hard, dirty and noisy working conditions compared to a former outdoor life.

The 1851 census shows only nine women at the Works, all employed as sheet and lining makers and paid between 12 and 15 shillings a week, and there were many examples of quite extraordinary lengths of duty. Mary Ann Mayger the earliest known woman employee lived at New Town as early as 1851. She continued working until she died in 1891. Another example of long service is provided by James Baker. In 1846 the first section of the locomotive shop was being erected and amongst the men employed was this twenty-one year old. He had been engaged by the contractors, Messrs Peto and Grissell, to excavate earth for the foundations and continued for some time in their employ. In January 1851 the South Eastern Railway

Company employed him in the locomotive shop that he had helped to build and it is recorded that 53 years later in January 1904 he was still there. By then in his 79th year he remained hale and hearty and was most regular in his timekeeping notwithstanding having lost the sight of one eye. In that year he was the oldest inhabitant working in the factory and his service may well have been an all-time record.

Chapter Two

CUDWORTH IS KING

The rich man has a carriage
Where no rude eye can flout him;
The poor man's bane
Is a third-class train,
With the daylight all about him.

Thomas Love Peacock

When Cudworth was appointed Locomotive Superintendent in 1845 he inherited a mixed bag of sixty-four engines some of which proved very unreliable. It was his good fortune however that over half came from the Sharp Roberts stable who provided a superb fleet of 2-2-2 locomotives which were smooth running, robust and performed well on their express duties. These beautiful little engines were the mainstay of the South Eastern, working splendidly for over 20 years. Developed from an original specification by Robert Stephenson and Joseph Locke their fine construction was considered a tribute to Robert's genius. Even so the expansion of the rail network, the unreliability of some pioneer engines and the fact that daily maintenance prevented even a twelve-hour working of these early machines resulted in Cudworth having to order 90 new locomotives during the first seven years of his reign.

By 1844 the South Eastern Board had decided to adopt the long-boilered type for all its new engines. This was a costly error as so many of them proved to be unsteady and even unsafe at more than modest speed. An early re-building programme became necessary creating a heavy workload for the new Ashford Works.

Seven Hicks Singles appeared in 1846 whose riding was so poor Cudworth had to re-build them all into 2-4-0s. Next in line came six four-coupled Forrester Goods engines. It quickly became apparent there were difficulties in permanently securing the cylinders to the frames, the only remedy being to re-build them. In addition four had to be re-boilered. Fifteen 2-2-2 Singles were ordered from Nasmyth Gaskell & Co and as with so many previous engines, they proved to be unstable at speed. In addition they suffered from loose cylinders, fractured steam pipes and leaking joints. After four had been received, an irate S.E.R. Chairman sent a letter to the makers who had to agree a number of modifications. Cudworth had most of them re-built within 30 months as either 2-4-0s or well tanks. The remaining six were sub-contracted to C. Tayleur & Company and although still not very successful, they were somewhat better than their predecessors.

Cudworth considered that 30 more locomotives would be required by 1847 and the Board agreed to approach Forresters to enquire if they could accept such a large order. At this time the huge upsurge in locomotive building had left the industry short of many materials, particularly copper plate and brass tubing. Consequently, Forresters would only accept an order for 15. These passenger 2-4-0s proved to be the best yet received from a manufacturer, apart from the Sharps. However in the same year the working of six new Bury Singles proved to be disastrous and an order for a further nine was cancelled. They suffered loose cylinders and broken frames and all had to be re-built, four of them twice over.

Finally three unusual engines, originally ordered by a Belgian railway were received from Tulk & Ley. They offered a Crampton design with a seven foot driving wheel behind the firebox but like so many other engines of the period, were also found wanting. It must have been with considerable thankfulness that Cudworth found the locomotives ordered from Robert Stephenson & Co during 1850 and 1851 to be more traffic-worthy. Ten Crampton 'Folkestone' class and five 'Bulldogs', together with an additional eight tried and trusted engines from Sharp Roberts brought relief to what must have been a very exasperated engineer.

The 'Folkestones' were inside cylinder engines of the latest Crampton design which performed quite well as lightly loaded expresses, most ably performing into the 1890s. The 'Bulldogs', robust and well constructed, were six coupled tanks and used to effect on Folkestone harbour and Whitstable branch services, while the smart express 2-2-2 Singles from Sharp Roberts showed themselves to be well capable of working the Dover expresses for more than a decade, in addition to undertaking excursion duties.

Accidents on the line were not rare and these could include boiler explosions. The boiler of a locomotive was inspected at Rye in March 1852 and pronounced sound by the Ashford Boilersmith. Tragedy followed – it was clearly not so for it blew up the following month killing the driver, John Hadley and wrecking the engine. The Forrester built locomotive owned by George Wythe, constructor of the line, was passing near Warehorne at the time hauling a night-time ballast train towards the as yet incomplete workings at Hastings. The South Eastern Gazette reported: 'The boiler burst with terrific violence a particle of which striking him (John Hadley), completely shattered his head and his death was instantaneous'. The remains of the engine were removed to Ashford Works for examination by a Board of Trade Inspector and later sold for scrap.

The extent of repair and maintenance work together with difficulties in obtaining a sufficient number of skilled men resulted in any Cudworth designed engine being delayed until 1853. Shortly before Christmas of that year the first Ashford built locomotive was proudly rolled out of its great shed. In an attractive livery of Holly Green, black bands lined out in white, red-brown frames, crimson buffer beams and embellished with oval brass number plates, the heavy 26 ton engine raised a cheer as she steamed into the open. This impressive symbol of power was destined for the Hastings line, which was heavily graded with severe curves. It possessed a very tall bell-mouthed chimney, large brass dome, long boiler, wheels five and a half feet in diameter and a six-wheeled tender. A 2-4-0 type carrying the number 157 she was the first of a series of ten to be built at Ashford and designated the 'Hastings' class.

Cudworth next turned his attention to the need for a standard goods engine and so in 1855 a rather smaller 0-6-0 locomotive with four and a half foot wheels made its appearance. In the first year four machines were produced with traditional coke-burning fireboxes but Cudworth, a man of inventive capability, devised a new system of steam distribution and a new type of firebox which made it possible for the first time to burn coal instead of coke without causing an emission of smoke. Cudworth claimed with justification that as a result Ashford Works spent less time on firebox maintenance than any other railway workshop. Such was the success of these exceptionally powerful engines, they were the fore-runners of another 49 of the same design all built at Ashford during the next twenty years and destined to give over 40 years service. The framing on the first four was later replaced with double framing with the extraordinary result that when the time came to withdraw the class, the primitive cutting equipment of the time proved incapable of reducing the iron plating to scrap.

An unusual decision was taken when the Works was instructed to build four six-wheeled singles to a design based largely upon that of eight engines delivered five years previously by Sharp Roberts. Because of their pedigree they were highly regarded, being particularly smart little engines in appearance and well suited for main-line working. They were originally known as the 'Mails' until the advent four years later of Cudworth's 2-2-2s, when they became known as 'Little Mails'. In an act of subterfuge Cudworth built two more, nos. 36 and 84, concealing his lack of authority by registering them as re-builds.

In the mid-1850s Cudworth was continuing to experience difficulty in finding sufficient steam engineers to build the engines he required.

Consequently he accepted a tender from E. B. Wilson & Co of the Railway Foundry, Leeds, for the supply of six 2-4-0s for secondary passenger services. They were well described by historian D. L. Bradley: 'Like all engines supplied by this manufacturer they were magnificently finished in an age when British engineering was unsurpassed in quality. All the well-known Wilson features were present, including highly polished mahogany sheathed boilers, tall copper-capped chimneys, brass dome covers in the style of Corinthian columns and radially-slotted driving wheel splashers. The latter were reputedly the creation of Mrs James Fenton, wife of the Works Manager.'

With the need for still more powerful locomotives Cudworth next used Ashford Works to re-build six of the 2-2-2 Sharp Roberts into virtually new 2-4-0 machines which promptly earned them the nickname 'Little Sharps', a curious choice of name since they were an improvement on the original design. The work extended their life into the Stirling era, the last one being withdrawn in 1884.

A class of engine which received too little recognition was Cudworth's 2-4-0 '118' class. Cudworth took his inspiration from the 'Wilsons' which had proved to be reliable, free-steaming, fast running and possibly the best coupled engines so far to grace South Eastern rails. Entering service in 1859, 68 were built at Ashford and judged to be an outstanding success. Designed to work every kind of passenger service with the exception of the Dover Mails and Folkestone Tidal expresses, the class, numbering 110 engines, eventually formed more than half the Company's entire locomotive stock.

What has rightfully been described as 'Cudworth's masterpiece' thundered down the metals in July 1861. Known as the 'Mail' class these large, powerful 2-2-2 express engines had a blunt-ended or handsome copper-capped chimney, a polished brass dome and a great seven-foot central driving wheel, which in appearance was reminiscent of a paddle steamer. Of the 16 produced, eight were built at Ashford and were an instant success.

Designed specifically for fast running as Continental Mail Expresses, they carried the Royal Mail from London to Dover's Admiralty Pier daily for onward transmission to the Continent and weekly to India and Australia. They proved to be the mainstay of the South Eastern main-line for the next twenty-five years and with justification were known among their admirers as 'Flyers' or 'Freewheelers'. It was said that for a short run requiring only one stop for water they were the fastest in England. They also performed well with their regular service for the Tidal expresses from Folkestone Harbour. Line working was difficult because the boat trains had to be fitted in to suit the tides but their fine running enabled them to cover the 69 mile journey from Folkestone junction to Cannon Street in 95 minutes. Good going, bearing in mind the gradients between Tonbridge and New Cross and their loads of 130 tons. Another example of their superb running comes from railway historian E.L.Ahrons who quotes a run of one express hauling 150 tons from Cannon Street to Ashford in 74 minutes. An unusual member of the class was No.81, built at Ashford in 1866, painted in Royal Blue, named the 'Flying Dutchman' and frequently called upon to haul the Royal Train. This was a task that it could handle with ease, since Queen Victoria refused to allow her train to travel at more than 40 m.p.h.

The 'Mail' class was the first to benefit from a system of electrical communication between driver and guard. In December 1864 the directors of the company instructed Cudworth to investigate means whereby communication on trains could be improved. Just over a year later after a series of experiments undertaken at Ashford, Cudworth was able to report that a coded bell system had been devised, replacing the primitive method of a cord outside the carriage, which connected to a gong or whistle on the engine. A short trial proved successful and orders were issued to begin equipping all main-line expresses with the system, a decision which subsequently prevented a number of accidents. The 'Mails' remained responsible for hauling continental expresses until 1884 and many continued with other duties until 1890. Number 197 achieved 913,684 miles during its working life, the highest mileage then recorded in the annals of the South Eastern Railway.

Because of requests from locomen Cudworth began to fit his engines with windshields. When the directors heard of this one of them exclaimed 'What! They'll be asking for armchairs next!'

In the mid-1860s Cudworth designed three small classes of engines known as 'Well Tanks', eight of these 0-4-2s being built at Ashford. Useful for modest but essential tasks, they were allocated mixed traffic duties.

Early Carriages

The superintendent of the carriage and wagon department was Richard Mansell. It was he who as early as 1848 brought distinction to Ashford with his invention of the 'Mansell Wheel' which produced a very pleasant and sound-deadening ride. His patent wheels for carriages were built of 16 teak segments all in symmetrical harmony, within iron tyres three feet six inches in diameter. Steel tyres were later substituted, their success being such they were accepted as a standard feature of South Eastern stock and their fine reputation quickly spread to almost every other railway company in Britain.

South Eastern Railway stock at this time comprised 134 three compartment first-class carriages, 45 composites, 121 second-class, 75 open thirds, 51 enclosed thirds and two saloons. The first-class carriages encompassed three compartments, each seating six passengers and styled in the manner of a road stagecoach. Mounted upon four wheels they were surprisingly comfortable. All were painted in 'Wellington Brown' in recognition of the 'Iron Duke' who was Lord Warden of the Cinque Ports.

The 'Seconds' (square wooden boxes with square windows) although spartan by any standard were superior to those of many other companies. This was part of a deliberate policy by the Company to offer better second-class comfort in order to coax the public away from the appalling 'cattle truck' third class and thus earn extra revenue. They had thin cushion seating together with an upholstered strip running along the boarded back. On the South Eastern the material used resembled that used for porters' uniform trousers, causing wits to ask whether the seats were covered with the porters' old pantaloons or whether the situation was to the contrary.

At first, third-class offered simple open wagons, with low four foot sides having doors to admit passengers to hard, narrow wooden benches but travellers soon benefited from the introduction of 'Parliamentary Trains' dubbed 'Parly Trains.' William Ewart Gladstone introduced a parliamentary bill obliging companies to provide '......on each weekday at least one train conveying third class passengers in carriages provided with seats and protected from the weather, at a speed of not less than twelve miles per hour, including stoppages, and at a fare not exceeding one penny a mile for adults, children under twelve half price and under three free. Fifty-six pounds of luggage allowed without charge.'

As a result of the Act the South Eastern introduced a four-wheel, roofed third class carriage for 48 passengers. The seats with a depth of only twelve inches, were placed around the sides of the carriage and back to back down the middle, light being obtained by means of four sliding shutters. Most uncomfortable, yet railway travel continued to increase in popularity. Folk at that time had a saying: 'Third class riding is better than First Class walking'.

A few years later two most unusual carriages were seen on South Eastern rails. One was a second-class hearse carriage containing a special compartment for the body and separate seating for sixteen passengers. The other was a first/second-class invalid carriage built in the Ashford Works and fitted up with a bed and washbasin. Despite the primitive standard of the early stock, one van built as early as 1845 gave 84 years of service – a tribute to its robust construction.

A writer at the time said: 'This is indeed the age of wonders. What would one of our simple-minded forefathers say if he were to return for four and twenty hours to the dull earth that he quitted some three or four hundred years ago? What would be his astonishment at seeing a score of carriages whisking along a railroad behind an immense tea-kettle somewhat after the fashion of a dog tail-piped?'

An early carriage achieved some fame. It had been built in 1838 by Joseph Wright and was subsequently re-built for the use of the Duke of Wellington. Its centre first-class compartment was considerably lower than the flanking 'seconds', giving it a novel appearance. It survived as a sort of exhibit in the yard at Ashford for many years.

Another 'ancient' was the 'Invicta' locomotive from the Canterbury and Whitstable Railway. Parked in a corner of the Works paint shop it enjoyed a number of outings to exhibitions both in this country and on the continent until given to Canterbury City Council in 1906.

In the summer of 1851 Richard Mansell unveiled what has been described as 'the most elaborate royal carriage of the time'. Mounted on six of his famous wheels the main compartment comprised a state saloon with a small vestibule at one end and an attendant's coupe at the other. The exterior of the coach was highly ornate with convex sides and curved mouldings decorated with four gilded carved lions. Painted in purple lake picked out with crimson, Richard Mansell described it as 'a coach of noble proportions'. The interior was unsurpassed. The walls were heavily padded and quilted in amber white and drab damask with coloured satin drapes above a floor covered with a velvet pile carpet. Two couches and two chairs accompanied the state chair with its carved maple front and covering of silk damask.

Fire! Fire!

The earliest record of fire fighting is contained in a report concerning a fire at the Works on 17th July 1852. Because of the way in which the fire was handled Cudworth was censured by the Board, however, the men who helped to extinguish the blaze were treated to an excursion to France. Clearly lessons had been learned when five years later on 6th July a fire broke out at the Railway Station. The fire in a building used as a carpenters' and paint shop, spread with great rapidity causing fears to be expressed for the safety of the Station. Two fire engines belonging to the South Eastern Company were quickly on the scene and the fire brought under control but not before the building had been completely destroyed. It was reported that 'further destruction was only prevented by the efficient working of the engines'.

In addition to their duties in protecting the Works, the South Eastern's fire brigade was often called upon to render assistance in dealing with a large number of incidents in the district. Six months after the fire at the railway station the brigade was called out at eleven o'clock on the evening of 26th January 1858. A blaze had broken out in a carpenter's shop behind the Queens Head public house at the bottom of East Hill. A strong wind that was blowing raised the fire to a fierceness, which, reaching a great height, could be seen for miles around. Neighbouring wooden buildings with their tarred or thatched roofs were threatened by the blaze and an adjoining house seemed certain to perish but was saved by the stream of water poured upon it by the South Eastern engine. There was some criticism at the time concerning the volunteer Ashford Town Brigade but commendation for the prompt arrival of the South Eastern engine from Alfred and their success in putting down the inferno.

It was perhaps natural that the railway itself should be used to transport fire engines from one locality to another. In 1865 what was probably the largest fire to have occurred in East Kent started in a cabinetmaker's workshop in Canterbury at Mercery Lane. Consternation reigned as it spread at an alarming rate. The combined engine power of the Kent Fire Office, City Police, Phoenix Fire Office, the Cathedral, the Barracks and the Station engines from the South Eastern Railway and London, Chatham and Dover Railway were not sufficient to cope with the outbreak. There were fears for the whole of Mercery Lane and a large part of the High Street as the fire raged with unabated fury.

Further engines were called from Faversham, Dover and Ramsgate and a telegraph message was sent to Ashford pleading for early assistance. The brigades here sprang into action. The South Eastern immediately made available a special train, the Works engine and that of the Town Brigade were quickly loaded and the fire-fighters set off at a smart pace down the line to Canterbury.

Four years later the Works brigade was again called upon to act the good neighbour. One of Ashford's most flourishing industries was the Lion Brewery in Dover Place. By 2 a.m. on the night of 16th October 1869 fire had gained a good hold. The glare was first noticed at New Town and the Works engine arrived whilst the Ashford Town Brigade was still being summoned. By the time of their arrival the building was doomed for the roof had fallen in and fire was belching out from all the iron-framed windows. In the midst of what had become a glaring furnace a huge tank supported on pillars swayed and finally collapsed, crashing to the ground amidst the bursting of large vats and casks. The South Eastern used the only available hydrant within reach and having finally exhausted the town's reservoir supply, drew water from the river.

One of the largest fires Ashford had experienced for many years occurred on Saturday 9th April 1870 engulfing the premises of Edward Burnett, carriage builder and harness maker at 30 High Street. The fire was first noticed in the paintshop on the top floor above the main workshop about 8 o'clock in the evening. It quickly enveloped the entire building in a blazing mass, the roof and floors falling in. The inferno was so fierce that neighbouring shopkeepers moved their stock and furniture to safety. There was to be some criticism of the Town Brigade for a late turnout but the South Eastern Works engine was on the scene within twenty minutes of being summoned. By this time one town engine was working from the North Street Corn Dealers yard of Hart & Tatnell and the other from the High Street. Owing to defective standpipes, a connection could not be made until the railwaymen attached their own canvas tank. A further arrival was the Godinton Park engine belonging to the 'fire' enthusiast Earl of Mount Charles. His Lordship accompanied his engine and together with Cudworth and Mansell who directed the Works engine, took an energetic part in bringing the fire under control after ten hours hard work. The damage done was immense, amounting to over £6,000.

The Works brigade was again in action of 23rd September 1881. An old 'Bulldog' locomotive used in a stationary capacity at the Works Sawmill was fired with a mixture of coke, wood-shavings and off-cuts from the Carriage Works. It appears that sparks from its chimney fell on a pile of seasoning timber which smouldered away for some hours when, following a change of wind, it suddenly burst into flames. Before the brigade could arrive the entire wood yard was ablaze with sparks setting fire to the main Carriage and Wagon Works building. It was the good fortune of all concerned that a sudden thunderstorm developed and the firemen's efforts were assisted by a torrential downpour of rain. The situation was brought under control but the 'Bulldog' was so badly damaged it was subsequently sold for scrap.

A famous fire was that of 26th October 1889 described as a day of disaster for the little town of Wye. A small fire, probably caused by a discarded cigarette, spread rapidly involving The King's Head hostelry, the Wye Brewery and adjoining houses. A huge blaze ensued which at its height sent a stream of sparks extending for fully half a mile. A strong north east wind drove the flames with such rapidity that it was impossible for rescuers to evacuate all the building's contents before being forced to retreat.

A telegram was despatched to Ashford Town Brigade at about a quarter to seven, help was sought from Colonel Hardy and his Chilham Castle Brigade and the Charing Brigade was telegraphed. Unfortunately Charing thought the message was a hoax and did not respond. In desperation an appeal was sent to the South Eastern Works Brigade. A special train was provided and the fire-fighters steamed down the line to Wye. Those at the scene of the fire had to rely on water from wells and pumps in the immediate neighbourhood. It was hoped that the railwaymen's additional leather hose would enable them to draw water from the river but the hose was faulty, bursting continually, and they had to resort to filling tubs and tanks at the riverside and bringing them to the fire by means of horse-drawn water barrels.

The fire was not fully mastered until midnight but the Ashford engines remained to play water on the ruins all next day. A contemporary report said: 'A huge area of ground which had been covered by buildings for hundreds of years was nothing but a smouldering heap of debris.'

Using a special train for an emergency was not confined to the fire service. In 1859 Walter Godfrey who was working in the cast-iron foundry at the Works slipped into machinery he was using and several of his toes were crushed. An engine and carriage were immediately made available to take him to hospital at Canterbury.

Mid-century Miscellany

A remarkable enterprise was the formation by railwaymen of a co-operative to provide good cheap bread. William Winsford came to Ashford from London at the age of 16 on 2nd February 1847 to take up an appointment in the Works for the sum of ten shillings per week. Upon arrival he strolled up Marsh Street and looking into a shop at the corner, kept by a man named Sims, was surprised to see the price of bread. He became incensed at the price and at the injustice of the bakers of the town in keeping their prices high. Determined to remedy the situation and having spoken to others in the Works, a well attended meeting was held in the engine men's mess room. At this time Alfred New Town was yet to be built and there were very few shops in the old Town. Everyone was at the mercy of one or two bakers.

The men at the meeting agreed that they should try to meet the requirements of the large influx of families attracted by the new railway works and also the wants of the local working men of the town. A strong committee was formed, an announcement made in the local newspaper and the society given the name of Ashford Co-operative Society. Capital was raised by ten-shilling shares, paid in instalments of two shillings and sixpence. The first act of the new society was to engage in bulk buying and after gauging requirements placed an advertisement in the local papers seeking a supply of loaves totalling 2,500 gallons.

The society changed its name in 1854 to the Alfred Joint Stock Bread and Flour Company Limited and a shop possessing an oven was obtained in New Street near the British Volunteers public house. In addition to keeping the price of bread low a bonus was paid to customers. They were urged to let their bonuses accumulate and then purchase a share, thus becoming a member of the society and entitled to take part in its management. Such was its success, despite bad managers and financial difficulties during the early years, they purchased their own property in North Street, erecting a shop, a fully-fledged bake-house and stabling. Here were kept a number of horses used for hauling carts making door-to-door deliveries. It was justifiably claimed that no better bread was made in the town and because of its strength the society was able to rule the price of bread and flour.

Three noteworthy events occurred in 1855. Charles Dickens was a regular user of the South Eastern line, declaring it to be his favourite. An invitation was therefore despatched to him suggesting that instead of simply passing through, he might visit the town. And so on 27th March Charles Dickens set foot in Ashford, arriving with his close friend Wilkie Collins. He had previously written to a friend – 'The train (an express one) leaves London Bridge Station at half past eleven in the forenoon. Fire and comfort are ordered to be in readiness at the Inn at Ashford. We shall have to return at half past two in the morning, getting to town before five'.

A large part of the huge carriage trimming department was cleared and fitted up for an occasion which attracted leading townspeople as well as railwaymen and their families. The great man read his 'Christmas Carol', delighting the crowded and attentive audience with the vitality of his ready and extraordinary dramatic powers. They listened spellbound as the voice of Dickens spoke the words of Bob Cratchet, the ghost of Jacob Marley, Mr and Mrs Fezziwig and Ebenezer Scrooge, concluding with the immortal words of Tiny Tim 'God Bless us, every one'.

In May of the same year a great banquet was given at the Saracens Head Hotel to honour a leading townsman, Charles Mercer. The chairman referred to the construction of the South Eastern line of railway and the radical extension of Ashford's establishments which had transformed the town, originally one of the quietest and most rural in Kent into a place of busy mechanical occupation and much commercial importance. The town was considered to be one of the most improving in the county with new streets forming and house building in every available spot. The construction of Bank Street made possible the opening of fields which lay to the south of the town and a new cattle market was being laid out ready for opening the following year. To this was attached a railway siding which would enable farmers to bring their cattle to market without recourse to the roads.

On 14th July Ashford was the scene of a small publishing marvel when its own local newspaper appeared. Henry Igglesden, owner of a modest printing and stationery business, founded the first provincial paper in the United Kingdom to be published at one penny. Until this time all newspapers had been subject to a heavy stamp duty. Now Mr Gladstone proposed to abolish what he called this 'tax upon knowledge'. Henry Igglesden was in the gallery of the House of Commons when Gladstone's Bill was passed without opposition. He rushed from the House, reached Ashford after travelling all night and made arrangements for immediate production.

The new paper appeared under the title The Ashford and Alfred News and General Advertiser and declared its intention to be 'a paper of high literary character and moral tone, the cheapness of its price putting it within reach of every working man'. Thus the coming of the railway and the expansion of the town had been the augury of further great change.

In a dramatic postscript to the year there was considerable excitement at the New Town. Thomas Clark, an engine fitter, went into the bathhouse and slashed himself with a razor. Fortunately he was rushed to a surgeon in time and his life was saved. It seems that the young man had suffered a disappointment in love, being enamoured of a young lady in Brussels who would not leave her own country for his. Some months previously he had placed his head on the railway line when he heard a train coming and again was discovered before he had succeeded in his purpose. What became of this unhappy young man can only be left to speculation.

Benefit societies were a common feature of Victorian life but the South Eastern Company seems to have been laggardly because by 1856 it was the only railway company without one. This state of affairs changed with the appointment of Samuel Smiles as Company Secretary. Smiles had interested himself in the railway industry since his association with George and Robert Stephenson in 1840. He had built an enormous reputation with lectures and books presented under the title 'Self Help', in which he championed workmen's benefit societies and state education. He showed how many poor men had benefited from the opportunities of knowledge and culture, demonstrating his firm beliefs by giving examples of men who had achieved wonderful results by their own efforts.

There was therefore great anticipation at the Works when news was received that Smiles was to visit and talk to the men. At a crowded meeting held at Alfred New Town in February of that year Samuel Smiles told of the advantages of a benefit society which provided for maintenance in times of sickness, accident, old age and death. He proclaimed that 'it made a man thrifty, and prevented him having recourse to the cold hand of charity. It also entitled him to respect for guarding against the calamities of life, for it is a sad reproach to a parent, when children cried for help and he had none to give through his own neglect in not providing for a rainy day when in his power'.

'Many men in the employ of the company were earning more money than some of our lieutenants and assistant-surgeons who were now before Sebastopol, they therefore ought to be as respectable but the cause of many not being so was the different modes of education. Many would spend their money in a beer shop rather than place it in a savings bank – it was a lamentable thing, but it was a fact'.

He did not wish to deprive a man of his pipe or his beer but he would caution against excess, for persons connected with the railways could not be too cautious. Benefit societies were well calculated to improve the social condition of members and set a good example to other workmen. He felt justified in stating that if they founded a society the Directors would subscribe liberally.

The Vicar of Ashford, Reverend Alcock, spoke as to the general good character and moral conduct of the workmen in the employ of the South Eastern Railway Company. He was acquainted with many of them, whom he was pleased to say were often contributors to the Savings Bank, but he warned against the use of intoxicating liquors as even moderation might lead them to excess.

Inspired by the words of high moral endeavour the meeting agreed to form a Benefit Society in conjunction with the South Eastern Railway and thereupon appointed a committee. There was quite a stir later on that year when it was learned that Samuel Smiles was to pay a further visit. He appeared to have been so impressed with what he found at Ashford that he decided to come down again to make a presentation of books for the library of the Mechanics' Institute.

That summer the increasing population of the town produced a further beneficial effect when it was decided to revive the Ashford Races after a lapse of eight years. A band played through the town and 3,000 people turned out for the event in a field adjoining the Works. The refreshments, provided by Mr Coomber of South Willesborough's Albion Tavern were reported as 'giving the greatest satisfaction'.

The year was also marked by a celebration in which Ashford and the New Town combined to commemorate the end of the Crimean War and a dinner for the school children of the two districts was held in the High Street. The districts again combined to celebrate the marriage of the Prince of Wales in 1863 when they arranged an athletic sports day and firework display. A further blending of functions occurred with the commencement of an annual Musical and Horticultural Fete. This was held in the fields between the cattle market and the railway station. Both the Ashford and New Town bands played and an enthusiastic welcome was given to the Royal Marines Band from Chatham.

The works' excursion always provoked great discussion, the Institute's negotiations with the Directors meeting with varying degrees of success. In 1857 a free excursion was provided to the Crystal Palace – the Institute being allowed to charge sixpence for adults and threepence for children thus raising £45 5s. 6d. for funds. A similar request the next year for a trip to Boulogne was refused but it was agreed that there should be a trip to Brighton accompanied by a band.

Despite the lack of a railway connection, a return cricket match was arranged between the Ashford Works and the Tenterden Club in 1859 on a ground adjoining the Albion Tavern. The Works team lost by two runs which was attributed to the skilful bowling of their opponents although Ashford's fielding attracted great praise. With the advantage of fine weather up to two thousand people attended joining in other amusements such as quoits, leapfrog and running. Younger people engaged themselves with polkas and quadrilles accompanied by Mr Harrenden's brass band. The local newspaper had cause to complain on one matter – 'The only drawback to the day's enjoyment was the dissatisfaction which the bad character of the viands provided called forth'. It was suggested that the host 'who reaped a proud harvest' would find it to his advantage to provide better on future occasions.

Railways had transformed the illegal sport of bare-knuckle prize fighting. Instead of small groups making their way to an isolated spot, hundreds, sometimes thousands could now take advantage of special trains and enjoy the spectacle. Great secrecy surrounded arrangements for a fight, the word being spread quietly through the London Pubs. The South Eastern declared its innocence of making any arrangement for special trains but the trains continued to run and knowledge of a coming 'Mill' would spread among railwaymen. No doubt the prospect of witnessing a slogging match was sufficient temptation to absent oneself from work and Ashford's men had the opportunity on two occasions to watch the future champion and national hero Tom Sayer in action.

Towards the end of 1854 'The London Fancy' as the fighting fraternity called themselves, boarded a monster train of some thirty carriages fronted by two locomotives and headed down the line towards Ashford. That town was not their final destination however, and the train swung southwards towards the Romney Marsh finally slowing to a halt close by the village of Appledore.

The fight began with the desolate Marsh still in the grip of a hard frost. The icy roads caused many locals to miss the start but they were repaid by the long slog between Sayer and his Midlands rival Poulson. The enthusiastic crowd roared their support through round after round until finally Poulson leaving his head unguarded received a right to the jaw and was down and out.

The delighted railwaymen and other local spectators had to wait five years before they were privileged to watch Sayer again. The opportunity came in the spring of 1859. Two huge trains disembarked nearly 1,000 characters in the neighbourhood of Headcorn. The 'Fancy', which included 'sporting' types together with roughs and other doubtful-looking individuals anticipated a reward worth their trouble. A ring was formed in a grass enclosure and Tom Sayer and William Bainge (alias Benjamin) commenced their pugilistic struggle for the championship of the prize ring. Those opposed to prize fighting called the next twenty-two minutes 'a disgusting exhibition'. The sheer thuggery of the game was certainly on display. The first few rounds were fought at a fierce pace, an onlooker describing them 'Like two tornadoes tearing one against the other'. Round seven was decisive. Benjamin's nose received a bone breaker, Sayer in turn received a left hook closing up his right eye and was knocked all over the ring but feinting and ducking, waited for his opportunity. Seizing his chance Sayer crooked his arm around Benjamin's neck, pulled him forward so that he was off balance and so helpless and repeatedly smashed his fist into his face until it was a mass of blood. Then in a feat of strength he lifted him up and dashed him against a ring stake.

Even this was not enough to end the fight. Three more rounds followed with both fighters in a blood-bespattered state, striking each other with the most vicious blows, which left their features barely recognisable as human. The blinded Benjamin finally fell in the eleventh round.

Two other prize fighters then came forward for a fight which lasted an hour and thirty-five minutes at the end of which time one of them succumbed in a dreadful state from bruises and exhaustion. Preparations for a third contest were brought to a sudden halt by the arrival of Superintendent Dewer and a body of police from Ashford, their having come up to Headcorn by train.

The town's close connection with the railway was given civic recognition when a design by local surveyor Thomas Thurston was accepted to represent the Arms of Ashford. This was incorporated into a 'common seal', which was made necessary following the formation of a Local Board to govern the town in 1861. Although not authorised by the College of Heralds the design was accepted and used thereafter. The traditional white horse as ascribed to Hengist, the fess and annulets from the amorial bearings of Sir John Fogge and the locomotive, were felt to properly represent the Ashford of Saxon, medieval and modern times. The presence of a locomotive on a town's coat of arms is believed to be unique. Representation on the Board was evidently regarded as important by the Company. Richard Mansell was elected upon its formation, he was joined the following year by James Cudworth and in later years William Wainwright and the stationmaster, William Elgar, also served.

In addition to the usual excitements of the festive season it was the custom to hold a concert and ball at the railway works every year during the evening of Boxing Day, and 1863 was no exception. This involved tremendous preparation by helpers who gave their time freely for an occasion which provided much pleasure and raised money for two local charities who provided relief to working people in Ashford and the neighbouring villages.

The numbers attending were in excess of 2,000 in what was probably the largest workshop in the county, its floor occupying a space of half an acre. Everyone was struck by the brilliant illuminations and the extensive and elaborate scale of the decorations. The rows of pillars supporting the roof were closely twined with laurel and floral decorations. Wreaths of evergreens and festoons of bright-hued flowers crossed and re-crossed each other overhead, even the gas pipes were bound in red cloth. The walls were decorated in similar fashion to the pillars together with gay flags and mottoes, which were the work of New Town Girls School teachers and other ladies. Above the orchestra a very large and graceful display comprised the Prince of Wales feathers and the arms of Great Britain and Denmark together with flags of other nations and the Union Flag. This was fronted by a star of gas jets.

Such was the setting for what was one of the town's premier social occasions and favoured by the presence and patronage of many of the gentry of the district. In addition to this event which was looked forward to with great anticipation, all employees sat down to an annual dinner in the Works each January whilst the coachbuilders also held their own dinner in the old town at the Royal Oak.

The Election

Having affected so many aspects of life it is not surprising that railways played a role in the political life of the country. In Ashford political feeling always ran high with farmers supporting the Conservatives and the tradesmen of the town voting Liberal. The latter party gained strength with the support of the many north countrymen who had joined the staff at the railway works. On polling day free fights were in abundance when farmers brought their tenants in wagons to the polling station in the High Street Assembly Rooms. There was no secret ballot and a running total was announced each hour.

1868 was a year to be remembered. Sir Brook Bridges who had been returned as Conservative MP (for the East Kent Division) for the past eleven years had been elevated to the peerage. Henry Tufton for the Liberals was challenging Edward Leigh Pemberton for the seat. Polling day arrived and there was an intense excitement in the town such as had not been known for many years. Flags were flown, the streets became thronged with country and townsfolk wearing their party favours and windows in the High Street were filled with ladies watching the free show.

At ten o'clock a procession of Liberal voters entered the town from the parishes to the east of Ashford. They were led by a band, which played them up the street to the market place. About eleven o'clock two processions arrived from the opposite sides of Ashford each headed by a band. The Liberals paraded Sir Edward Dering MP and Henry Tufton with leading supporters while the Conservatives boasted Sir Edward Knatchbull, well supported by gentlemen, yeomanry and farmers on horseback.

It was at this point that the day's proceedings became unpleasant and remembered for many years to come. Unbeknown to the town, a Conservative supporter had paid a score of hefty pugilists a fee to come by rail from Chatham, allegedly to prevent local Liberals from voting. An onlooker described them as 'villainous looking rascals, apparently prize fighters or ruffians of a still worse description'. Wearing party favours they joined the Conservative procession and later took their stand outside the committee rooms opposite the Saracens Head. Conservatives defended their action. It was, they said, in response to a previous election incident when Sir Norton Knatchbull's coachman was set upon and three of his teeth knocked out by a gang of assailants.

By the middle of the afternoon, Ashford's railwaymen, infuriated by the roughs, were engaged in a free fight. A large force of police were present to keep the peace but the prize-fighters received such a drubbing that it was they who became in need of police protection. A water cart was brought in to clear a way to the polling station and the prize fighters took the opportunity to try to escape but they were spotted and the railwaymen supported by a large crowd went in hot pursuit.

The prize-fighters first attempted to take refuge in the Saracens Head Tap but the door was closed against them. While they were frantically trying to force it open the furious crowd were upon them and another fierce fight broke out with bloody faces and bruises resulting on both sides. Again the strong force of police were needed to restore order and after some further scuffling, booing and hooting the ruffians got away to the Somerset Arms where they obtained shelter.

The streets continued to the be the scene of turmoil and excitement with many engaging in the pastime then prevalent of pelting the 'other side' with eggs. It became known the prize-fighters had left their shelter and so a search got under way at the Saracens Head stables and other places, with the crowd of Ashfordians eager to inflict further punishment. Many ran down to the railway station to waylay them on their departure. Again the police intervened and the ruffians were taken in a large van under heavy escort back to their train but not without another rough struggle in the station yard.

Shortly afterwards the Ashford result was declared with the other county figures and it became clear that the Conservatives had held their East Kent seat.

Tufton, defeated but defiant, arrived at the railway station that evening about eight o'clock to an enthusiastic reception. The horses were removed from his carriage and it was drawn to the Saracens Head by his supporters, whom he then addressed from the balcony. Later that evening an effigy of Pemberton was burnt in front of the house of the Conservative agent William Burra and a number of fights took place in different parts of the town but it was not until a very late hour that the town returned to peace.

If this were not enough excitement for one year, within six months a general election was called and Pemberton and Tufton clashed again. A

Conservative meeting was called for eight o'clock on Tuesday 27th October to take place in the new Corn Exchange. A huge crowd of at least 2,000, including large numbers of railwaymen, collected outside to await the opening of the doors. It quickly became evident that there was still much ill feeling concerning the introduction of prize-fighters to the town at the previous election.

With the doors open at last the crowd, surging and swaying, entered the hall carrying all before them. Trouble started at once which led a new local newspaper, the Ashford Guardian, to headline its report 'Disgraceful Riot at the Ashford Corn Exchange' and alleging that it was 'one of the most disgraceful election riots which have occurred for a long time in any part of the country'. With the hall densely packed trouble started at once with a scene of noise, disorder and confusion that was absolutely indescribable.

Uproar greeted the appearance of the chairman Sir Edward Knatchbull. His attempts to speak were greeted with hisses, catcalls and continual noise. He called for fair play but his words were lost in the din. Pemberton then tried to speak but the disorderly chorus of shouts and noises of all kinds made it impossible for one word to be heard. He was met with cries of 'Put him out', 'Where are the Chatham bull dogs?' and a shower of rotten potatoes, pieces of chewed tobacco and other abominable missiles. Much in evidence at this point was a prominent local railway official.

Noise mounted to a crescendo when the speaker claimed – 'You may depend upon this, that the Conservatives are the real and true friends of the working classes'. Laughter, shouting and booing lasted for several minutes accompanied by shouts of 'Tufton for ever' and 'Three cheers for Gladstone'. The Conservative agent tried his hand but to no avail. 'Men of Ashford' he cried 'is this what you call fair play?' but his words were drowned by cries of 'Get down', 'Where's your fighting bullies?' and another shower of acorns, rotten eggs and potatoes. Burra declared 'If you call this the fair play of Ashford I think it is a disgraceful town'. A voice 'Did you call it fair play to bring your roughs down here?'

Renewed uproar swept the hall when the next speaker revealed himself to be an engine-smith from Faversham, working for the London, Chatham and Dover Railway. This was too much for an already over-heated audience. Why the Conservatives should have brought a speaker from the much-hated 'Chatham' railway to a South Eastern Railway town is something of a mystery.

Speakers continued to attempt to address the meeting but it was hopeless. The turmoil at this time was beyond description with hundreds of people all shouting at once and the platform party in a state of complete disorganisation, walking about the stage and gesticulating at the crowd. A Colonel Groves attempted to speak but was shouted down. Sir Edward Knatchbull again tried his luck but failed, Pemberton tried to present his case but with constant barracking retired amidst a din of groans and yelling. The Honourable George Milles made an attempt to speak but it was impossible.

William Burra again came forward and declared that the meeting was a discredit to the town of Ashford. This resulted in ominous signs of movement by the crowd in front of the platform. At once the gas was lowered and the platform party rushed for the exit pursued by the crowd who laughing and shouting surged out behind them.

As a consequence of the disturbances in the town caused by the importation of the prize-fighters and because feeling was still running high there was a large augmentation of police on polling day. One hundred constables, eight sergeants and three superintendents were on hand. Sure enough during the morning a train arrived from Canterbury containing fifty roughs who had come to 'help' the Conservative cause. They were immediate apprehended by the police, taken to a public house where they were locked up and later sent packing on the afternoon train.

The election result announced later that day showed that Tufton had swept Ashford Town with 217 votes to Pemberton's 79 but when the votes from the other East Kent districts were in, Pemberton was in too.

Tribulations and Expansion

By 1871 the locomotive repair shops had grown by some 50% and a second engine shed had been added to the west of the main range. The addition of 13 bays to the locomotive shop matched the design of the original arcades while the detail of the new engine shed echoed that of the original 1850 carriage works. In addition a new carriage works was erected near the main gate. The building, of yellow brick with its round-headed windows, double pitched roof, cast iron columns and timber trusses with queen posts, is today one of the least altered structurally of all the buildings in the Works.

The Ordnance Survey map of 1871, the work of Captain H.S.Palmer of the Royal Engineers, shows that by this time Ashford had developed three thriving railway communities. The oldest was New Town with all houses owned by the South Eastern Company exclusively for its workers and comprising some 150 properties with a population of 1,000. Adjacent was the settlement of South Willesborough. Here were opportunities for artisans to own their own homes and an early feature of the village was the provision of large garden areas attached to many of the 140 houses which had been built during the previous 20 years. An entirely different character was stamped on the third community at South Ashford. Over 300 mostly terraced cottages had been packed into a very compact area by local builders working on behalf of private landlords. Small by any standard, most gardens were but narrow strips and with communal rear ways there was little privacy to be enjoyed.

The likely hazard of building on land known as the Ashford Marshes was shown all too clearly in October 1865 when atrocious weather conditions hit the district. It had been raining continuously for two weeks but during the final three days the downpour was tremendous. During Tuesday 29th the river finally burst its banks and the low lying area of South Ashford was flooded. Houses in Goldmead Street and Rugby Road were inundated, the water filling the ground floors to a depth of two or three feet. The railway families beat a hasty retreat with their furniture to their upper floors. One railwayman in Goldmead Street had to remove his pigs from the garden and take them into his bedroom to save them from drowning.

That night the water rose still higher and by Wednesday morning the Beaver fields and those between South Ashford and the Railway Station resembled a vast lake, with patches of high land standing out here and there. Beaver Road was flooded but an entrepreneur provided a horse and cart, which conveyed passengers through the water for a small charge. That this was not the first time that an inundation had affected the district was revealed by a report to the local Board referring to similar floods in both 1847 and 1857.

The experience so alarmed tenants in Goldmead Street and Rugby Road that by the end of the week there were signs of a general exodus, so alarming the landlord that he sought to persuade tenants to remain with the offer of a month's free rent and four hundredweight of coal. These two streets remained particularly vulnerable to flooding until well into the next century when their condition had become such that they were demolished.

An interesting story of these times concerns the local Mather family. William Mather, who was born in Newcastle, came to Ashford in 1848 with his wife Elizabeth and two year old daughter Jane. Records in the Railway Works wages books show him employed as a fitter from 10th July that year and as a patternmaker when he retired aged 70 on 31st December 1892. During this entire period his pay remained exactly the same.

In 1859 building had commenced in Beaver Road and William Mather's family moved into one of the first four cottages to be completed. As the first tenant he thus became the pioneer of the district known as South Ashford. Shortly afterwards he built himself a house in Torrington Road for his enlarged family which now included three young sons – William, George and John. His new house also provided a home for his retired father, who being a widower had come down from Northumberland having previously followed the trade of millwright and patternmaker.

In the mid 1860s young George joined his father in the Works as an apprentice patternmaker and foundryman. He continued in the Foundry for the next twenty years before being offered the appointment of foreman in the foundry and ironworks in St. John's Lane. In 1889 its owner, John Udall Bugler, put the business up for sale and John Mather, seizing his opportunity, became the new owner.

That George was able to put his railway training and experience to good use was shown five years later when he was awarded a Certificate of Merit for engine castings. Laudatory comment at the time referred to 'his careful competent hands which had gained a sterling reputation for high class work to the entire satisfaction of engineers, mill owners, agriculturists and builders.'

This remarkable family record was to continue through the generations, passing from George to his son Douglas, who moved the foundry to a site near the railway off Godinton Road, to his grandson, James, and finally in the 1990s to his great grandson Douglas.

The need for an additional parish church to provide for the increased population had been acknowledged for many years. South of the railway a community of more than 2,000 had sprung up on the open fields between the town and the hamlet of Beaver. The boys' schoolroom at New Town where morning service was held every Sunday was no longer adequate. In 1861, George Jemmett, Lord of the Manor, provided a site in Beaver Road and a committee of eminent persons launched a financial appeal. Over 4,000 appeal letters were dispatched, every shareholder of the South Eastern Railway Company was approached and the sum of £2,900 was raised.

Designed by H. J. Austin of Bayswater and erected by local builders Steddy, Joy and Steddy, the church opened for divine service on May 1st, 1867.

In his appeal letter the Reverend Alcock, said 'We are all willing to acknowledge the convenience and comfort of railways and that there is no class of men on whom we are more dependent than those who labour in providing those comforts and conveniences for us. We are all ready to confess that it is our Christian duty to promote their spiritual welfare. I earnestly ask for your kind help in such a duty.'

The main work of construction having been completed, local railwaymen were active in beautifying the church of which they were so proud. A clergyman wrote – 'Few churches in the English Communion could point to such beautiful and withal artistic painting and decoration and be able to say " this adornment is the handiwork of the men of our congregation, who after a day of labour and toil have spent their evenings in the church beautifying the Sanctuary." This we can say at Ashford.'

A few years later a large and handsome building was erected next to the church for the use of the clergyman in charge. A stone erected at the front entrance of the house reads – 'This house is a gift of Marsh Pierson Piety of the S.E.R. Works, to be for all time occupied by the clergy for the time being serving in the district of South Ashford and conducting services in Christ Church.' A unique gift from a working man.

Emigration to America continued to be an attraction for many during the nineteenth century. John Wheatley, a hard working man at the Ashford Works for upwards of twenty-one years, received the good wishes of over one hundred workmates at the Denmark Arms in South Ashford, prior to his leaving the town for the States. Having been presented with an elegant writing desk in recognition of his service as Secretary of the Locomotive Friendly Society, ernest wishes were expressed for his safe voyage across the Atlantic.

Emigration did not always result in a happy outcome. Robert Bennett, son of the Locomotive Department's chief foremen, left his job at the Works for a lucrative appointment as foreman of the Great Southern Railway of India. Six months after arriving in that country he became ill and had to undergo an operation, following which he died. His wife and child followed out on a later boat but having reached India found that he was dead and had been buried.

The casualness with which many treated railways was again demonstrated by the action of a young man who lost his life whilst attempting to board a passing goods train at Ashford Station. The engine driver, James Rand, who lived at 76 New Town, described how the deceased jumped at the engine simply in order to ride the short distance of 300 yards between the station and his home at Hempsted Terrace. Misjudging his leap he fell between the platform and the tender of the engine following which his body was completely severed as the wheels of twenty-one goods trucks passed over him. His melancholy death inspired a sermon from a local parson the following Sunday drawn from the Book of Samuel: 'There is but a step between me and death.'

 News of a shocking murder gripped the district in June 1872 when the body of a 51 year old woman was found in a barley field at Bybrook. The husband, Thomas Moore, who had been employed at the Railway Works was arrested. It seems he was separated from his wife but following a casual meeting on that fateful day had attacked and strangled her. Evidence was given that she had suffered his ill treatment in the past. At first Moore denied all knowledge of the crime, unsurprising since he had a most unfortunate reputation as a notorious liar, both in the Works and among his acquaintances. Later, realising the weakness of his defence, he made a full confession. Rumour swept the town that Moore had been responsible for the murder of a young woman at New Town some years previously but Moore denied most strenuously he had been responsible.

On 13th August Moore was privately hanged at Maidstone Jail. Public hangings were no longer allowed, denying the public an 'entertainment' that had previously drawn huge crowds. In the execution yard the hangman grasped Moore's hand in a final farewell, his limbs were tightly bound and a white hood drawn over his head. The hangman sprang the trap-door and Moore 'fell without a quiver.'

Cudworth Departs

In August 1876 Cudworth resigned from his position with the South Eastern. The circumstances surrounding his leaving are illustrative not only of his Quaker patience in the face of adversity but also yet another revelation of the abrasive and bullying character of Sir Edward Watkin, the then Chairman, of whom it was said – 'Everywhere he went controversy and acrimony reigned, fuelled by a blunt and aggressive personality which was intolerant of criticism'.

In order to cope with faster schedules and heavier six-wheeled carriages Watkin wanted new and more powerful locomotives. Cudworth believed he could improve still further on the capability of his 2-2-2 Mails and would not be moved from his belief. After a chaotic 1875 summer season and without giving warning to Cudworth, Watkin invited John Ramsbottom, formerly of the London and North Western, to report on both the locomotive department and the line and present a written report within 15 days.

In the event Ramsbottom praised Cudworth's management observing that – 'I was received courteously by Mr. Cudworth at London Bridge on 2nd October and with him I visited Bricklayers Arms shed before taking a fast train to Tonbridge where the goods yards and installations were inspected before continuing to Ashford Works via Hastings. The return to London was by boat train from Dover Pier. All trains ran to schedule and I was greatly impressed by the mechanical order and cleanliness of all the engines and carriages observed as well as the manner of the various grades of railwaymen. The Works at Ashford were well organised and equipped.' Nevertheless he recommended more powerful engines and in due course Cudworth was ordered to seek outside tenders for 20 new locomotives.

Cudworth's position was further undermined with the appointment by Sir Edward of his son Alfred as Traffic Superintendent. At the Board meeting of 3rd August 1876 Sir Charles Whetham complained that Alfred Watkin already held an appointment with another railway company and that this situation did not accord with Company rules. He also complained that Cudworth, who had for so long been a valuable officer of the Company, should be placed in a subordinate position to a young man who, whatever his ability, had not the experience. Furthermore, on occasions when Royalty travelled on the line, Mr. Watkin would then have his name before the public and receive any presents which might be given.

To this Sir Edward replied – 'I had a great respect for Mr. Cudworth but I saw clearly that if you were to have safety and efficiency you must have some younger man with more zeal and energy.'

It was in consequence of those remarks that James Cudworth resigned. The Railway News remarked 'They were of such a character that, in the absence of a complete retraction, Mr. Cudworth could not with due regard to his self-respect continue to occupy his position.'

During the November Board meeting at London Bridge Station Cudworth was presented with a magnificent silver tea and coffee service which was inscribed – 'Presented by the Chairman, Deputy Chairman and Directors of the South Eastern Railway Company to James l'Anson Cudworth Esq. as a token of their regard and esteem on his resignation of the office of Locomotive Engineer which he had held for a period of 31 years.' It must have been with tongue in cheek that Watkin expressed his 'great regret at the severance of a connection which had been so long and honourably maintained' adding that he had much pleasure in testifying to Mr. Cudworth's eminent and valuable services.

The dismay of the staff at the prospect of Cudworth's departure was demonstrated by the large sum that was raised towards a testimonial, which included a gold watch and other valuable articles. In response, Cudworth, in token of remembrance of the good feelings which had existed between the employees and himself since the establishment of the Locomotive Works, offered to the S.E.R. Mechanics Institute his 75 shares in the Ashford Swimming Bath Company.

The sadness that was felt at Cudworth's going can only be imagined. He had been a foundation stone and inspiration for so long that any idea of change seemed unthinkable. His many talents had not been confined to the Works. Since 1864 he had been an elected member of the Local Board and from 1872 to 1874 served as its Chairman. He had arrived in Ashford a bachelor, had married a young Dover lady, and set up home at No 1 Barrow Hill Place. His only child was the railway. Now with the heartfelt good wishes of the Local Board, the Works and the townspeople, James Cudworth and his wife departed to a retirement at Reigate where they would live quietly together for the next twenty-two years. The 240 locomotives he had designed whilst at Ashford were his true memorial.

Braking systems were still very rudimentary and so prior to his departure Cudworth had sought ways to employ continuous brakes on passenger trains. In the late summer of 1874 trials had been carried out between Ashford and London testing the vacuum brake system. The trial's success resulted in Cudworth being instructed to fit the new brakes to the Folkestone Tidal express and the greater safety and speed that resulted led to all prestige expresses being similarly equipped. It was to the Directors' credit that putting safety before cash, they extended the system to the suburban services as well.

In 1877 the Board of Trade demanded that all major railways provide details of their braking systems which were often still of the hand or chain variety. The South Eastern was able to primly reply 'All the Company's important expresses are equipped with Smith's vacuum brake which has proved efficient, reliable and inexpensive.'

The Board of Trade preferred the fully automatic brake because this applied itself if by chance the train divided, although it was more expensive to fit and maintain. Ten years later the foreman of the erecting shop at Ashford devised an inexpensive and mechanically simple solution, which enabled the engine's automatic vacuum equipment to operate the brakes of carriages thus solving the problem.

With Cudworth gone, Alfred Watkin promptly filled his chair but not for long. During the following summer he was elected Member of Parliament for Great Grimsby. Such a public defiance of Company rules could not be accepted and in the subsequent uproar he was forced to resign, only ten months after his appointment. At the time of Cudworth's leaving, three 0-6-0 tank engines were under construction at Ashford. Intended for the Folkestone Harbour branch, they pursued their unassuming tasks for fifteen years, one ended up supplying steam for the Works' steam hammer.

Meanwhile Richard Mansell, who had been promoted to the position of locomotive engineer, asked for nine new engines to replace a similar number of worn out locomotives. Known as the Mansell 'Gunboats' these 0-4-4 tanks performed well on their north and mid-Kent passenger services.

Finally Richard Mansell ordered three 0-6-0 tanks, designated '59s' for working goods traffic from Redhill to London. Twenty years later two finished up at Ashford on ballasting and similar light duties.

Chapter Three

THE STIRLING ERA

*He thought in all his thirty years of service it was strange
His wages never were increased. 'Twas time to make a change,
He meant to try another calling earlier or later,
So went at once to Spiers and Pond who turned him to a waiter!*
                                                    Victorian Music Hall Song

1878 saw the arrival of the South Eastern's new chief engineer who would preside at Ashford for the next twenty years. James Stirling, a truly dour Scotsman and son of an Ayrshire rector, had spent most of his working life in railway service, most latterly as locomotive superintendent of the Glasgow and South Western Railway. As a result of the influence of his railway engineer brother Patrick, he brought to his new post what have been described as his family heirlooms – the domeless boiler and the Stirling cab. The cab was a much welcomed innovation providing a weather protection for engine crews that had been noticeably absent. The very hardiness of the South Eastern's footplatemen can be appreciated when it is realised that in spite of increasing speeds of locomotives, most had no protection other than a small windshield.

Despite Stirling's stern ways he soon came to be admired by his staff although it was said that 'He was a man who saw no necessity for the outer world to be notified of what was going on within the confines of his Works and he paid his small son pocket money to look for news items in any technical journal naming Ashford, in order that he might call down fire and slaughter upon the heads of the offending editors'.

He at once reviewed the South Eastern's locomotive stock and deciding on a policy of standardisation, introduced only six classes of engines, four of which had interchangeable boilers. In appearance they reflected their designer's character, being described as 'austere, gaunt and functional'.

Deciding that the most urgent need was for an engine capable of hauling secondary passenger, excursion and goods traffic, Stirling introduced his 'O' class 0-6-0. For reasons of urgency the first batches were ordered in from outside sources, but within four years Ashford was entrusted with their production, building 87 of the 122 that came into service. The engines, with their simple robust design and free-steaming boilers, found favour with running shed staff and footplatemen alike. The latter also appreciated the Stirling-designed steam-operated reverser, which replaced a much-maligned hand-worked appliance used previously.

Meanwhile and ironically, the supposedly more powerful locomotives introduced by Ramsbottom, known as 'Ironclads', were unsuccessful compared with Cudworth's 'Mails' and had been downgraded to semi-fast services. In order to reinforce this class Stirling introduced his 4-4-0 'A's which were judged creditable though not outstanding. He had hoped they might provide some improvement for main line services but their indifferent performance, particularly between Tonbridge and Ashford where maximum speed was required, resulted in Cudworth's 'Mails' being recalled for these prestige duties. The class of twelve were all built at Ashford and were significant in being the first engines on the South Eastern to feature a leading bogie.

Although tank engines had not previously been much in evidence on South Eastern rails, Stirling identified a need for such engines on the by now extensive London Suburban services. The result was the 'Q' class 0-4-4s and of the 118 built, Ashford Works produced 48

Given their lively acceleration and steady riding they were well appreciated by their footplatemen.

Rival Line

By the early 1880s the picture of Ashford as a town loyal only to the South Eastern Railway had begun to change. Consternation swept the district when it was rumoured that the entire locomotive and carriage works were to be closed and moved elsewhere. Rumour followed upon rumour. They were to be moved to Blackfriars – they were to be moved to Grove Park, some held quite definitely that the new site would be Sevenoaks.

In the midst of this worry and uncertainty building in the town came to a virtual standstill and trade began to fall off. The railway works had transformed the character of Ashford, giving it the largest industrial element in east Kent. Its population had swollen, new suburbs had been erected to house the skilled artisans, and the township community of New Town was something unique to south-eastern England. It would be no exaggeration to say that the loss of the 'Works' would have left Ashford a ghost town.

These fears later received confirmation when Sir Edward Watkin, addressing a House of Commons committee, agreed that the board had the matter of removal under consideration. Although the plans were to come to nought it is little wonder that many looked to their new friends in the form of the London, Chatham and Dover Railway, who were building a new line from Maidstone to Ashford.

James Bugler, chairman of the local board, openly hoped the new railway would 'alter the present state of affairs and help to bring resuscitation to the town'. He also hoped that 'They would be able to get their goods conveyed much cheaper than they had been able to do hitherto'.

Nor was he alone in making known his views. The local newspaper, the Kentish Express and Ashford News, said that Ashford might well feel proud of the coming of the new line 'placing Ashford in direct communication with the county town, opening up a most beautiful and fruitful agricultural district and stimulating the prosperity of both centres'.

Public services on the new line commenced on Tuesday July 1st, 1884. The local newspaper lamented: 'No salvos of guns or strains of music or chiming bells or applauding shouts greeted its opening'. During the morning the first train made its appearance and Ashford was introduced to a new railway livery – black locomotives and teak coloured wooden carriages. This first train, drawn by four heavy engines, had made slow progress from Maidstone, its primary task being to provide a final test for the bridges by having the weight of four engines upon them.

The new station, to be called Ashford West, was approached from Chart Terrace (now a part of Godinton Road) and overlooked a wide station yard. It was a spacious and handsome affair with an ornamental shelter at its front. The platforms were long and covered with glass roofs supported by two rows of ornamental pillars. The original idea had been to enclose the entire station with a glass canopy but this idea was abandoned. One feature about which the locals seem to have been particularly proud was the provision of a gentleman's toilet, which, it was claimed, was the only one to exist at an inland local railway station in the entire country. The lavatories were lined with glazed brick, a novelty in this part of England.

An engine shed spread along the entire length of the platform on the north side and there was a large goods shed situated at its west end. On the south side were several coal depots and four sets of rails, one running into the cattle market. It was announced that six locomotives were to be based at Ashford and that the terminus would be supported by a staff of fifty. The LC&DR immediately showed that it meant business. The third class fare to London was to be seven shillings and fourpence, undercutting the South Eastern's charge of eight shillings and sixpence and excursions to the Crystal Palace were to cost only four shillings, this to include admission.

Such an event could not pass without being properly marked and so a month later official celebrations were held. The new station was decorated with flowers, plants, evergreens and bunting. The main streets of the town were alive with flags strung across the thoroughfares. A 'Festival Field' at the western end of the town offered all kinds of sporting activities and entertainments. During the two previous weeks the district had enjoyed balmy weather with warm nights and hot sunny days. Temperatures had continued to soar and this 'day of days' was a real scorcher.

At three o'clock the Ashford Rifle Band played through the town whilst the Ashford Drum and Fife Band led the way to the field. Here there was high excitement and the numbers of people so great that many shrieking and fainting females had their dresses torn in the crush. Celebrations were not confined to local inhabitants. The railway laid on excursion trains from Swanley Junction calling at every town and village along the line and charging only a single fare for the return journey.

Promptly at 5pm a special train arrived carrying distinguished guests, its locomotive decorated with a profuse display of gorgeous roses. This first-class express had journeyed from London and covered the new line from Maidstone to Ashford in 28 minutes allowing a single stop at Lenham. In Ashford the guests were received on the platform of the new station by James Bugler, Chairman of the Local Board. This was a cherished moment for the 'Chathams' Chairman, James Forbes. After years of battling with Sir Edward Watkin, he was arriving in the very heartland of his rival's territory, Ashford being the South Eastern's holy of holies. If that was a surprising event, even more surprising was the welcome that he and his company were receiving. There must have been a taste of bitter aloes in Watkin's mouth that day.

The New Ashford

For the first 42 years of the nineteenth century, life in Ashford had meandered along. The second 42 years had seen dramatic change, with the population soaring to 10,000. The town now boasted an impressive range of religious, educational, commercial, industrial and social facilities. Residential development in the form of high-class villas and smaller houses was spreading across the fields and a fine, broad, tree-lined thoroughfare linked the railway station and the town.

Where once Ashford's High Street had contained many private residences, commercial activity now predominated. Instead of a few higgledy-piggledy shops with small windows and mean little doorways, fine shop fronts, often replete with lanterns, welcomed the public. Grocers, cheesemongers, bakers, tea merchants, drapers, furnishers, stationers, ironmongers, leather merchants and bazaars for glass and china all competed for the increased trade.

Many of the traders enjoyed Warrants of Appointment to their Royal Highnesses the Duke and Duchess of Edinburgh. The Duke had leased

Eastwell Park following his marriage to the Imperial Grand Duchess Marie Alexandrovna, daughter of the Czar of Russia. Their decision caused a frisson of excitement to run through the inhabitants of the town, which was well rewarded by the continual arrival of aristocratic visitors. The Prince and Princess of Wales were frequent visitors, travelling down from London in a saloon carriage attached to an express train, and on to Eastwell by carriage and pair. With the country house party such a feature in Victorian times there was a constant parade of British and foreign royalty between the railway station and Eastwell, together with all manner of Earls, Viscounts, Marquesses, Admirals and Captains and their ladies, giving sightseers many an opportunity to provide a cheering audience.

The increased movement of goods and people brought about by the railway resulted in a great increase of horse-drawn traffic. Twenty carriers now operated between the town and the surrounding villages and in addition there were a number of omnibuses, one of which met every train in order to convey passengers and their luggage to the High Street.

Regular and speedy railway services enabled the Royal Mail to provide a quite exceptional service. Letters and parcels were delivered in the town at 7.55am, 10.15am, 2.45pm and 6.45pm. Mail was despatched at set times between 7.55am and 10.45pm. In addition there was a box for late mail on the railway station platform, which was cleared before each train departure.

An elegant building housed the new General Post Office in Bank Street and railwaymen benefited from a Money Order, Telegraph Office and Savings Bank at New Town.

Many manufacturing enterprises were also contributing to Ashford's wealth. One of the most conspicuous landmarks was provided by the Lion Brewery in Dover Place, whose speciality was their pale and bitter ale. Owners Chapman & Company possessed a fine stud of horses and their 'Lion' drays and vans were a feature of the district's roads. The Ashford 'Original Brewery' operated from its malthouse in Brewer Street, while Lyle Mineral Water Manufactory flourished in New Street, producing hundreds of dozens of bottles each day.

With such hot and heavy work it is little wonder that inns and taverns serving Ashford's railwaymen flourished. The Alfred Arms was the only public house at New Town and its landlord clearly prospered because later on he opened the Victoria Hotel opposite the railway station in competition with the Kent Arms on the opposite side of the bridge. This, together with the Market Hotel and the Fernley Temperance added to the town's establishments catering for private and commercial travellers.

The railway community at South Willesborough could boast an ancient Inn in the form of the Albion which dated back to the days of the Aylesford Green hamlet and two new licensed houses, the Bricklayers Arms and the Crown and Anchor. The Beaver Inn had previously been the only hostelry south of the town serving the tiny hamlet of Beaver. Now it was joined by others serving the railwaymen's suburb around Christchurch: the Locomotive, South Eastern Tavern, The Foresters Arms, Denmark Arms and John Elgar's beer house on Beaver Road. His was another success story as he later moved to the Fountain Inn on the High Street. Should anyone manage to pass any of these on their way home, there was always the Railway Light and the Royal Oak Tap in Marsh Street in addition to a profusion of other pubs and beer houses in the rest of the town.

Compared with pre-railway days the town was abuzz with trade and industry. Three iron and brass foundries competed for trade. Hill and Sons' Bewdley Works were to be found in New Street and Frederick Clarke's Elwick Ironworks operated next to the Market but the largest was that of James Bugler in St. John's Lane, shortly to pass to the ownership of former railway foundryman George Mather. There were a number of small carriage works and pre-eminent among these was that of J.D.Skinner in Marsh Street, which provided a superb range of hand-built carriages, pony traps, vans and dogcarts.

William Leeson, 'one of the best shots in the country', had a gun manufacturing business which enjoyed the patronage of HRH the Duke of Edinburgh. John Broad had a candle factory producing huge quantities of wax candles in addition to soap-making, creating the most atrocious smells on a Friday when tallow was being melted, to the great distress of the inhabitants. Ashford's famous oak-bark tannery lay alongside the river, another producer of unpleasant odour. With a history going back for over two hundred years its nineteenth century owners, Greenhill and Dorman, maintained a reputation for producing large quantities of tough high quality leather. The town's newspaper was well established and continued to flourish but now faced competition from a newcomer, the Kent Examiner and Ashford Chronicle, launched by two local businessmen, Herbert and Burgess Headley, from their High Street printing works.

The growth of the town gave rise to a rapidly expanding building trade providing opportunities for individuals offering their services as painters, sign writers, guilders, paperhangers, plumbers and roofers. Harry Knock in New Street and George Davis in Godinton Road were leading builders, both with steam sawing and joinery works. Expansion was set to continue. Within a few years, Henry Pledge built a huge steam mill on the Railway Company's land near the station for his flour milling business. Francis Heathfield specialised in farm waggons at his new 'Gold Medal Waggon, Van and Cart Works' in Godinton Road from which he was destined to produce thousands of vehicles. A railwayman who made good was Charles Hayward who, having previously been a turner in the Works, opened a business in New Street making bicycles. Borrowing the South Eastern Railway Motto, he christened his enterprise 'the "Onward" Cycle Works'.

To accommodate the growing needs of families, additional schools were built. A new grammar school opened in Hythe Road, a local authority run 'Board School' was built nearby the railway station, and a large, new 'British School' was provided in West Street, primarily for non-conformists. Churches too had increased. Over the previous fifteen years no fewer than nine new buildings had been erected, many for the non-conformist persuasion.

Leading townsmen had been active in promoting the provision of hospitals, the earliest being the isolation hospital near the Warren in 1860. Ten years later, public minded subscribers were able to fund a fourteen-bed cottage hospital in Station Road, but within a few years, thanks to the generosity of William Pomfret Burra, a much larger and most picturesque cottage hospital opened in Wellesley Road.

The town was well endowed with social facilities and offered the Temperance Institute, YMCA, Benevolent Society, Mechanics' Institute, Conservative Club, Liberal Club, Choral and Orchestral Society, and three bands, including the railwaymen's New Town Brass Band. For the academically minded lectures were offered at the High Street Assembly Room on both scientific and popular subjects.

Ashford was responsible for raising 'F' Troop of the East Kent Yeomanry and 'H' Company of the East Kent Volunteers. It is related that the first drills of 'H' Company were held in the Railway Station Yard and the men, being so keen, could be seen morning after morning practising military movements as early as six o'clock. Dressed in a uniform of dark green, in contrast to the grey of other units, they were known as the 'Devil's Own' and glorified in being the crack company of the battalion.

Apart from the shops, an interesting trading feature at New Town were the stalls set up outside the main gate of the Works every Friday evening – this being 'Pay Night'. One stall sold fresh fish, another fruit and yet another hot faggots and gravy. This last was a great favourite, selling at three pence per head. A popular character was 'Bricky' Pope, whose stall in season was piled high with fresh herrings at one penny each. During the summer months another trader trundled his hand-cart around New Town offering ice-cream at one half-penny per cup with a single wafer.

The sporting enthusiasm of the railwaymen led to the forming of the first senior football team in Ashford. Appropriately named the South Eastern Rangers, its beginning dated from the period following the arrival of James Stirling and a number of Scottish families. Matches were played on the well-groomed Green at New Town and shared according to season with the Works cricketers, both teams using the Alfred Arms as dressing rooms.

A rival team was that of the Kentish Express Football Club but in the summer of 1891 the two clubs amalgamated and became Ashford United, with a ground behind the Victoria Hotel in Beaver Road. 700 people were present for the new club's first game against a strong Highland Light Infantry side when the Ashford men were beaten 5-1. That the result was not received in a sportsmanlike manner is shown by a newspaper report, which deprecated the 'insulting remarks passed by the onlookers to one or two of the players who were off colour'.

The high point of the club's history came on April 9th 1893 when they met Chatham in the final of the Kent Cup. Despite the unfairness of a decision that the match be played on the Chathams' ground, a number of supporters set out for the scene of combat, detraining at Maidstone and then facing 'a dusty six mile drive'. With Ashford winning 2-1, surprise and astonishment was expressed the length and breadth of the County. Commenting upon the unexpected result, the Kentish Express sports writer referred to the 'plucky railway lads' adding 'Happy Ashford! Well may you be proud of your success. I heartily congratulate you'.

Scenes of immense enthusiasm prevailed at Ashford when news of United's victory reached the town by telegram. Called to his duty, the Town Crier paraded the streets proclaiming the good news, causing an immense crowd to gather at the London, Chatham and Dover Railway Station to welcome the team home. The players were carried shoulder-high to a four-in-hand and then to the stirring strains of a brass band the triumphal procession wound its way through the principal streets of the town with the trophy being exhibited en route. Coloured lights were burned, and in the High Street Dr. Coke, the club's President made a congratulatory speech and later entertained the team to a champagne supper at the Victoria Hotel. It was a matter of great satisfaction that with one or two exceptions every member of the Ashford team had learnt the rudiments of the game in the railway town.

The club's next home was an enclosed ground at Godinton Road just beyond the railway bridge. This boasted a spacious timber-built stand with dressing rooms beneath. Its great drawback was its inaccessibility, the only conveyances available being the old 'Pride of Ashford' horse bus and various other wagonettes which ran on match days from the New Town and other outlying districts.

Heavy debts caused the club to close in 1907 but hard on the heels of this misfortune and with the support of the Railway Company, a new club, 'Ashford Railway Works', was formed. A new ground, rent free, was obtained, possibly from the Company, access being under the railway arch from the New Town Road. With the club colours of green and red it was now that the cry of 'Come on the Nuts and Bolts!' was heard from supporters behind the goal near the river and from the commanding viewpoint on the railway banking. The most memorable games were when train loads of supporters from Folkestone accompanied their team. It was said 'feeling sometimes outran discretion'. After the First World War the club became

Ashford Town but remained at the New Town ground until its move a few years later to Essella Park.

It was perhaps to be expected that many of the town's sensations should have a railway connection. On one occasion both excitement and indignation were reported from New Town where an intended bride, daughter of a Works foreman found herself 'let down' at the last minute. The prospective groom had formerly been an employee in the Works but now held a good position at York. He was expected down on the Saturday, but wrote some excuse stating he would be at Ashford on Monday in time for the marriage. In a state of great excitement the bride, bridesmaids, family and friends made preparations for the occasion; the wedding breakfast was spread and the wedding presents displayed. But they waited and waited as hour after hour passed by without the appearance of the bridegroom. A telegram was sent to York seeking news of the recreant swain but the disappointing reply was that the young man had gone to his business in the usual way that morning instead of coming to Ashford.

A surprising insight into the times was provided by the experience of a young married woman who was travelling from London to Rye when she became ill and upon arriving at Ashford Station was taken to the first class waiting room. There to the consternation of the staff she gave birth to a child. It was fortunate that a local doctor was on the station platform at the time and was able to attend to her. He endeavoured to secure her admission to the Cottage Hospital but the matron was adamant – the rules of the hospital debarred the admission of maternity cases. The unfortunate mother, who seems to have been in a shockingly destitute condition, having eaten nothing but a crust of bread for several hours prior to her arrival at Ashford, was immediately the subject of much sympathy and practical support from local ladies. But one week later, she and her baby daughter were still confined to the first class waiting room.

Fatal accidents on the railway were all too frequent and Ashford Railway Works was no exception either in its indoor or outdoor work. 33 year old Joseph Winter was a shunter, much liked and known as a thoroughly competent and trustworthy man. On that fateful day he was standing on the step of an engine close to a tender which was used to carry refuse iron from the sidings to the rolling mill. The custom in coupling tenders to engines differed from that in coupling wagons or carriages. In the latter case a man stands between the rails but in the case of a tender, which has no buffers at the front, the coupling is performed from the top of the tender through a panel in the floor.

In a moment of thoughtlessness, the shunter jumped down from his engine, went between the engine and tender to couple it, and was squeezed to death. Men came running to the spot but Joseph Winter was dead 'and never uttered a sound'. The body was taken to the Albion Inn at South Willesborough where an inquest was held next day. A juryman remarked that the duty appeared very perilous but the locomotive foreman said it was a necessary one, which the deceased well understood. While his widow and three young children mourned their loss, the jury returned a verdict that 'the deceased came by his death purely by accident'.

Perhaps the most memorable of all the facilities provided by the railway company were those for the scholars of the town. Each year the company had provided a train to take the children of the National School on an outing. One such was on August 17th 1888, to Margate. An account of the trip was written as a school exercise by Robert Hunter, an elder boy in the Sixth Standard. To this may be added from the records that 'the children were paired, an elder child being responsible for the safety of a younger one.' and that 'the amusements included alfresco performances of clowns, niggers, conjurers and acrobats, whilst some of the girls gathered shells and seaweed.'

'We assembled at school at eight o'clock, where the flags and orders were given out. At eight thirty we started for the station, and arrived there just before nine o'clock. We were then put into the train, special carriages being set aside for the teachers and some of the parents. As we went along we passed the Great Asylum at Chartham, the Cathedral at Canterbury, and as we passed St Lawrence we saw some of the English Fleet lying in the Downs. After about an hour's ride we arrived at Margate. We then dispersed and went onto the sands to play until one o'clock. There we amused ourselves in donkey riding, paddling in the sea and crab catching, some of us being bitten by them, while others were too sharp to let the crabs bite them. When we had spent the morning in this way, we assembled at one o'clock for our dinner, which was quickly given us in the shape of one large pasty each. After we had eaten our pasty we went into the town to see the sights. The first thing we saw was the Jetty, which juts out into the sea for some considerable distance. Next we saw the stone pier with the Lighthouse at the end of it. On the top of the cliff stands a cannon from Sevastopol and presented to the Mayor. As we went along we came to the Arcade, where there were sweet shops, shooting galleries and china shops. Another interesting place was the Menagerie belonging to Mr. Sanger.'

'We assembled outside the station at five o'clock. We then went into the station yard where we were given two buns each. While we were there cheers were given for the master, teachers and governesses. We left Margate at six o'clock, and on our homeward journey songs were sung. Shortly after seven o'clock we arrived at Ashford, safe and sound. Before we departed we gave cheers for the S.E.R.Company, the Vicar and Mr. and Mrs. Perkins and then went away perfectly satisfied with our treat'.

Struggling to Improve

At this time the long drawn-out feud between the South Eastern and the London, Chatham and Dover Railway was at its most fierce and the S.E.R. Directors determined upon a series of changes to wrest traffic from their deadly rival. These included improvements at their London Termini and at Folkestone, modernised signalling between Tonbridge and Ashford and new rolling stock. The heavier carriages to be employed on the Kent Coast and Continental services brought a need for larger and more powerful engines finally signalling the end for Cudworth's 'Mails'.

Once more Stirling drew upon his Scottish experience in which he had distinguished himself as a pioneer of the leading bogie with his 4-4-0 designs. Now in December 1883 his latest creation emerged from Ashford Works. Designated 'F' class, it was neat and attractive, with domeless boiler, rounded cab, narrow tender, seven-foot driving wheels and of course, leading bogies. But what first caught the eye was the livery that would ever after be associated with Stirling's reign. Now no longer Cudworth's holly green but a sombre black. This was partly relieved by an attractive lining out scheme, boiler bands lined with red, wheel splashers with red, yellow and white and the Company's coat of arms decorating the leading splashers. Completing the changes were the valences, now red/brown lined with yellow.

Despite their changed appearance the engines were popular with their crews. Steaming was good and controlling them required little need for enginemanship. Drivers had no difficulty taking charge of the Tidal Expresses and the Day and Night Mails, their engines coming to be recognised as Stirling's most renowned locomotives. They were known to both railwaymen and travellers by the affectionate name of 'Jumbos'. 88 of the class entered service, all built at Ashford. The final accolade came when No. 240 was specially painted out in umber livery with fine yellow lining, named 'Onward' and displayed at the Paris Exhibition of 1889, winning a Gold Medal award.

With the exception of six shunting engines placed in service by Cudworth, the South Eastern had paid little attention to the increasing need for this type of locomotive. Footplate crews increasingly complained at the unsuitable engines with which they were provided to deal with the heavy volume of goods traffic and so in 1888, Stirling produced his 'R' class, in effect a tank version of his 'O' class. In addition to shunting duties they were also useful in undertaking light passenger work on Kentish branch lines and found to be particularly useful for hauling the heavy boat trains up the steep gradient from Folkestone Harbour to the Junction, a tough task necessitating two or sometimes three engines working in tandem. All 25 of the class were built at Ashford, their robust character being demonstrated by their long life, the last being withdrawn in March 1960.

The final contribution of James Stirling to his adopted Company was the 4-4-0 'B' class introduced in 1898. Here was an engine, sturdily constructed and a joy to behold. Extremely handsome, magnificently finished but most surprising of all, its' livery. Prussian Green fine-lined in vermilion and yellow, its frames deep red lined out in vermilion and pink whilst the leading splashers were embellished with the Company's coat-of-arms. Stirling had based his new design on his 'F' class, giving the new locomotive a slightly larger boiler, improved cab and higher frames, thus improving its appearance. In service they gave little mechanical trouble but unfortunately contributed little to the South Eastern's growing need for engines with increased power.

Even so, the smooth and eager riding of the 'B' class was illustrated some years later when driver Ben Adams, in charge of Ashford-built No. 34, was severely reprimanded and fined £2 for running from Redhill to Ashford in 44? minutes instead of the booked 52. In his defence Adams pleaded: 'It was such a lovely evening with all the signals showing for miles ahead that I let the old girl have her head.'

Of the 29 put into service, Ashford built nine, No. 217 being immediately rostered for the Granville Express which ran non-stop from Cannon Street to Margate and No. 21 being placed on regular duty with the luxurious American Car Trains. By the conclusion of its 52 years of service, No. 217 had clocked up 1,320,917 miles.

The Company had not been idle in taking steps to improve its carriage stock which had become a pressing task. Richard Mansell as Carriage and Wagon Superintendent was famous for his patent wheel with solid wooden segments and iron tyre. His carriages, built of teak, had a propensity never to wear out which suited the South Eastern in its impoverished state. Some disgruntled passengers claimed that as Chairman, Watkin continued using antiquated third class stock in order to drive passengers into paying for a more expensive class. Others said that Watkin felt it was his duty to protect third-class passengers from the depraving effects of comfort. The fact is that advancing standards in carriage design had left the South Eastern far behind.

The Kentish Express and Ashford News complained: 'Many of the cramped, stuffy, ill-made carriages into which the third-class passengers are now made to enter seem vehicles designed for inflicting the greatest amount of discomfort. There is absolutely no width between the seats and getting in or out is a task of considerable difficulty and danger. Nor are the second-class carriages now running, by any means what they ought to be.' The newspaper would have been justified if it had also commented on carriage lighting. At this time illumination was by means of rape oil lamps which were lit at the start of a journey by a lamplighter, walking along the roof and attending to the lamp pots. In the third class there were usually only two lamps to a carriage, which had a beastly habit of dripping oil onto the unsuspecting passengers below.

The passengers themselves could be the cause of discomfort. In Victorian times personal hygiene often left something to be desired, hence the problem of fleas in carriages. Within the Works, the trimming shop was responsible for the renovation of carriage cushions. These were stuffed with horsehair which from time-to-time were removed, steam cleaned, machine combed and then replaced within the cushion. A side effect of this job was that all those employed on it became infected with fleas and these were carried to their homes. Wherever a trimmer lived there was likely to be a flea problem and for some reason, Bridge Street in particular had a reputation for being 'lousy'.

When William Wainwright took over from Mansell he made plans for immediate improvements and in November 1888 produced what the local newspaper described as: 'a magnificent innovation' whilst also claiming: 'The journey will be undertaken in the easiest manner possible, not the slightest motion being noticeable.' Wainwright's resourcefulness had produced an arc-roofed carriage mounted on a steel frame with six pairs of wheels and providing four first-class and three second-class compartments. Lighting throughout was by gas. The fittings and furniture were of a luxurious quality, the carriage being lined out in birds-eye maple and its sprung seats being covered in blue cloth and Morocco.

Thrusting itself to the forefront, the South Eastern Railway was among the first to introduce lavatories into second-class main-line carriages. Previously these travellers had the choice of either purchasing certain discreet appliances from Victorian surgical stores or suffering some distress until a station was reached. It is said that the third-class passengers were less modest and would 'unashamedly add a pot to their visible luggage'.

A revolutionary enterprise in 1891 was the South Eastern's Pullman carriage order from the American Gilbert Car Company. Lavishly appointed, they set an unheard standard for public services in Britain. Supplied in sections from New York and assembled at Ashford, the four Drawing Room carriages were furnished with 14 revolving chairs, two single chairs and a couch. A smoking compartment was available and also separate ladies' and gentlemen's toilets. A 28-seater buffet car and a baggage car completed the set, which was painted dark lake.

Despite William Wainwright's efforts at new design, the Company continued to build six-wheeled carriages in large numbers and it was 1899 before the South Eastern finally abandoned their manufacture.

William Wainwright was succeeded by his son Harry, who pressed forward with the work of upgrading the carriage stock. Gas lighting gave way to electric, steam heating was introduced, patent draught excluders and air extractors were fitted. First-class compartments were furnished in Tashmere tapestry and second-class in Tashmere velvet. Also introduced was the Wainwright 'trademark', the distinctive 'bird-cage' carriage ends. His greatest accomplishment as Carriage Superintendent was surely to have designed the extravagantly luxurious parlour cars for the service known as 'The Folkestone Vestibuled Limited'. Clearly inspired by the previous order of parlour cars from America, Harry Wainwright's eight coach creation resulted in the South Eastern possessing the only complete train of vestibuled coaches in the United Kingdom. Although the contract for this train was given to the Metropolitan Railway Carriage and Wagon Company, an additional first-class vestibuled Drawing Room car was ordered from America, erected at Ashford in 1897 and placed in service on the London – Tunbridge Wells run.

This car was over 32 feet in length and accommodated 18 passengers. It included a ladies saloon, which provided upholstery in a cream-coloured tapestry with embossed flowers, the facings and sides of the chairs being of crimson plush velvet. The floor was covered with a rich Axminster carpet while window blinds were of old gold brocaded silk falling beneath a festooned valance of pale blue to match the upper panels of the partition. Italian walnut was used for the woodwork in the style of Louis XV. In the other first-class car the style was Louis XVI and the woodwork Spanish mahogany with beautiful mottled panels. Here, all chairs and settees were upholstered in goblin green. Even the second-class and third-class cars were noted for their richness and elegance and their superb comfort.

Smooth running in the Works was not always matched elsewhere. Good Friday, April 8th 1898 was anything but, following a most extraordinary sequence of accidents. At 7.45pm the Folkestone excursion, returning to London, arrived at Ashford's up-platform with its sixteen carriages. Being short of steam the engine driver whistled for a replacement engine. Fortunately, another locomotive was standing in the nearby running shed with a full head of steam and was summoned as a substitute. In order to reach the head of the excursion it had to run up the line close to the rear carriage, cross to the through line, pass the entire train and finally cross back to the platform line before backing up to the leading carriage. Unfortunately the signalman failed to warn the relief engine's driver that the last excursion carriage was only 40 yards clear of the cross-over, with the result that the relief engine crashed into it at some speed.

This engine was then removed back to the Work's shed and a further relief engine was sent but before it could reach the station one of its driving wheel tyres fractured and this too had to be returned. Yet another relief engine was sent for but again the confused signalman was too agitated to warn of the excursion train's position and in a scene familiar to all film comedy buffs, this engine also crashed into the last carriage. As a result of these shenanigans twenty-eight passengers were shaken and bruised. So battered was the excursion stock by now that the entire train was removed and a complete replacement sought. The wretched holidaymakers eventually reached London at midnight – three hours late.

Following a subsequent investigation the Inspection Officer, in a classic understatement, said he was of the opinion that 'the circumstances went to show that the instructions for station yard working at Ashford required reconsideration.'

Two years later the Works was to witness another curious incident in which the Continental mail train narrowly escaped being wrecked. A heavy roll of matting had fallen from a goods train obstructing the down line close to the Sevington bridge. The engine and three front carriages jumped the obstruction but the next carriage, the Ostend mail van, was derailed. The train was only stopped through the presence of mind of the postal officials who pulled the communication cord. With the engine brought to a standstill it was found that the mail van's front wheels were damaged and a breakdown gang removed it to the Ashford Works. The engine and three front carriages, being undamaged, proceeded on to Dover.

The coming of the new century set in motion a series of notable events, the most astonishing being the ending of the long-running feud between the South Eastern Railway and the London, Chatham and Dover Railway. Encouraged by the retirement of Sir Edward Watkin as South Eastern chairman and the appointment of the more amenable H. Cosmo Bonsor, the impossible was about to happen. Towards the end of June 1898 a letter was sent to the Stock Exchange Committee in London giving details of a draft agreement between the two companies.

It was not to be a total merger, perish the thought! The proposal was to set up a working union that would mean that the two companies would operate as one in matters of traffic and engineering but would remain independent in matters of finance.

The position was clearly stated in the act of association: 'With a view to avoiding undue competition and unnecessary expense and delays and other inconveniences arising from diversity of interests, and turning to the best account the respective powers and resources of the two companies ...... with a view also to the improvement and extension of the services between England and the Continent it is expedient and will be for the public advantage that ...... the undertakings of the two companies should be used, worked, managed , maintained and improved ...... as one undertaking.'

Thus the reason for the new operation bearing the title 'South Eastern and Chatham Managing Committee.' Net receipts would be divided 59% to the South Eastern and 41% to their former rivals. The first day of January 1899 saw the new arrangement put into practice although, because of the opposition of some City interests, Parliamentary approval was not secured until the following August. Ashford West station was closed and passengers from the Maidstone line were taken directly into the main town station. There can have been little regret from travellers, who would now be spared the tiresome walk between the two places. The former LC&DR buildings continued to be of service for many years as a parcels depot.

The end of 1898 saw the retirement of James Stirling. The coming upheavals may well have played a part in his decision to leave but he departed with a notable record – 384 of the Company's 459 locomotives in service being of his design. He continued to take a keen interest in matters concerning the railway, often visiting the Works and remaining in the town until his death in 1917 at the age of 81.

Chapter Four

WAINWRIGHT ELEGANCE

The steam is up, the engine bright as gold;
The fire-king echoes back the guards shrill cry,
The roaring vapour shrieks out fierce and bold
A moment – and like lightning on we fly.

Anon

Stirling's retirement from the South Eastern was matched by that of William Kirtley from the London, Chatham and Dover, clearing the way for the appointment of a new Chief Superintendent for the combined companies. The choice fell upon Harry Wainwright but there was universal surprise when the Board announced that both the locomotive and the carriage and wagon departments would be placed under his management. It was Wainwright's task to weld the Kentish railways together, and to plan and carry through their reorganisation. A massive task, and one that would finally prove to be too much for one man's shoulders.

Wainwright was first involved in a decision to centralise the carriage and wagon shops of both companies. At a cost of over £81,000 smart businesslike buildings were situated between the Ashford main Works and the Hastings line, covering 132,000 square feet. Named respectively Klondyke and Kimberley, possibly after contemporary events in the Yukon and Cape Province, they were urgently needed for the conversion of the 'Chatham' fleet, as well as all new carriage and wagon construction.

The former carriage shop near the Works main entrance would now function as a sawmill. Alongside this a huge water tower in Italianate style was erected and remains a prominent landmark to this day. Equipped with tanks 55 feet above floor level it provided a head of water to power the automatic sprinkler fire extinguishing system. A railway magazine that year stated that this was the only railway workshop of its kind in England to be fitted with such a system.

The new chief next had to get to grips with the need for more powerful locomotives, the 'Chatham' section in particular being in need of increased motive power. Although an accomplished engineer, Wainwright had no great experience of all aspects of locomotive design, but fortunately could call upon the services of Robert Surtees of the 'Chatham'.

Surtees was undoubtedly influenced by his father when he decided to enter the railway industry, Robert Surtees Snr. being Chief Foundryman for Robert Stephenson and Co. at their Newcastle Works. He it was who cast the first metal wheels replacing the wooden ones on George Stephenson's 'Rocket'. Young Robert joined his father at the Works as a draughtsman before moving on to the London, Chatham & Dover Railway in 1878. As Chief Draughstman under William Kirtley, the 'Chatham's' engineer, Surtees would polish his skills, which contributed greatly to that company's locomotive designs, although he would always be overshadowed by his chief. Now, with the linking of the South Eastern and the 'Chatham', Surtees' talents were at the disposal of Wainwright.

New locomotives were urgently needed for suburban working and as an immediate expedient, five Pickergill class 'G' 4-4-0s were purchased from Neilson, Reed & Company, by arrangement with the Great North of Scotland Railway. 15 class 'R1' 0?4?4 were also obtained, these tank engines being based upon a 'Chatham' design of 1879, but improved upon by Surtees before being ordered from Sharp Stewart. Drawing further upon Surtees' knowledge, Wainwright then produced his first locomotive, a simple, robust and well-designed 0-6-0 main-line goods engine, whose easy firing and free-steaming boilers produced such a fine turn of speed that they were often used for secondary passenger and excursion work. Classified 'C' class, 109 were built, 70 of them at Ashford. 60 years later large numbers of these massively built engines were still in service.

Edwardian Glory

The following year (1901) saw the appearance of the magnificent class 'D' 4-4-0 express locomotives, perhaps the most beautiful engines ever to grace the rails of Great Britain. It was said of them: '…. the artistic hand of Wainwright was apparent and a first rate mechanical design was clothed in a unity of outward style and "line" that made one of these engines a true objet d'art.' Tribute must be paid to Surtees' engineering skills which were a major contribution to a design which produced a popular machine with a first-rate reputation for fine running and punctuality. Many drivers claimed the 'Coppertop' as their favourite engine.

The new century was thus ushered in with gorgeous style, the new locomotives having highly polished brass domes, copper sheathed chimney tops and a selection of resplendent colours: Brunswick green lined out with light green, yellow, red, black and vermilion together with dark red underframes.

More than 50 of these wonderful and beautiful machines were built, 22 of them at Ashford. Such were their extraordinarily high standards they would offer complete dependability during a lifetime's work of over 50 years. Accompanying their exuberant appearance, a new livery was introduced for carriages, sovereign purple lake, fine lined with gold.

More honour came to Ashford with a seven-carriage Royal train, also designed by Harry Wainwright. The most sumptuous effects were reserved for the King's saloon which, enhanced by silken cushions and drapes in a colour scheme of beautiful apple green, lay beneath a graceful clerestory roof, adjacent to a smoking room trimmed with leather upholstery. The Adams styling of the interior, together with its elaborate facilities, which included closets of gilt queensware, earned it acclaim as 'the most meritorious of any of England's Royal trains.' It was stored at Ashford Works in a special train shed where its imperial splendour was a source of great pride among the workforce.

If Wainwright's locomotive liveries were considered flamboyant, they merely reflected his own splendid appearance – waxed moustache, wing collar, cravat and stylish overcoat. One of the first people to own a motor car, he drove to work each day. His hospitality was legendary even though his social circle was far removed from the staff at Ashford. A sensitive man, concerned at his men's working conditions, he had a reputation for always seeking out any railwayman who had fallen upon hard times. A member of the Royal Automobile Club and the Royal Society of Arts, he was also Honorary Secretary of the Association of Railway Locomotive Engineers of Great Britain and Ireland.

Surtees demonstrated a completely different personality. Anti-social to the point of being able to walk through the Works without a word spoken to anyone, yet greatly admired for his engineering skills by the men, who believed he deserved shared praise for the excellence of the Wainwright engines.

The high esteem in which Harry Wainwright was held was amply demonstrated on 29th December 1900, when the workforce welcomed him home with his bride. He had married eighteen days previously at what was undoubtedly one of the high society weddings of the year in St. Margaret's, Westminster. At the conclusion of their honeymoon the happy pair left Hastings with the station staff giving them a hearty send off, accompanied by the explosion of fog signals and shrieking of engine whistles. Mounting excitement at Ashford produced a welcome that would not have disgraced royalty. As the Wainwrights' train arrived, enthusiastic cheering erupted from the large crowd that had gathered. Outside the station a carriage stood ready for the 'happy pair' to be drawn to New Town by the men from the Works, accompanied by a torchlight procession led by the New Town Band. Boys from the Railway school paraded with their banner and the Church Lads Brigade were given the privilege of forming a guard of honour.

Processing under the Hastings Bridge with its message of 'Welcome', the Wainwrights were confronted with the familiar roadway leading up to the Works but now lined, unbelievably, with Venetian masts flying streamers, pennants and flags and overshadowed by a heavily decorated clock tower. Wooden stands had been erected on either side of the road and were filled to overflowing with families and friends of the workforce, whose cheering roared out another exuberant welcome.

Upon his arrival, Wainwright was presented with an elaborately illuminated address on vellum, framed in gold – ' ...on behalf of the foremen, clerks and fellow workmen employed in the Locomotive, Carriage and Wagon Departments of the South Eastern and Chatham Railway Works at Ashford, Kent, (we) beg your acceptance of this address as a souvenir of your marriage and desire to express on the occasion of this auspicious event our appreciation and gratitude for the unvarying kindness we have at all times received from you and the kind genial manner you have at all times shown to the employees under you...'

Wainwright, quite overcome by the magnificence of his reception said he had 'tried to act in a wise manner and in as kind a manner as possible......no railway company could be successful without a good staff......he was thankful he had an excellent staff, whether foremen, clerks or workmen, and he was proud of them. It was only by unity, good feeling and good fellowship that they could make a success of any undertaking.'

As the children sang 'Noel' and 'Home Sweet Home' the Wainwrights' carriage was drawn into the grounds of Alfred House, their future home, which had been illuminated with fairy lights, the house itself being draped with flags and a banner proclaiming 'Hearty Welcome Home'. To add to the occasion the band of the Buffs Volunteers entertained by playing a programme of music throughout the evening. It had been a wonderful tribute, demonstrating the warm feelings of Ashford's railway folk towards their revered chief.

Cheers and Tears

Turn of the century changes at Ashford were overshadowed by the Boer War. As the brutal conflict raged on, volunteers were called for from towns and villages all over the country. Responding in an atmosphere of intense patriotism, Ashford's 'H' Company of the East Kent Volunteers rose to the occasion, as a number of its members opted for service in South Africa. Together with members of the East Kent Yeomanry, they received an ecstatic send-off at the Railway Station with a band playing, torches flaring and a huge crowd frantically trying to gain access to the station platform to to cheer them on.

Every week the Kentish Express devoted long columns of print to news from the front, which was not always good. Anxieties grew as lists of casualties were posted and the spirited enthusiasm of the early days gave way to a fervent wish for an end to the fighting. Thus, the 2nd June 1902 would long be remembered. Shortly after seven o'clock on that Sunday evening word was received by telephone at the Ashford Railway Station of victory over the Boers. A message was immediately sent to the Vicar who, after announcing the news from his pulpit, led the congregation in a heartfelt singing of the hymn 'Now thank we all our God' and an enthusiastic rendering of the National Anthem.

In celebration the next evening coloured fire was lit on the church tower and rockets were fired from the Barrow Hill water tower which were visible for several miles around. Fires were lit in neighbouring villages while sky rockets could be seen being fired from Rye and the Wye Downs. Shops were quickly decorated and salutes of bombs were given in the old London, Chatham and Dover Railway yard. Speeches were made and a band played in the High Street amidst general rejoicing.

Within a few hours of the news being received the elements put on their own colourful show. A violent storm of great intensity swept Ashford and the Weald. The cannonade of thunder was accompanied by a widespread display of the most vivid lightning. As the storm reached its' peak the signalman in the Hastings line junction box noticed that one of the sheds of the newly-built Kimberley works was alight. Mr. Wainwright was sent for, the alarm bell was sounded and two engines of the South Eastern Fire Brigade were soon at work. Ashford Town Brigade firemen were roused from their beds at 3.30am and were ready in four minutes. Meanwhile at the Works, burning carriages were being hauled out of the shed to help confine the fire to the roof. The blaze was soon brought under control but not before two carriages were destroyed and a further three damaged. Lightning was blamed for the fire.

In the new century trades unionism began to make itself heard. Craft unions such as the Amalgamated Society of Engineers, the Society of Boilermakers and the Amalgamated Society of Carpenters had been represented in Ashford since the 1850s but generally growth had been slow. It was not until December 1st 1889, that a meeting had been held to inaugurate a branch of the Amalgamated Society of Railway Servants. Now, in June 1902, a number of visiting union men addressed railwaymen and their wives in the Corn Exchange, the intention being: 'to infuse a little more life into those outside the Society' and claiming: 'If there were 250,000 members instead of 60,000 there would be no more seven-day a week men on the railway.'

The society's object was announced as being: 'to improve the conditions and to promote railway workers' interests, to maintain reasonable hours of duty and fair wages, to assist the unemployed, injured and aged members, to provide for orphans, provide legal assistance, obtain compensation for accidents and promote greater safety in railway work.' The leading speaker remarked that having spent 16 years as a goods guard, he knew something of the railway service. 'It is a regrettable affair that it is still necessary to teach the principles of combination to the working classes of this country. The workman was really a partner in a concern and he had a right to say what his interest in the shape of wages should be. The capitalist simply invested his cash but railway servants invested their lives and limbs, and the loss of life and limb was a greater loss than any money invested.'

Very little came from the meeting and the weakness of the unions was demonstrated the following year when the Company chairman declared the need to reduce expenses. Wagon construction was cut back and part of the locomotive and carriage shops at both Ashford and Longbridge were closed on Saturdays.

Despite the need for economy the requirement for new locomotives persisted and in 1904 the first of Wainwright's 'H' class 0-4-4 tanks began to appear. Designed for semi-fast passenger and suburban services they proved well suited to the wear and tear to which they were subject. With their gay and colourful livery and a profusion of shining brass and copper they were greatly admired. All sixty-six of the class were built at Ashford.

In the autumn of 1905, Ashford received a Cudworth '118' class which had been based at Redhill. This engine, No 247, built in 1874 to an 1859 design was the last of its class to remain in service. Highly venerated by men who always kept it beautifully groomed, there was great anxiety concerning its future. Thus it was that a number of locomen and other employees approached the Company asking for its preservation. Unfortunately the idea received no backing from Wainwright. An approach was made to the Ashford Urban District Council, which also met with disinterest. Tragically the last of the 'Cudworths' went to the sidings for breaking up in March 1907. An unbelievable loss.

Wainwright's introduction of heavier, steam-heated carriages led him to instruct his Ashford design team to improve still further on the celebrated 'D' class locomotives. The result was the splendid 'E' class 4-4-0. Ashford was entrusted with building the entire class of 26 at an average cost of £2,895 per engine. They proved to be an exciting addition to the South Eastern and Chatham stable and with the 'D' class were given the heaviest work on the system, including being placed in charge of the Continental Boat Expresses. They demonstrated an easy ability to haul loadings of up to 350 tons, a weighty task for the period.

The class was so highly regarded by the Company that No 516 was chosen for exhibition at the 1908 Franco-British Exhibition in London and subsequently, because of its magnificent finish was invariably scheduled for special duties, gaining the accolade the 'Royal E'. It would certainly have been able to satisfy the King's passion for speed, which was revealed by his request to railway companies to always make his train go as fast as possible.

Paint shop records reveal the care taken to hand produce the fine finish for a 'special'. Numerous coats of flat, undercoat and gloss were applied, well rubbed down, followed by four coats of Brunswick green, over which five coats of copal varnish were carefully brushed. The engine and tender were then left some days to dry in a warmed paint shop, after which they were wax polished.

Short time working was again in evidence in 1907. At the half-yearly meeting of the Company, Cosmo Bonsor observed that in common with every other railway in England, they had had a bad half-year. Receipts from both passenger and goods services were down and the coal-bill was up, at a cost to the Company of £80,000. He regretted that a feeling of insecurity existed, affecting the railways, but all British industry was affected. There had been complaints about working conditions in many of the railway companies and a demand for union recognition, although there had been few complaints at Ashford. Only the last-minute intervention of Lloyd George as President of the Board of Trade averted an attempted national railway strike. He negotiated an agreement to set up conciliation boards to recognise unions. Cosmo Bonsor claimed nevertheless that relations with the men were excellent and that the Company was paying full market value for their labour.

1908 brought better times and in particular a chance to celebrate what the local newspaper called 'An Ashford Triumph'. The New Town Band was now the Ashford Railway Works Band and in a spirit of optimism had entered for the National Band Festival championship at the Crystal Palace, although few considered their chances as being favourable.

The Company laid on a special train and, it being a Saturday, close on 300 enthusiastic supporters accompanied the bandsmen. The contingent included supporters of two other Ashford bands who were also entering the contest, the 5th Buffs (Volunteers) under the baton of Bandmaster Thorne and the Kingsnorth Industrial School Band under Bandmaster Clinton. During the afternoon the competitors each took their place at the Crystal Fountain Bandstand. The Buffs and the railwaymen were competing directly with each other whilst the school band competed in the boys' section.

At the conclusion of the massed band concert that evening before an audience estimated at 60,000 the Ashford Buffs were proclaimed Reed Champions for an unparalleled third consecutive year, whilst Ashford Railway Works Band under Bandmaster Street excelled themselves by winning second place. To complete the triumphant evening the school band won third place in its section, causing the Kentish Express to proclaim:

'The fact that three bands from a comparatively small place as Ashford should compete was unique in the contest, but that each should be named in the first three prize-winners is a proud distinction for the competition and the Town.'

The result was received with cheers and immediately telegraphed to Ashford, where it was known soon after nine o'clock. The news spread like wildfire and what seemed like the entire population poured out of their homes to await the homecoming train. As the victors swept into the station the enormous crowd roared their appreciation. There were frantic appeals for speeches and Bandmaster Thorne attempted to respond on behalf of the three bands, but was unable to make himself heard in the din. The result had also been telegraphed to Harry Wainwright, the president of the Works band, who arrived and made a presentation of a musical instrument.

The school band played the victorious bands through the station, striking up the regimental march of the Buffs and the 'Onward' march for the works. Three brakes had been made ready to process the performers round the town but they had great difficulty in making their way through the thousands of excited well-wishers who, singing and cheering, demonstrated their sheer delight. During the next few days letters and telegrams of congratulation poured in to mark a day of pride that would be remembered and spoken of for years to come.

After all the excitement it was back to business. The following year saw a class of fussy little engines introduced. Eight small 0-6-0 tanks, classified 'P' class, were built at Ashford, destined for the most minor of branch lines. Their mode of operation was to be placed between two carriages and then to operate in a forward or reverse direction. In this they proved to be rather more successful than Wainwright's 'Kitson built' steam railcars introduced four years previously.

Long service was still a feature of the workforce and although there might be some grumbles amongst the men, most valued the fact that they had a permanent job. In addition, those who had given loyal service for many years could hope for recognition. Alfred Goldsmith, a fitter, had worked at Ashford works for 59 years and at the age of 76 applied to retire. His wages had been 34 shillings per week and he also received the new government Old Age Pension of five shillings. The Board agreed to make him a weekly allowance of ten shillings, which in those days was regarded as generous.

If the atmosphere at Ashford was fairly placid it contrasted strongly with other parts of the country where there had been further industrial tension with an increasing number of wild-cat strikes. The conciliation boards set up in 1907 had failed to resolve matters in dispute and this had led to growing restiveness. Finally, in August 1911 'the pot boiled over' and the national leaders of the four main railway unions issued an ultimatum to the companies – 'agree within 24 hours to meet and negotiate or face a national railway stoppage.' The government response was to make what appeared to be an indifferent offer, which did not impress the men, but they also, provocatively, called out the military, particularly in London, the Midlands and the North.

At five o'clock on the afternoon of 17th August a telegram was sent out by union leaders to nearly 2000 rail centres calling the first national railway strike: 'Your liberty is at stake. All railwaymen must strike at once. The loyalty of each means victory for all.' Again Lloyd George intervened securing an agreement within 48 hours that would improve working conditions, in return for which railway companies would be allowed to increase charges. In addition a commission of inquiry was to investigate the men's grievances and although a union official would be allowed to represent the men on the conciliation boards there would still be no formal union recognition.

The amenable attitude of Ashford's railwaymen was a tribute to the liberal management of their company, none of the local men having joined the strike. Although the dispute provoked considerable activity in the enrolling of new union members, the men themselves admitted the South Eastern Company had dealt with them very fairly on the whole, and the few petty grievances were capable of amicable settlement. Some of the union men said they would not come out on strike even if ordered to, as they were perfectly satisfied with their conditions. Evidence of this is shown by the fact that SE&CR receipts were down by only 2.7% during the dispute period.

In an attempt to drum up membership, a well-attended meeting was later held in Ashford' High Street, with speeches by national officials of the Railway Workers Union. Insisting on the right to organise and fight for social justice and bargain with their labour, they claimed the men's weapons were the strike and the vote.

The strike was seen to have been a major catalyst when the following year, three of the leading unions merged into the National Union of Railwaymen, although much trade disunity continued. The craft unions refused to recognise the right of the NUR to speak for shopmen whilst the NUR refused to abandon its interest in them.

The task which placed the greatest burden upon Wainwright followed the decision to close the 'Chatham's' Longhedge Works at Battersea except for maintenance work, and concentrate production and repairs at Ashford. This was a tremendous undertaking, which placed a great strain upon the Company's resources. The proposals provided for the extension of every department at Ashford by fifty per cent. The principle new building was a 580 foot erecting shop running parallel to the main line alongside the existing one and capable of dealing with 28 locomotives at any one time. It featured a central running road with longitudinal pits in place of the old method of single pits served by a transverser. These features were also provided in the 154 foot long tender shop. The machine and fitting shop was increased in size and a new building was added for the extension of the boiler-making and repairing departments.

In addition, the new coppersmith's shop had central fires and flues, whilst the larger paint shop was equipped with new heating apparatus to maintain even temperatures. An additional engine house, a new tool room and new patternmakers' shop were also planned. There was to be additional machinery including pneumatic machine tools, although much of this would come from Longhedge, their equipment being more modern than that at Ashford.

Included in the improvements was the renovation of the clocktower, together with the fitting of a new clock. Having seen nearly half-a-century of service the old turret clock was removed and replaced with one with four faces instead of two. Larger in diameter, the clock face was illuminated by an automatic gas and reflector arrangement. Great satisfaction was expressed to the makers, Thwaites and Reed of London, who had produced the timepiece at a cost of £66.7s.6d.

The decision to introduce electricity into the Works posed a problem, as there was no generating facility in the district. There were wrangles for many years on the Ashford Council concerning this new power source, the Council fearing competition to its own Gas Works. A power house was therefore built in 1912 close to the boiler shop and equipped with two oil-driven DC generators to provide lighting and power for the workshops, offices and yards. Previously, overhead cranes throughout the shops had been driven by means of continuous ropes running along the walls. Now modern, electrically-driven cranes were installed, increasing both lifting and traversing speeds.

Much change was afoot, with the expected arrival of over 200 families from Battersea. New Town, having remained unchanged since its early days, would witness the erection of another 126 houses and a new school. Railway schools had been a feature of life in railway villages throughout the country – New Town was to provide the last example of this branch of philanthropy.

Company architect, Charles Mercer, was made responsible for the school's design and he succeeded in producing a style in tune with the Edwardian era. Borrowing features from the past, he embellished his work with Portland stone facing, richly modelled pediments, shingles, medieval-style timbers and the whole presided over by a climactic lantern, replete with classical mouldings. A brick wall with substantial pillars and strong iron railings provided an enclosure. Happily, the houses picked up, in modest form, some of the school's architectural features, with their gable ends and hung tiles and mouldings, producing a certain harmonisation.

Twelve firms were invited to tender for the school, and local builder, C.I Epps, with a bid of £4,700, was successful. Accepted in November 1912, construction was completed within the year, opening on 8th October, 1913.

Sir William Hart- Dyke took an intense interest in the school for many years. Director of the South Eastern and Chatham Railway and Chairman of the School Managers, he had at one time been Vice-President of the Board of Education and typified the paternalistic attitude that had so often been in evidence on the South Eastern.

With Wainwright residing in Alfred House, it is unsurprising that a pristine smartness pervaded the village. Houses were kept well decorated, the Green looked like velvet and a smart white fence surrounded this treasured space. Nothing was allowed to offend the eye. With well-kept gardens and flowers in profusion, New Town attracted folk from Ashford who had decided upon a gentle Sunday afternoon walk. The highlight of the summer season was the Flower Show on the Green, accompanied by a small fun fair. Music for these occasions was always provided by the Ashford Railway Works Band.

The hallowed Green still provided an excellent pitch for a fine cricket team, one member distinguishing himself by knocking a ball through the pub window. In 1912 the three pumps, one at each corner of the Green, remained, although they had not been used for some time, the residents now enjoying piped water.

New Town's businesses continued to flourish. Nestling in the shadow of the great Bath House was the Alfred Arms, where reigned Stephen Bailey and his wife, who enjoyed a grand reputation with their support of community events. Close by was the well known Alfred Stores and Post Office, owned by Thomas Headley, proprietor of a number of such establishments both in the town and the surrounding villages. The popular Mr. and Mrs. Robins had a shop selling sweets, greengrocery and general odds and ends, whilst next to the Alfred Arms was a butchery owned by Arthur Hurford. Joining him, having moved down from Longhedge, was Archie Ridout, who helped during the evenings. Having been in the trade before joining the railway, he taught the owner how to make black puddings, which were hugely popular.

A feature of the locality were the locomotive road crossings. One set of lines crossed the road by the clock tower enabling engines and wagons to cross from the main Works to the Kimberley Sheds. Another set crossed New Town Road to the Gas Works and in each case there was a warning bell to halt road traffic.

A welcome tradition was observed by the Ancient Order of Hooligans. Formed many years previously, their most memorable event each year was an outing known as the 'Hooligans' Beano', always taking place on the last Saturday of June. Men gathered outside the Alfred Arms at 9 o'clock on the appointed morning and it was the custom for each to wear a white peaked cap. The reason for this is not known for certain but it is thought that it helped in recognising the wearer if he strayed at any point during the journey. Conveyance was by horse-drawn brake and two of these were usually provided. A typical outing would be to the Royal Oak at Newingreen, thence via Lyminge to Elham and on to Barham for lunch. This landlord always showed pleasure when his hostelry was chosen for the venue by providing fresh vegetables from his own garden. The horse-brakes rolled on towards Canterbury and here a stop was made for tea. The journey home was punctuated by stops at wayside inns, the rule being one drink only at each house. The tired but happy party arrived back at New Town in the late evening.

Of course, everything was not always sweetness and light. A railwayman's daughter from South Willesborough found herself in court after 'using' the railway for what was described as 'a series of impudent frauds'. The girl had obtained money for railway fares and expenses by answering advertisements in the Kentish Express for servants wanted in the resort of Ramsgate, then pocketing the money instead of travelling for an interview. For this deception she was sentenced to six weeks hard labour.

Wainwright's Departure

Ever since the announcement of changes affecting the Longhedge Works, dismay had been growing there. Many were going to lose their jobs, and of those who were not, there was resentment at having to pull up roots and move away from family and friends to Ashford. It was also unfortunate that the Company had been looking for a financial saving in merging the two Works and had failed to grasp the true cost of their plans, with the result that, despite the extensions at Ashford, there was insufficient manpower or machinery for the combined workload. Longhedge had been allowed to run down since 1910 and the Board's over-eagerness to close the Works before Ashford was ready for the extra work created a crisis. A key factor was that whilst 70 Boilermakers were lost in London only 24 were gained at Ashford. With the Company seeking to compromise their expansion with economies, the wonder is that Wainwright was able to achieve what he did. The task facing him had been made even more formidable and his reputation suffered as a consequence.

At the time of the merger, additional and more powerful locomotives had been needed, and all the Chatham oil-lit carriages required conversion to electric lighting, steam heating and automatic brakes. 200 new bogie carriages had to be ordered and 300 wagons built to meet a severe shortage. The immediate situation was so desperate that 500 wagons had to be hired in. Urgent construction work was necessary at Victoria, Slades Green, Dover Marine and Folkestone Harbour. Parts of the system, particularly the 'Chatham' section needed upgrading as the rails were too light and the bridges needed strengthening. In addition to all this were the costs of the new extensions at Ashford Works, together with the expansion of New Town. With insufficient funds being made available to carry through all the improvements necessary to a previously cash-starved system, a serious situation was bound to emerge.

Wainwright's saddest year was 1913. All the difficulties that had been building up came to a head. The new outdoor locomotive superintendent was instructed by the directors to report on the difficulties that had been experienced in working trains during the previous summer season. He complained at the condition of many of the engines in service, claiming that there was a backlog of repairs at the Works and an increase in engine failures. The position had worsened since the previous December when 138 of the locomotives were at work although in need of a major overhaul.

There should have been little surprise at this state of affairs. True, there had been some 50 locomotive re-builds during the previous three years but no additional engines had been built. The 1910 funding had been used to pay off a heavy deficit on the carriage programme and Wainwright's request to use outside manufacturers for the supply of new boilers and the repair of old ones was refused, thus exacerbating an already difficult situation. In a period of increasing and heavier traffic loads, too many ageing locomotives were having to be either patched up or sent out in an unacceptable condition. The lack of repair facilities at Ashford Works together with the absence of new locomotive orders had led inevitably to a shortage of motive power.

As far back as 1910 double heading had been introduced on trains in an attempt to cope with the heavier loads. Anticipating the problem four years earlier, Wainwright had his Ashford team design an inside cylinder 4-4-2 Atlantic locomotive as well as two 4?6?0s with weights of up to 108 tons. These designs were followed by another 4-6-0 and an 0-8-0 but the Company's Civil Engineer refused to countenance such weighty locomotives on the system. Wainwright was able to introduce a robust and attractive 0?6?4 tank engine, designated 'J' class for outer suburban work but only five were built, all at Ashford.

Finally the Board were forced to face up to the serious situation. 40 boilers were ordered in from outside manufacturers, the capacity of the Ashford boiler shop was doubled and an additional workforce recruited. Structural changes were made to the erecting shop, making room for a further ten engines and overtime and weekend working introduced. With improvements now promised to the main-line permanent way, Wainwright was instructed to produce drawings for the largest possible 4-4-0 passenger express. Meanwhile, to meet the crisis, fifteen 2-4-0 locomotives were secured on immediate loan from the Great Northern Railway.

Against this burdensome background, Wainwright suffered severe personal problems. He was not a physically robust man and had developed a weak heart condition. In October 1913 his wife made clear that she was leaving him, ostensibly to live with her mother. With his life in disarray, possibly affecting his work, the Chairman, Cosmo Bonsor, quietly approached him the following month and tactfully suggested early retirement. A sad end for someone who, although not a strong administrator, deserved better from the Board, having transformed the combined companies in little more than a decade.

He faced further personal trials the following year when his wife's disloyalty became evident and, in what amounted to a mocking challenge of – 'If you want the evidence, here it is!' – took her millionaire lover to the Great Eastern Hotel in London and ensured that the receptionist, waiter and chambermaid all knew of her adultery. Wainwright had no other course than to divorce her.

After his retirement he remained in Ashford for a further two years before moving to Richmond in Surrey and later to St. Leonards, where he died in 1925 at the early age of sixty. A cultured man with a kindly and sympathetic nature who deserved a better deal of the cards, his name would live on in his beautifully designed locomotives.

Chapter Five

MAUNSELL ARRIVES

A green eye – and a red – in the dark,
Thunder – smoke – and a spark,
It is there – it is here – flashed by,
Whither will the wild thing fly?

Mary Coleridge

Wainwright's successor was the redoubtable Richard Edward Lloyd Maunsell, son of a Dublin lawyer, who had trained as an engineer at the Inchicore Works of the Great Southern and Western Railway of Ireland, returning there after a spell with the East Indian Railway. Bristling with enthusiasm and full of ideas he arrived in Ashford, taking up residence at Northbrooke House on Gore Hill, and set to work to reshape the South Eastern and Chatham. In a rearrangement of duties, the previous post of Locomotive, Carriage and Wagon Superintendent was discarded and Maunsell was appointed Chief Mechanical Engineer.

Within six months of his arrival he had made a clean sweep of the former engineering team and appointed new and able young men to provide the backbone of his department. It has been claimed that almost the whole success of Southern Railway practice up to 1937 can be traced back to the momentous reorganisation that took place at Ashford in the early months of 1914.

Surtees was due for retirement, and to succeed him as Chief Locomotive Draughtsman Maunsell selected James Clayton. He now returned to Ashford from Derby, having previously left the town in 1903 after acquiring experience under Surtees. Three top men were recruited from Swindon, George Pearson as Maunsell's assistant and Works Manager, Harold Holcroft whose task it was to further modernise the Works and Lionel Lynes for Carriage and Wagon Design. To complete the new team, Harry Hicks was brought over from Inchicore as Assistant Works Manager.

Although there were changes at the top, the Works base was strong. It has rightly been said that Ashford was always fortunate in its shop foremen, who were all sound, capable and conscientious men.

Maunsell was not long in making his presence felt, decrying: 'The shops at Ashford are not adequate to keep the present stock.' A reference surely to the Board's previous shortcomings. He also tackled the slack administration that had resulted in the parts for two engines going missing. A total of 66 0-4-4 'H' class passenger tank engines had been authorised but only 64 were completed, the last one in 1910. No doubt the 'lost parts' had been borrowed for use as spares but this was not the kind of irregularity that Maunsell would tolerate. The story is told that he turned Ashford Works upside down to get the missing parts found and the engines constructed. During the early months of 1915 the engines, at last completed, took their place on the line.

One of Maunsell's first responsibilities was to meet a need for more powerful locomotives. Upon arrival, he found he had inherited a new large 4-4-0 design from Wainwright, designated 'L' class. This had been modified by Surtees and, following a few alterations, was accepted.

The Chairman explained the introduction of a more weighty locomotive at a SE&CR shareholders' meeting: 'When we took over the undertakings of the two companies neither of the roads was up to date. We have on them more bridges than there are on any other line of similar mileage in the country and those bridges were built to carry an axle-load of only sixteen tons. The rails were light and would not bear heavy traffic. Since then we have been renewing the bridges to carry a twenty ton axle-load and we have renewed almost the whole of our main line with heavier rails. The time has now arrived when we can order and use heavier locomotives.' This did not in fact apply to the 'Chatham' section and sadly for the Company the country was about to be caught up in an horrendous European conflict that would force the postponement of all thoughts of improvement.

Two weeks before the beginning of that fateful year, management had placed an order with Beyer, Peacock & Company for twelve 'L' class locomotives. A further ten were to be built at Ashford but because of the difficulties still facing the Works, Maunsell advised seeking an outside contractor. Unable to find any British manufacturer able to deliver in the time required, an order was finally placed with the Berlin firm of Borsig. Between 24th May and 12th June, the German-built engines were unloaded at Dover docks and towed to Ashford, where Borsig's fitters prepared them for service. Because of the subsequent outbreak of war, Borsig's account could not be paid. The money was demanded by the British Government and not subsequently transferred to the German firm until May 1920. The London Evening News later rejoiced at the thought 'that the engines have helped to move millions of troops to the Front'.

The Great War

The Great War began on 4th August 1914 and immediately made its' presence felt. Under an Act of Parliament which enabled the Government to take control of railways in the event of war, the SE&CR, along with all the other British railway companies, was to be administered by the state for the duration of hostilities. An official statement was issued which declared the Act's purpose 'to ensure that the railways, locomotives, rolling stock and staff be used as one complete unit in the best interests of the State for the movement of troops, stores and food supplies'.

The sudden and unexpected outbreak of war caused what was described as 'a state of subdued excitement' in Ashford, more so than in any other town in mid-Kent. Local soldiery was on the move. The 5th Buffs speedily returned from camp following a nine-hour train journey and proceeded on to Dover next day. Ashford Section 2nd Home Counties Field Ambulance was mustered at Canterbury. 'D' Squadron, Royal East Kent Mounted Rifles, having mobilised on the Wednesday at the town's Drill Hall, could later be seen at the centre of animated groups in the High Street. The following day, this smartly turned out, khaki-clad cavalry clattered out of town bound for Sturry, each man on his charger and leading a spare mount.

In the Railway Works empty places began to appear as large numbers of men were called to the colours for service in the Army or Naval reserve. Ashford now entered into the spirit of war with great enthusiasm, and the Works band was in great demand at the many events that were quickly organised. A Promenade Concert in the High Street raised £9.10s. 7?d for the Sick and Wounded Fund. At a recruiting evening, patriotic tunes were played and leading townsmen gave rousing speeches on behalf of the 5th Buffs, which were heartily cheered. A concert in the Corn Exchange attracted a large audience in response to an appeal for the Prince of Wales Relief Fund. Many were anxious to help in the provision of VAD hospitals and early offers were made in respect of the Congregational Church Hall and Eastwell Park Mansion.

That war was not all flag waving soon became clear. Train services were reduced, railwaymen's privilege tickets were cancelled, three of the bandsmen found themselves whisked into the Army and early lists of casualties began to appear with former Works employees prominent among them. But these were early days and letters poured back from France all couched in the most enthusiastic terms.

Train crews were heavily engaged in the early days with the running of special trains for the thousands of Belgian refugees arriving by steam packet at Dover. At the same time they were under intensive pressure moving the British Expeditionary Force to the front. Throughout the war, large numbers of trains would pass through Ashford, carrying troops and armaments to the coastal ports. Going in the opposite direction were the leave trains to Victoria and ambulance trains carrying the wounded to Charing Cross, or in the event of heavy casualties at the front, to hospitals in the Midlands.

Ashford was a key point in the railway system, with long lines of stock in every available siding. Fully equipped ambulance trains waited here until ordered forward to Dover. Storage was provided for heavy materials, munitions and equipment for onward transmission by rail. Loaded into barges, this traffic was taken across the Channel and directly through French canals to our troops in the field. As the war progressed a new port was constructed at Richborough, to enable cross-Channel barges and ferry steamers to receive ever increasing train loads of Army stores and materials.

From the commencement of hostilities, the War Office requested the South Eastern & Chatham to have ready at all times engines and carriages for the rapid conveyance of high ranking figures and couriers to and from France. These trains, known as Imperial Specials (A) were hauled by Wainwright 'D' class expresses and guaranteed clear fast runs. As they normally consisted of a pullman and a van, Ashford was witness to the very fast timings that were achieved, Admiralty Pier at Dover being reached within 1 hour 20 minutes of leaving Charing Cross.

In the Works much effort was put into War manufacture. The first order had been received as war clouds were gathering and on the Sunday and Bank Holiday Monday before the fateful 4th August, conversion work was urgently carried out on a number of troop trains for the War Office and two ambulance trains for the Admiralty. Consisting of eleven vans comprising brake vans and brake thirds, the ambulance vans were fitted up with two tiers of cots and fittings for drinking water tanks. Many unusual tasks would be undertaken during the next four years but the most testing and one which summoned every ounce of skill from the workforce was the need to supply spare parts for Belgian locomotives. Despite the speed of the German advance, most of the rolling stock of Belgian railways had been safely withdrawn to France, but this left them without spare parts and servicing facilities. Maunsell, who at the outbreak of war became Chief Mechanical Engineer to the government's Railway Executive Committee undertook to provide parts and awarded the task to Ashford. Special tools were often necessary to produce those items quite unusual to Britain, but as always the skill of the Ashford men rose to the occasion.

Other contracts called for large numbers of railway wagons, scores of Army horse lorries and 1,000 ambulance stretchers for the War Office, together with the production of thousands of six inch high explosive nose caps, fuse plugs and 60-pounder cartridge-box linings for the Ministry of Munitions.

The Company's expertise was needed when it was called upon to lay out and control an extensive rail system to serve the Army's ammunition, clothing and food depots at Boulogne. It was also required to supply the permanent way and signalling, together with twelve locomotives to assist with the construction work around the base. This was an unexpected hour of glory for two of Ashford's 'P' class. Taken from their usual routine in April 1915, these modest little tank engines were now painted in Army style olive green and shipped across the Channel for their wartime duties.

Two 'P' class engines also proved their worth later in the war when they were based at Ashford in order to work the military railway from Westenhanger to Lympne Camp and the military spur line to Manston aerodrome. Here they serviced the often overcrowded sidings which were full of bogie aircraft vans, fuel tankers and flat wagons carrying aircraft engines. All this together with a steady stream of work for the Army's Boulogne base, including the repair and maintenance of ambulance carriages, kept the Works busy during the war years.

Early on it became increasingly difficult to supply suitable motive power for the heavy military traffic. Maunsell approached the Ministry of Munitions requesting the loan of 14 goods engines, with the result that the Hull & Barnley Railway agreed to transfer their surplus 0-6-0s to relieve a situation that was becoming critical.

An unexpected effect of the war had been the immediate increase in food prices, which pressed heavily upon the budgets of railway families. Faced with such a rapid surge in the cost of living, increases in rates of pay became an urgent necessity. By early 1915, the price of bread had risen from 5?d to 8d a quartern loaf. Sugar had gone from 2d a pound to 3?d, butter from 1/4d to 1/6d, cheese from 9d to 11d, bacon from 10d to 1s and flour had increased from 1/8d to 2/6d. To feelings of widespread dismay, food prices in Ashford as in other towns across the country had risen by nearly 20 per cent.

The South Eastern & Chatham Railway led the way with the idea of giving a war bonus to offset the price increases. This welcome and understanding decision cut across any need for protracted negotiations, in accordance with the usual accepted procedures concerning rates of pay. Such a speedy solution was seized upon by the Unions, who, upon approaching the government, were promised that financial support would be given in order that all other railway companies could follow suit. Unbeknown to all concerned, the war bonus would become a matter of contention when hostilities ceased.

New Town was often the scene of military activity, ringing to shouts of command as numerous RSMs drilled their men. Kitchener was raising his 'New Armies' and raw recruits were put through their paces on the Green. The local district became their 'home', the soldiers being billeted with local families. Columns of men on route marches, led by their Colonel on a white horse, became a familiar scene in the neighbourhood. Men from the King's Regiment (10th Battalion) Liverpool Scottish and from the Canadian Army Ordnance Depot were much in evidence. The Canadians erected timber clad buildings in Station Road and along the southern perimeter of the railway station yard, the latter being used throughout the time of their long stay in Ashford as a cook-house. After the war they were used as railway offices.

The nearest the locality came to the fighting was as a result of a number of intrusions by German aerial raiders. The beginning of 1915 had seen the frequent use of airships in attempts to bomb English towns, but without much success. From 17th May, air raids were carried out by an improved type of zeppelin. Built in the great works of Friedrichshafen, the new 'Luftschiffs' were 536 feet long, 61 feet in diameter, powered by four 210 hp engines and capable of carrying two tons of bombs. Ten of these giants were allocated to the Naval Airships Division based at Nordholz near Cuxhaven.

On the night of 17th August, the menacing drone of an airship was heard approaching Ashford. Four zeppelins had set out for southern England but two developed mechanical problems and had to turn back. Of the remaining two, one crossed the coast and chose to use the railway line from Dungeness as a navigational aid, no doubt hoping to pick up the lights from a train to guide him towards London. The 17th was a beautiful night. Many people, after a hot day, were enjoying the cool air in their gardens before retiring for the night. Some had remarked – 'What a perfect night for a zep raid'.

Shortly after ten o'clock a faint hum of engines was heard and a zeppelin was spotted, presenting an awesome spectacle against the pale light of the stars. The great ship, under the command of Oberleutnant zur Horst Baron von Buttlar, was riding high in the southern sky and flying quite leisurely towards Ashford.

Although a black-out was in force glimmers of light from many bedrooms caused men from the locally stationed Liverpool Scottish to go round the streets shouting 'Lights out'. Fortunately the airship commander turned to the west and again using the railway line as his guide headed towards London.

However, the night's excitement was not over. At about 10.30pm the sound of engines heralded the return of the machine. The airship was seen high up almost directly over the parish church 'like a giant cigar'. Buttlar seemed to onlookers to be uncertain of his position – he shut off his engines and appeared to hesitate as to which direction to take. Finally the zeppelin's engines roared and its Captain steered northward. A star shell fell near the Cottage Hospital in Wellesley Road, lighting up the area like day. Almost immediately there was an explosion as an incendiary bomb fell on Lower Queens Road, followed by a high explosive bomb on the fields beyond. By now the airship was travelling fast and dropped another bomb on the old golf links at Bybrook as it headed towards Faversham. The airship was picked up by a searchlight but escaped and later dropped a further twelve bombs but without causing damage.

The raid, which was part of a wider zeppelin attack on London, Kent and Essex, caused considerable panic in official quarters. A special national committee was set up to consider the problem of railway lighting, which resulted in a decision to bring trains to a standstill, with no glare permitted from the firebox if air-raid reports indicated that hostile aircraft were endeavouring to find their way to London. The Home Secretary later issued a 'Defence of the Realm' Order which called for the intensity of light at railway stations, sidings, goods yards and docks to be reduced to a minimum and for passengers to keep window blinds lowered in carriages. During subsequent raids the order's severe restrictions brought all railway traffic to a halt over a wide area and caused more chaos than the efforts of the enemy raiders. At the request of the railway authorities the order was relaxed but the lighting restrictions continued.

During the next two years, Dungeness Point proved to be a useful navigational aid for zeppelins as they criss-crossed Kent, following either the coast or inland railway lines.

Von Buttlar was one of the few zeppelin commanders who survived the entire war. In Germany he was hailed as a national hero and was one of only two members of the force who was awarded the 'Pour la Merité', popularly known as 'The Blue Max'.

During those dark years the war cast its shadow over everyone. None more than the relatives whose constant dread was a knock on the door, to be confronted by a telegraph boy bringing tidings that were universally feared.

Lance-Corporal A.G.Chittenden, aged 30, was killed in action. Before the war he worked in the Works Boiler Shop. His commanding officer wrote: 'He surely was a splendid man and an excellent soldier and he died a hero's death.'

Private G.Button of the Buffs aged 30 was also killed. Prior to joining the Army he had served his apprenticeship in the Works as a coach builder. He was drafted to France where he was killed by shrapnel.

Seaman Edward King aged 18 had finished his education at the New Town School and was afterwards employed in the Railway Works. He lost his life in the great naval battle off Jutland while serving in the luckless 'Invincible'.

Private David Reid 'died a hero's death' serving with the Kent Cyclists Battalion. He was previously a fitter's apprentice in the Locomotive Department, in which his father was one of the foremen, and was described as 'a fine handsome fellow of over six feet who had been through some very fierce fighting'. The chaplain of the regiment wrote to his bereaved parents: 'He has died the noblest of all deaths but that does not fill the empty place in your home. But at any rate we thank you for giving him to the country when England needed him and you have made the greatest of all sacrifices as well as he himself...... "God bless the old folks at home" were the last words he said and he died quietly and peacefully and painlessly.'

Sapper J. Cook of the Kent Fortress Royal Engineers, aged 18, was struck in the head with shrapnel and died almost instantly. Prior to enlisting he had been a fitter's apprentice.

Corporal Alfred Campion of the 1st Buffs was seriously wounded. Hit by shrapnel just before Christmas, his elbow was so terribly shattered it needed amputation. Whilst previously serving in the reserve he was employed in the coppersmith's shop. His father also worked in the Works as a trimmer.

Sergeant-Major Gowing died from pneumonia while on active service with the Kent Fortress Royal Engineers. He had been employed in the Works and upon the outbreak of war had volunteered for the Army.

And so the anguish went on through four long years of war. Young men struck down in that most terrible of conflicts.

In 1917 Ashford was caught up in a drama which had horrific implications for the future. In one of the best kept secrets of the war, the Germans had assembled a fleet of heavy Gotha bombers in Belgium. The German High Command named the new force the Luftstreitkrafte and believed that it would achieve a swift and decisive victory, bringing Britain to its knees. 24 aircraft formed the 'England Squadron' under the command of Kapitanleutnant Ernst Brandenberg, who was to become a national idol. By May all was ready, and on the 25th of that month at 4pm the giant planes, which were capable of 80 miles per hour, carried a bomb load of both 60lb and 110lb bombs and which could achieve a height of 15,000 feet, lifted off to carry out their first strike.

Leaving their base at Ghent behind them they headed out across the North Sea for London, but the weather over the city protected the capital. Cloud banks and heavy mist made bombing impossible, so over the Thames estuary Brandenburg turned his force south for Folkestone following the main railway line across Kent.

People were in holiday mood, the balmy weather along the south coast had replaced that of a gloomy winter and spring. The Whitsun weekend beckoned. In Ashford the church clock struck 6 o'clock. Work had mostly finished for the day although shops were still open. The inhabitants became aware of the humming of aircraft and they searched the skies with some considerable curiosity. The raiders were flying at a great height and, with the sun shining through a light haze, it was some time before they could be detected.

As the formation came into view onlookers watched in awe as they counted 21 heavy two-engined machines, the most powerful squadron of German warplanes yet seen in the skies over England. The shout went up 'They're Germans!' Despite the obvious danger, people gathered in the streets to witness the spectacle. Quite suddenly, five bombs came crashing down. Undoubtedly aimed at the Works, they landed in the open near Musgrove Farm and between New Town and Providence Street. Shrapnel wounds were caused to two men and a child but, most pathetically, 18 year-old Gladys Sparkes, daughter of railwayman Charles Sparkes of 13 Providence Street, was killed. She had been out shopping, had hurried to get home and then called to her two younger brothers who were playing in the street. She was caught by a piece of shrapnel and her father, on removing her hat, saw that her brains were protruding from her skull.

Ten year-old Fred Chandler, son of a Works fitter, was playing in the street. 'I was playing quite innocently,' he said, 'along with Jack and Bill Sparks and Ernie Burden. Suddenly there were a series of loud bangs, Ernie was struck with shrapnel and everything seemed to go red and become engulfed in fire. I felt that I couldn't breathe. I just ran from the scene. Windows in Torrington Road and Denmark Road were broken and chimney pots were down.'

A neighbour saw the bomb explode at chimney height. 'There was a loud bang, followed by a wheel of fire,' she said. Another witness described a flash 'like a fork of lightning' and said a darkness like a black cloud followed although there was no smoke.' Fred Chandler recalled that by the time he had returned home, Providence Street and the area around was packed tight with people who had arrived on foot and on bicycles to witness the scene. The incident would be a curtain-raiser to German bombs causing civilian casualties in the district around the Works during the next war.

Having passed over the town, the German warplanes continued flying down the line and decided to test their skill on an express that had just left Ashford. The driver slowed down so as to avoid the emission of smoke and with the idea of keeping behind the aircraft but upon approaching Smeeth Station six bombs exploded on both sides of the line within 200 yards. The driver said later 'I noticed the bombers and one seemed right above us. They meant to get us if they could but happily missed, but not by a very large margin.'

The bombers' route down the main railway line led them to Folkestone, where they were responsible for an infamous attack, which left the town stricken with over 200 dead or injured. For years afterwards, Ashford's inhabitants would recall the horror of that town's Tontine Street, which was packed with late shoppers. A Canadian Army sergeant, just returned from the battle at Vimy Ridge, said the havoc was worse than anything he had seen on the Western Front. 'The whole street seemed to explode – smoke and flames all over – worst were the screams of the wounded and dying.' There were demolished buildings with people fatally entombed, mothers looking frantically for their children, an entire queue outside a shop with all either killed or seriously wounded, explosively-bursting glass and people making a desperate but hopeless attempt to flee. There was a sense of outrage throughout the country.

The Admiralty later reported: 'The raiders were met over the Channel by fighting squadrons of the Royal Naval Air Service from Dunkirk who shot down three German machines' although the reality was that one was shot down and one crashed on landing. A further report was later issued – 'Naval aeroplanes carried out an attack on the German aerodrome at St. Denis Westram, near Ghent, yesterday morning. Many bombs were dropped.'

Three months later the war intruded upon another Bank Holiday when the railway sidings at Ashford became denuded of waiting ambulance trains. A great battle was raging in France on this, the third anniversary of the outbreak of war. Despite the changeable weather, crowds of people had descended upon the various seaside resorts, including, of course, railway families enjoying their 'privilege' quarter-fare tickets. Those that paused to listen above the seaside jollity could sometimes catch a faint booming carried on the wind. On the Western front the noise was horrific. There had been two weeks of intense artillery bombardment followed by 'a big push'. In the hell that followed, hundreds of soldiers met their death, blown to bits, mown down by machine-gun fire or drowned in the gurgling mud that encompassed everything. The battle was officially called 'Third Ypres' but became known simply as Passchendaele.

Steamers were arriving at Dover loaded to the gunnels with wounded. They were quickly transferred to the waiting ambulance trains, a succession of which made their way on the main line through Ashford every hour to Charing Cross.

The exploits of a Willesborough man, a former scholar at the New Town railway school now came to the attention of the public. A few months previously, Ernest Crust had won the Military Medal whilst serving as a corporal. Raised to the rank of lieutenant, he now had the unique experience of being awarded the Military Cross 'for successfully and skilfully leading a surprise attack on a German trench on the Western Front, bringing his men back with scarcely any loss'. On leave to his home town his bravery was recognised in a ceremony held in the grounds of the school, where he was presented with a silver watch by South Willesborough's Wesleyan Church at which he had been a member of the Sunday School.

By now the war was pressing heavily on daily life. Food shortages and long queues at the shops had first appeared early in 1917. Submarine warfare was at its height and German U-boats were sinking one in every four ships sailing from British ports. Margarine, fats, milk, bacon and potatoes became scarce, while sugar and butter were virtually unobtainable. There was a patriotic call for everyone to limit themselves to 4lb of bread and 2½lb meat per week. Matters were made worse by huge increases in prices with a steep rise in bread prices hitting poorer families the hardest. The 20 per cent price increases of 1915 had now increased to 65 per cent. In an attempt to bring about some stability, the government introduced controls on a range of items as diverse as bread, meat, potatoes, jam, matches and coal. The following year would see the introduction of strict rationing.

On the railway the military call-up and competing manpower demands had left the South Eastern and Chatham short of over 5,000 men, nearly a quarter of the usual workforce. Drivers for goods shunting were desperately short and so guards, ticket collectors, lamp men and porters were pressed into service. Little used signal boxes were closed, as were a number of minor lines. Locally neither the Appledore – Lydd, Sandling Junction – Sandgate, Paddock Wood – Hawkhurst, Elham Valley or Canterbury – Whitstable lines saw any more traffic until the end of hostilities.

Despite the difficult conditions, Maunsell had been putting Ashford Works in order after the doldrums of the latter part of the Wainwright era. Modern machinery had been introduced and improved efficiency resulted with Ashford's engine repair costs becoming very much lower than those of neighbouring companies at Brighton and Eastleigh. The Boiler Shop in particular was held in high esteem and locomotive mileages between repairs rose considerably. A chemical laboratory was opened for metal, coal, oils and paint analysis and general metallurgical research. A Physical Laboratory for research into materials and failed components would follow in the twenties.

The need for more powerful yet fewer classes of locomotive had exercised the minds of Maunsell and his team from the moment of their appointment. Now, in 1917, they were able to demonstrate the fruits of their labour by revealing single examples of two engines, this in accordance with Maunsell's wish to satisfy himself of the suitability of a new class before proceeding further.

The first, a 2-6-0 Mogul 'N' class for both fast goods and passenger traffic, proved hugely successful when it went into full production after the war. It gave rise to a whole family of Moguls which finally numbered 172, of which 118 were built at Ashford. The Works was always particularly proud of these engines, which were destined to earn a wonderful reputation on Southern lines during the next 40 years, proving their worth on both main lines and cross-country routes, hauling heavy loads and running very high mileages between visits to the maintenance shops.

The second, a 2-6-4 passenger express tank engine, designated 'K' class, was a variation of the class 'N' but designed to haul the boat trains and operate without the need to replenish its water supply en-route. Because of the war, production was delayed until as late as 1925.

The military port of Richborough was now further extended to improve shipment of railway locomotives, armoured vehicles, aircraft, artillery and other heavy equipment destined for the Western Front. A powerful shunter was urgently needed by the War Department, but a new design was out of the question, Ashford being fully committed to repairs and the production of shell cases. Maunsell decided to modify a 1900 'C' class goods locomotive and a quite extraordinary number of changes were carried out in order to produce a highly successful saddle tank engine quite unlike its progenitor – designated Special Tank Shunter class 'G'.

Even while meeting the demands of war, the South Eastern and Chatham continued with its coach-building programme, the Ashford shops producing 36 coaches between 1914 and 1917. Steam heated, with electric lighting and lavatories, their smooth running was highly admired. Even so, there was a considerable difference in the comfort offered by the two classes, the first class being described as 'Examples of Edwardian opulence with wide reclining seats that could so easily cradle the unwary beyond their destination.' The third class simply offered a strip of blue leatherette to lean back on, with the minimum of padding.

In addition, an energetic programme of equipping all main line carriages with steam heating was carried through. With Wainwright gone, the practice of fitting roof observatories was reconsidered, and upon the recommendation of the Superintendent of the Line, they were dispensed with on all coaching stock built from 1915 onward.

That many in the industry were looking beyond the war was evident at a meeting of railwaymen held one Sunday evening at the Co-operative Hall. A speaker from Ashford's No.1 branch of the NUR declared; 'We are on the threshold of a new era; we are at the dawn of a new democracy. After the war many problems will have to be faced, including the reconstruction of industry, where the workers will have to reshape the destiny of the nation and will have to think politically as well as industrially.' He also spoke on the question of war bonus being converted into wages, little realising the struggle that railwaymen would have to bring this into effect when the war was over.

For most of the war there was much socialising between the Canadian soldiers stationed in Ashford and local people, many events being arranged for the troops' benefit. Not unnaturally, with such strapping young men in their midst, the inevitable happened. Dozens of excited young girls were present when a member of the Canadian Ordnance Corps Band married Mabel Stone, daughter of a railwayman, at the parish church. In addition, a great many of the bridegroom's comrades were in the congregation, who after the service gathered outside and greeted the happy couple with a rousing reception.

A scandal that caused a local sensation occurred when civil and Canadian Military Police carried out a raid on wearers of Canadian army boots, 300 pairs of which had been found missing from the Canadian Ordnance corps depot in the town during the previous three months. Most of the men concerned were employed in the Railway Works and were summoned to appear before the local magistrates' court, which held special sittings lasting the entire week.

Most of the defendants accounted for their possession of the boots either by claiming they had purchased them from Canadian soldiers, 7/6d appearing to be the going rate, or that they had been left behind at their homes when Canadian soldiers had been billeted with them. Many pleaded extenuating circumstances but many others were not so lucky and were fined £5.

An accident that could have had the most serious consequences occurred on the foggy night of 4th November 1917. The main line had seen heavy military traffic throughout the war and the marvel is perhaps that there had been no incident until then. A special goods with military supplies and headed for the port of Richborough, had stopped on the down through line to change crews, but on getting away the last seven wagons and two brake vans parted company from the rest of the train. Before the signalman could be warned, two class 'O' locomotives stormed out of the fog with a train of armoured vehicles and crashed into the other goods, smashing it to one side and reducing its wagons to matchwood. Extraordinarily, no-one was hurt and damage to the two engines was minimal but the line was blocked for some hours.

A brilliant 'Bombers Moon' set the scene for a crucial air attack in May 1918. Ernst Brandenburg, as England Squadron commander, had assembled a force of 43 German bombers and now launched the biggest air fleet ever against England, intending to achieve decisive results. But Germany's increased air power was being countered by Britain's stronger anti-aircraft defences, as they would learn to their cost.

Between 10.30pm and midnight a succession of raiders began crossing the coast between Dover and Blackwater. Thirteen bombers penetrated to the capital but others dumped their bombs over Kent and Sussex and headed for home. Unsurprisingly some found the South Eastern railway line beckoning the way, and just before midnight on Whit Sunday the sound of Gotha bombers was heard over Ashford. They were at once assailed by a barrage from the 18 guns around the town and the whole area was lit up by searchlights, star shells and flashes from the guns. The heavy barrage made the very earth quiver while the air resounded with explosions and the screech of shells and shrapnel.

Also seeking to bar their way were the night fighter squadrons of the newly-formed Royal Air Force. 112 Squadron, flying Sopwith Camels and operating out of Throwley Aerodrome had a patrol from their landing ground across to Ashford, guarding the way across the rail corridor from Folkestone to London.

The fighters and anti-aircraft guns across south-eastern England had a good night, claiming a total of seven aircraft shot down. These losses, together with the fact that only thirteen bombers had managed to reach London, finally caused the Germans to abandon their air assault on this country. Ashford, having been witness to the first of the Gotha bomber raids the previous Whitsun, had now been witness to the last.

The end of the war came with comparative swiftness, the news being received in Ashford with general rejoicing. Church bells rang, shops and houses were decorated with flags and bunting, people paraded the streets singing and cheering and school children were given an impromptu holiday. That evening the railway station was illuminated and army searchlights sent their beams across the night sky playing upon the low clouds, which with the misty atmosphere provided the most remarkable scenic effects. Bands played in the High Street and an effigy of the Kaiser was hung from a lamp post and later dragged through the town.

Shortly afterwards, at the annual prize giving in the railway school at New Town the headmaster, Frederick Durtnall, spoke of their difficulties during the war years and of the contribution that the school had made to the fighting forces. Nearly 400 old boys had joined the army or navy and 46 had lost their lives. Four of the teachers had joined the army, two had obtained commissions and one had died a captive in Germany. In the Works, memorials recorded the names of all those railwaymen who had been killed in action during those dreadful years.

The Great Railway Strike

With the war over, demobilisation began, allowing former railwaymen to return to their jobs, a relief for a company faced with a shortage of engines and a backlog of repairs. In accordance with wartime promises to trades unions, working hours were reduced. They would now commence at 7.30am and finish at 5.30pm other than Saturday, when work would cease at noon. Despite this concession, there was clearly much discontent among the country's workforce. Promises of a better life for the men who had fought for their country were being forgotten.

Matters blew up when the government refused to make permanent the higher rates of pay introduced during the war, which were an ordinary wage of 18s. plus war bonus of 33s. The rail unions complained of unfairness and anomalies in rates, claiming lower grades would suffer a pay cut. They called for a minimum wage of £3. Negotiations between trades unions and the government had been going on since the previous March and had reached stalemate. It had been said there would be serious trouble in the railway world and these fears were now about to come true.

Quite unexpectedly, at midnight on Friday 26th September 1919, the unions called a general rail strike, throwing the country into a state of chaos. In Ashford, meetings held over the weekend brought out the entire workforce of the National Union of Railwaymen, comprising 2,400 men. They were joined by the 300 members of the Associated Society of Enginemen and Firemen and the 50 men employed at the goods depot. One man was permitted to remain to attend to livestock on rail and three others to feed and water the Company's horses but even this concession was withdrawn on the Monday.

The Kentish Express reported: 'On Saturday morning the railway station presented a deserted appearance with a few officials standing about discussing the situation, one or two passengers seeking in vain for a train and a few men in khaki who were not unhappy at this unexpected extension of leave, being unable to return to their regiments. The booking clerks were there but no trains to issue tickets for, the refreshment rooms were open but there was no-one to eat the station buns. The station sparrows flew down on the line in search of stray grain or crumbs of food, whilst the station cat, realising that there was now no danger from passing trains, wandered on to the line in the hope of catching one of the birds. At one point a Continental mails train went cautiously through the station in the charge of a locomotive foreman. Little else disturbed the quiet.'

On Sunday the railway station was entirely closed but in the station yard there was a lone newsagent selling newspapers that he had brought down from London by car. There was also an interchange of milk churns brought in from the country and put into lorries which had been pressed into service. When the strike broke out there were over 200 vans in the railway goods depot, containing consignments of foodstuffs for Ashford and neighbouring towns. None of this was touched during the weekend but during the week following, tradesmen were allowed to unload and take away their own goods.

A railwaymen's meeting held in the Corn Exchange on that first Saturday was packed to capacity and this would be only the first of a series of rallies during the strike period.

On Monday the strikers were joined by men from the Amalgamated Society of Engineers, the Boilermakers Union, the Operative Bricklayers Society and the United Kingdom Society of Coachmakers. This action finally shut down the Works as far as actual work was concerned.

The whole town was reported as being affected, particularly in South Ashford and Willesborough, where there was scarcely a house in which husbands and sons had not left their work. Ashford town centre presented quite a holiday appearance with the men standing about in groups wearing their best clothes.

The strike committee representing the various unions set up joint headquarters in the Liberal Association Rooms in the High Street. The scene was one of continuous activity with men coming and going at all hours of the day. During the morning there was great enthusiasm shown when a message from London union headquarters was read to the crowd from the committee room window. That evening, clerks still working in the Superintendent's office were working by candlelight, the gas supply having been cut when the Works Gas House workers joined the strike.

The Governments response to the unions was in direct contrast to the attitude of the railwaymen. In an ominous move on Sunday morning a detachment of men from the East Kent Regiment – the Buffs – arrived, in full service order and steel helmets, for emergency duties and was quartered in Ashford's Drill Hall. That day also saw a large convoy of 29 lorries filled with troops pass through the town heading for London. In addition to troops in Ashford, soldiers were standing guard at Maidstone, Marines were on duty at Chatham, Dover Pier was picketed by soldiers with fixed bayonets and a machine gun had been erected at Folkestone junction. The strikers, meantime, proclaimed their Christian ideals and the leaders asked the men to conduct themselves in a quiet and orderly manner.

On the following Wednesday over 1,000 railwaymen processed through the streets of Ashford singing, headed up by a rag-time band playing 'Tipperary' as they made their way to a rally in Victoria Park. A succession of speakers addressed the men, the keynote being solidarity and endurance, in support of claims that they were fighting to win a better country for the working classes of England. The Government was attacked for failing to look after the country's maimed soldiers, having promised so much.

Declaring that it was the strikers who were trying to make England a land fit for heroes to live in and thanking the pickets, who were composed of men who had learnt discipline on the plains of France, a speaker urged them to fight cleanly and prove they were men and gentlemen.

The rally was followed during the evening by a further mass meeting in the Corn Exchange and there was yet another meeting on the Saturday following, which again attracted a packed audience. One of the speakers claimed: 'If the Government reduces the wages of the railwaymen, all labour organisations will go to the wall.' It was announced that the distress fund now amounted to £33 and an appeal was made for gifts of vegetables for a soup kitchen that was to be opened at Willesborough.

The town was alive with people again on Sunday when hundreds of men again marched in procession through the streets, this time headed by the Ashford Railway Works Band. Winding their way towards Victoria Park they were greeted by an immense crowd of well-wishers. Perhaps out of respect for the Sabbath, a speaker said: 'Trade Unionism was the essence of life and God was in the movement.' He referred to Moses receiving an order from God to lead the Israelites into the Land of Promise. 'If it was a crime to be poor then surely God would have made us all rich. The sooner the rich realised this, the quicker they would make this land what God meant it to be.'

By early evening rumours were circulating in the town that there was to be a settlement favourable to the men. At 7.40pm, Ted Bumstead, Chairman of the Ashford Strike Committee appeared at the High Street window of Strike Headquarters and in a dramatic announcement gave the news that the strike was over. Faced with the possibility of its extension to other trades, the Cabinet had capitulated. Amidst a scene of intense excitement the crowd that had gathered cheered frantically, whereupon the Chairman assembled all the locomotive men he could find and led them in ordered ranks down to the Works to report for duty. The railwaymen had won full recognition of their unions by the companies and a system of joint discussion for wages and conditions.

Next day all the men employed in the Works reported for work at 7.30am. With the same readiness that they left work, the men now returned. Later that week, a Victory Concert was held in the Corn Exchange with entertainment being provided for the men, their wives and children. The evening concluded with votes of thanks, acclamations and cheers and everyone singing 'We all go the same way home'.

Ashford Works was caught up in an echo of the war in the spring of 1919. The SE&CR had recognised the need to replace their aging stock of vans. In a radical departure from previous Victorian styling, the prototype had a steel underframe, 21-foot wheelbase, 2 sets of double doors and an elliptical roof. The new design soon became a common sight on the southern network, whether on minor lines or attached to prestige expresses. Production was destined to last for over 30 years and exceed 1,600 vehicles.

The first van, numbered 132, was outshopped from the Works in a dark umber livery with bold yellow lettering. It immediately entered history by being sent to Dover Marine Station on 14th May to receive the body of Nurse Edith Cavell, which had been returned from Belgium.

Edith Cavell had achieved fame as a result of becoming involved in the wartime situation. As matron of a training hospital in Brussels she had elected to remain when Belgium was over-run by the German Army in 1914. She was soon playing an important part in organising a support network for escaping British soldiers. By mid-1915 the suspicions of the German secret police were thoroughly aroused. She was arrested and a few days later the German authorities published a confession. With 26 other defendants she was brought before a German military court, and together with four others who were considered to be the leaders, sentenced to death. In the event, she was one of two who were executed by firing squad in the early hours of 12th October 1915. Neutral and Allied public opinion was outraged and Edith Cavell was hailed as a martyr.

Now her body had been exhumed from the execution ground and was being returned to England with full military honours. Her coffin was brought by train from Brussels to Ostend where it was taken aboard the destroyer HMS Rowena, which was accompanied across the channel by HMS Rigorous. At Dover the flag-draped coffin was landed at the pierhead and then preceded a procession of military, nursing and civic representatives, watched in silence by a large crowd. The band of the Royal Marines, Deal, played solemn music and the parish church rang a peal of muffled bells.

At the recently completed Marine Station, Van 132 freshly arrived from Ashford was standing suitably prepared for the coffin. It was hung with drapes, wreaths were placed in it and it remained there overnight with a guard provided by the Buffs Regiment.

The following day the van, with a special saloon for the funeral party, proceeded to Victoria Station and, as befitting a day of national mourning, was escorted to Westminster Abbey by the bands of the Coldstream, Welsh and Grenadier Guards. This poignant introduction to service by Van 132 resulted in all subsequent vans of this type being known to the railwaymen as Cavell Vans.

In December 1919, Maunsell initiated an annual dinner for the Ashford & District Foreman's Association, the first being held in the George Hotel. They were destined to become an institution, with 'The Chief' revealing the programme of works for the months ahead. Awaited with both concern and anticipation, his news could herald a period of either short-time working or full employment. Maunsell revealed his fellow feeling for the railwaymen when he declared that conditions should not and could not remain as they were. 'Men should be able to be proud to work in our great industrial centres.'

During the two years following the war, Ashford continued to adjust. Organisation and methods further improved and a steady stream of new machinery came in to replace obsolete plant. Proposals to group the railways into four major companies were being floated, but Maunsell, in a spirit of optimism, considered Ashford could build or repair engines, carriages and wagons as well as any other workshop.

The plans of Maunsell and his team for improved locomotives were now beginning to bear fruit. Facing them was the perennial problem of producing engines that were more powerful, yet light enough to be used over 'Chatham' lines. Plans for bridge strengthening and track-renewal were still some years from completion. The need for a speedy remedy resulted in a decision to completely rebuild Wainwright's 'E' class with parts interchangeable with those of the new 'N' class. No 179 was rebuilt at Ashford in 1919, and perhaps unsurprisingly given its pedigree, was an immediate success, so much so that a further ten were sent to Beyer-Peacock &

Company for immediate conversion. The secret of their new ability lay in the fitting of a superheater, modernising the design of the valve-gear and reducing weight wherever possible, resulting in an engine of greatly enhanced capability yet no heavier then the original. It was the view of railway historian O.S.Nock that they ranked among Maunsell's most brilliant successes. Now classed 'E1's they were given the prestige job of working the boat trains between Victoria and Dover.

Thoughts naturally turned to the possibility of re-building some of Wainwright's 'D' class and they proved to be as amenable to conversion and improved running as their 'sisters'. Again Beyer-Peacock re-built ten but a further eleven were dealt with in the Ashford Works. They distinguished themselves as 'D1's in charge of expresses between London and the Kent coast and 30 years later were still being used for fast passenger work.

Production of the 'N' class began in earnest in 1920 and during the next three years, fifteen were constructed at Ashford, bringing much needed relief to a war-worn railway. Of significance was the building of No.822, with three cylinders instead of two as with the rest of the class, giving it a greatly superior performance. Being completed in December 1922, No.822 can also lay claim to being the last South Eastern and Chatham engine to be built.

The Southern

The grouping of the railway systems came into effect on 1st January 1923, the new Southern Railway being created from the South Eastern & Chatham, the London, Brighton & South Coast and the London & South Western railways. Maunsell was appointed Chief Mechanical Engineer and moved his office to Waterloo but made sure that the brilliant Ashford design team was retained. He also decided that the principal locomotive and carriage drawing offices would be located at Eastleigh, resulting in the Ashford office being reduced in status.

The changes included a break in the link between the New Town School and the company. Much sadness attended the take-over by Kent County Council as former pupils recalled their happy days at the railway school.

The 1922 Dinner was typical of many when three of the Ashford foremen retired after long service. John Woodworth had been born at 101 New Town in 1853, his father having been a patternmaker at the Works since 1848. As a foreman fitter in the locomotive shop he had served under six superintendents. Albert Harrison had also been born at New Town, in 1859, the son of Lancashire parents, and could boast a record of 49 years continuous service to the Company. He had risen to foreman coach trimmer, succeeding his father in that position in 1899. His father had by then served for 53 years. The third retiring foreman was a smith, John Cole, who had commenced his long service with an apprenticeship in 1873 at the age of 15. His father was another early pioneer at the Works, having come down from Manchester in 1846.

Six years later another example of long service came to the public's attention, following a report on the death of a Mrs. Jane Stupples at Ashford. Her father, William Curry, had driven George Stephenson's Rocket and later the first express train between Dover and London. Her husband and several of her descendants and relations had followed in William's footsteps, all giving long service to the South Eastern Railway in various capacities.

Other locomotive works always looked at Ashford with some bemusement with its reputation of being a 'family Works'. Fathers, sons, uncles, nephews and cousins, generation upon generation, were to be found throughout the workforce. There was one 'Spanish custom' which left the other works gaping. As the fruit picking and hop picking seasons approached, large numbers of the labouring force simply took off. There seemed little the management could do about this and so they worked around the problem in such a way that the services of the labourers could be temporarily dispensed with. At the end of their time in the orchards and hop gardens the labourers returned and were duly reinstated on the payroll. This appears to have been an old Kentish custom, examples of such behaviour having been recorded since the 17th century in the dockyard towns of Deptford and Chatham.

An astonishing admission was made by Maunsell at the 1922 Dinner when he revealed that no scheme of working for the amalgamated railways had yet been considered, much less put into operation. Electrification of some of the lines was still going ahead but no instructions had come to him either for new construction or conversion of rolling stock. The unsettled state of affairs in connection with the railways generally had led to fewer orders and short time working. In this atmosphere of uncertainty fears about the future of the Works again arose.

It was the best part of two years before the situation was seen to have changed and for the better. Maunsell was confident that in the long run, efficiency was the key which would settle where work would be carried out and certainly work was now flowing in as the new Southern Railway management got into their stride. There now appeared to be enough construction and conversion work on the order book to keep the shops in full time working for some years to come.

Attempts to return to pre-war conditions had been agonisingly slow with locomotives continuing to appear in their drab funeral grey wartime livery because of difficulties in obtaining supplies of suitable green paint. It had been to universal approval that the new company revealed its choice of livery, sage green for both locomotives and carriages with the smartly turned out engines having a tasteful lining out in black and white and the simple title 'Southern' emblazoned in yellow on their tenders. Finally, on 8th November 1923, Stirling goods No.170 became the last locomotive to leave the paint shop in grey uniform.

At the 1924 Dinner, Maunsell reminded the foremen that the following year would see the 100th anniversary of the first public railway and of the amazing development in the power of the steam engine. As regards electrification on the multiple unit system, Maunsell's view was that it was not yet a serious rival for main-line work and was not likely to be so as long as its power was transmitted from central generating stations by means of conductors.

It was during this year that the Southern was involved in the unusual circumstance of purchasing 50 sets of locomotive parts for assembly at Ashford. Following the Armistice in 1918, the Government decided to create employment for the otherwise redundant workers at Woolwich Arsenal by producing a standard engine suitable for use across the national network. Following abortive attempts by the Association of Railway Engineers to design such a locomotive, the choice fell on Maunsell's class 'N' 2-6-0.

The government scheme proved to be a disaster. Doubts were cast upon the mathematical ability of those at Woolwich to properly use drawings supplied by Ashford Works. To help resolve the muddle, it was decided that the boilers would have to be supplied by a specialist manufacturer but finally inferior workshop organisation, ineffective costing and total lack of knowledge of steam locomotive construction led to miserable failure. Poor output was compounded by partially assembled engines being stored in the open with little protection from either pilfering or the elements.

The Southern purchased 20 partly assembled engines in 1924 but their passage under tow, which began on 25th May, was so beset with difficulties that Ashford was not reached until eight days later. Only two were in a complete condition, the remainder, travelling in trains of four at a time, were described as being 'no more than boilers on frames with the pony truck, leading and coupled wheels in place'. The condition of some was such that they had to be transported on wagons. They were unable to enter into traffic until Ashford's men had worked on them for 24 days continuously. Another 30 engines were purchased later in the year and again the skill of the Ashford men was called for in righting the problems of the Woolwich product.

The government had initially envisaged the railways would be nationalised and in need of a standard locomotive design, but with the grouping of railways into four private companies the scheme went awry. The authorities had to sell the Woolwich parts where they could and they were sold off at bargain prices, the Southern paying only £4,000 for each locomotive compared with a normal cost of £9,000. Railway wags promptly nicknamed them 'Woolworths'. The Woolwich scheme resulted in a loss to public funds of well over £1 million.

After the work fears two years previously, prospects at Ashford were now extremely buoyant. Authority had been given for the erection of 20 of Maunsell's 'K' class but Ashford was too busy to carry out the task. Finished parts from Ashford were therefore sent to Brighton Works and to Armstrong Whitworth at Newcastle, who completed the job with the exception of No.890 which Ashford erected as a three-cylinder engine, designated class 'K1'.

The mid-twenties was a period when the correspondence columns of newspapers began to feature complaints from passengers, reminiscent of the dark days of the South Eastern. Complaints were made that the Southern had been unsympathetic to passengers' grievances and it was claimed: 'Under the old regime complaints from the public were received with courtesy and sympathy'. Complainants were particularly agitated by dirty carriages and the condition of lavatories. 'The condition of the rolling stock generally is bad' it was said and 'the service lacked punctuality'. An Ashford passenger wrote that the carriage he went up to London in was icy cold. His grievance was magnified by finding the same cold conditions on his return journey. He pleaded 'I do ask the Southern Railway to provide foot warmers if they cannot heat their carriages any other way'. When three Sussex MPs who were all Cabinet Ministers associated themselves with the complaints, the Southern had to respond.

With some justification the Company strongly defended itself with Press advertisements entitled 'The Truth about the Southern'. They reminded the public of the pummeling the system had taken during the war. 'Locomotives already overtaxed were made to pound just a little bit harder, carriages which had more than "done their bit" did just a "bit" more, trucks which were never built to take them took guns and parts of guns, great Howitzers and long range monsters; cattle trucks were patched and repatched so that the horses and mules might reach their destinations on time and the track itself, used to a more normal traffic of peace time proportions, bore the weight and stood the racket of hundreds and hundreds of troop trains thundering by day and night over them.'

After this appeal to patriotic sentiment, they pointed to the fact that railways were only freed from government war-time control in 1921, that the amalgamation scheme for the Southern companies only followed in 1923 and that try as they might, it would take time to repair the ravages of war. There followed an announcement of a new programme of locomotive and carriage construction, which must surely have brought joy to the men in the

Railway Works, as well as to passengers. In order to provide evidence of the efforts being made, a representative group of national journalists was invited to visit the Works at Ashford. The local newspaper enthused at the visit, claiming that the visitors found every indication of hustle. 'The vast Works were traversed and everybody was enthralled and astonished at the speed work is now being carried out and the wonderful machinery, which seems in its subtlety to possess almost a human touch. The Ashford Works are thoroughly up to date and pressure is being placed upon the staff to provide the new electric trains. The preliminary work of making the new electrical carriages is done at Ashford, where steel frames are constructed. Then comes the erection of the coach bodies on the under-frames, on which 600 men are engaged and the installation of the electric motors in the tractor carriages. When the coaches reach this stage, they are sent to Brighton Works for completion.' Certainly the local newspaper's headline 'The Awakening of the Southern Railway – Gigantic Projects' appeared to be undeniable. Keen to further improve its image, the Southern now selected a Maunsell 'N' class locomotive, No.866 newly built at Ashford, for showing at the British Empire Exhibition at Wembley.

The year also saw the emergence of the first of Maunsell's class 'N15' "King Arthur" locomotives, which would bring a new prestige to the Southern. Although all the class were built at Eastleigh, they owed much of their success to Ashford influences. Basically a London & South Western Railway Urie 2-6-0, Maunsell and his staff carried out a number of Ashfordising modifications. The valve gear was modified, the smokebox, draughting and superheating was altered and the boiler pressure increased. The result was a brilliant locomotive in which Ashford could take shared pride.

July 1925 saw the official opening of a much-appreciated facility at Ashford by the Company's General Manager, Sir Herbert Walker. The Southern had provided land known locally as Bath Meadows, together with a gift of £2,000 in order to provide hard tennis courts and a bowling green, adding to the cricket ground, band stand and dancing green which already existed. The new pavilion was a masterpiece of innovation, which had been made entirely out of scrap materials. Together with the Works football club, the 500 members of the Railway Institute were now set to enjoy a wide range of activities.

The General Strike

1926 witnessed the drama of the General Strike. Provoked by a final decision on Friday 30th April to reduce miners' wages, the coal industry ceased work the next day. The General Council of the TUC called for the support of other trades and in response the government declared a State of Emergency. Fruitless negotiations continued during the weekend as the industrial temper rose. On Monday, Sir Herbert Walker, General Manager of the Southern Railway issued a statement – 'At this moment of National Emergency I earnestly appeal to every member of the Company's staff to continue at work and remain loyal to his conditions of service'. The drama continued to unfold during the day and at 11.15 that evening the message came over the wireless – 'All negotiations have failed'. At midnight the message was – 'The General Strike takes effect from now'.

Just before midnight a train was heard to rumble slowly into Ashford station – after that, all was quiet. The peace of the night was unbroken by the usual noise of shunting and no train entered the station until one arrived bringing the few abbreviated morning papers that had been published.

The official strike announcement had been preceded in Ashford by a mass meeting in the town's Corn Exchange. Basil Noble, speaking for the railwaymen, said that although they had not been directly attacked, as soon as the miners were forced to accept worse conditions, they would be faced with the same problem. He pledged solidarity and the Chairman, Ebenezer Tong, called for work to cease that evening. A message was received from the local branch of the A.E.U. union that members had been ordered to cease work. The National Union of Vehicle Workers, representing wagon makers, reported that their members were ordered out. A telegram was received from the Railway Clerks Association that they were acting jointly with the National Union of Railwaymen. A representative of the Clerks said that he had just left a meeting of nearly 160 railway clerks, who had passed a resolution pledging support. In Ashford the strike was solid, the only members of regular staff remaining at work being the station-master, two inspectors, a shunter and a guard.

The Government's belligerent attitude was demonstrated by Sir John Simon in the House of Commons, who, declaring the strike to be illegal, said that: 'Every trade union leader and every striker is liable in damages to the uttermost farthing of his personal possessions'.

Ashford saw little excitement during the strike period but following its sudden and dramatic end on 12th May it was some days before working returned to normal. The absent workforce, numbering between two and three thousand had to await instructions from the railway management. A notice was posted outside the railway station which read: 'Work will be recommenced in the Company's workshops on Friday morning but for the present there will not be sufficient work for the whole of the men who were previously employed'. In the event the Works did not open until the Monday morning, although it was only on the Southern Railway that there was a complete re-instatement of men.

The previous Sunday afternoon the strikers, headed by a band, had marched around the principal streets of the town finishing with a meeting in Victoria Park, where they concluded with the hymn 'O God our help in ages past' after being addressed by a number of local speakers. During the months following, new arrangements were set up between the railway companies and trade unions to deal with rates of pay and sundry other matters.

The country's difficulties of the past few months had kept the Works short of materials and this restriction on output had again aroused fears for the future, but Maunsell was adamant: 'There is no intention of either closing or lessening the activities of the Works'. To emphasise this he announced a programme of further improvements, which comprised the erection of a travelling Goliath crane, enabling them to move and store complete boilers, wheel centres and tyres in much less space, a new running shed, a new wheel shop and an electric transverser.

Now, with industrial difficulties receding, full-time working was resumed on the locomotive side but the electrification programme was proving to be a mixed blessing, the cause of overtime in some shops but short-time working in others.

More Change

Excitement mounted during the year at the prospect of an official visit by the Duke and Duchess of York, the townspeople little realising that ten years later the popular couple would be King and Queen. The boat train from London was specially stopped at the station and the Duke and Duchess, upon passing through the booking hall into the station yard, were confronted by a battery of cameramen and cinema newsmen. The playing of the National Anthem by the Southern Railway Institute Band announced their arrival to both the waiting crowd and a contingent of civic dignitaries.

As part of his loyal address, James Hogg, Chairman of the local council, noted that the Duke was president of the Industrial Welfare Society and by his intense interest in the welfare of the community he was endeavouring to raise the whole standard of industrial life. 'We are glad' he said 'that you are to visit the important Works of the Southern Railway Company with which the life of this town is inseparably bound.'

Having first inaugurated the town's electricity supply from the new generating station, the royal couple proceeded to the Railway Works. They first saw the steam hammers at work, after which it became clear that they were especially interested in the making of rivets and nuts by an automatic machine. In the locomotive machine shop, the Duchess was impressed with the making of copper fire-box stays, asking for an explanation from the foreman. Having watched the huge engines being lifted by crane in the erecting shop, the Duchess twice returned to the boiler shop to see stays being riveted to a boiler. So engrossed was she in the riveting operations that she thrust her head into a fire-box to see how the rivets were treated on the inside. Having passed through the carriage paint shop they inspected the Southern's latest Eastleigh-built engine 'Lord Nelson' – the most powerful locomotive in the United Kingdom.

At this point the Duke and Duchess embarked on an adventure that would be recalled in the Works and the town for many years to come. Mounting the footplate, the Duke opened the regulator – smothering all the photographers in specks of soot – and set the giant locomotive in motion which, amidst rousing cheers from the railway workers, steamed majestically out of the Works towards the station.

After visiting the parish church and town centre there remained a ceremony to lay the foundation stone for a new hospital in King's Avenue. The Duke concluded his visit with the words: 'I understand that a scheme for a special contribution to the new hospital is about to be launched by the Southern Railway employees at Ashford, to which the Board of the Southern Railway has promised to contribute. I hope that the scheme will meet with a warm response and that your efforts to erect and equip the hospital will meet with the success they so richly deserve.'

Everyone was shocked when, on 21st August 1927, news came through that 'K' class "River Cray" had left the track when approaching Sevenoaks at the head of the Charing Cross – Deal pullman car express (first stop – Ashford). 13 passengers had lost their lives and 43 were badly injured. There had been numerous complaints from drivers about the instability of these engines at speed and now the inevitable had happened.

The entire class was immediately withdrawn from service but Maunsell was subsequently vindicated, an inquiry finding that the fault lay with the poor standard of the permanent way. Previously, shingle ballast from Dungeness laid on a foundation of ash had been used. With the heavier rolling stock coming into use this was no longer adequate and so the Directors decided to replace shingle with Meldon granite on all main lines, and to improve drainage. To further restore confidence, a re-building programme was launched which resulted in the ill-fated 2-6-4 'K' class tank engines being converted to 2-6-0 tender locomotives. Ashford was charged with the re-building of twenty of them and they were re-classified as 'U' class.

The Works was cheered when it learned of the decision to replace 105 six-coupled tank engines of various ages and classes with a new 0-6-0 tank locomotive, designated 'Y' class. Based upon construction at Ashford, costs were estimated at £3,125 each and the hope was that the home Works would get the lion's share of the work. Sadly, with a worsening world economic climate and a drop in traffic receipts, the plan was shelved until better days. In the event, with the later appearance of diesel shunters, the class was cancelled.

A further disappointment was the decision to build all the new Schools 'V' class at Eastleigh. The opportunity to build this most glittering of Maunsell's locomotives was snatched from Ashford by the need to have all the first ten in traffic by mid-1930. To achieve this it was found necessary to concentrate their construction at a single Works and Eastleigh was the chosen Works.

It was some consolation to Ashford that an order for a further five class 'N1's remained outstanding but this was soon offset by the loss of an order for five of the new and powerful 2-6-4 'W' class tank engines. Intended for handling goods traffic in the London electrified area, this latest locomotive was a version of the class 'K1' and would prove to be the final member of the Maunsell Mogul family. Drawings had been prepared by the Ashford drawing office and by March 1929 had been accepted by the Locomotive Committee, but because of the poor economic situation the order was set aside and the frames and cylinders that had already been prepared by Ashford were placed in store at Eastleigh. Unfortunately, when it was later decided to go ahead with their erection in 1932, it was Eastleigh that was awarded the task.

Towards the end of 1929, Maunsell introduced changes that were to bring about an upheaval in the lives of many. The Southern's main workshops were to be reorganised. Brighton was to be run down over ten years with locomotive construction and repairs concentrated at Eastleigh and Ashford. Carriage work was to cease at Ashford, new construction being transferred to Eastleigh and repair work to Lancing. Building of wagons would be centred at Ashford.

The changes took account of the fact that Eastleigh, which had opened in 1910, was the largest, most modern and best equipped of the Southern workshops. Ashford had a reliable and distinctive record but part of its carriage works could only handle four- and six-wheelers and Brighton suffered continual problems caused by a lack of space on its small site. The consequence of these alterations was a major re-shuffle of manpower, with many families being wrenched apart. Much of Brighton's machinery was moved to Ashford, including a 35-ton crane for the erecting shop, but in the event Brighton was re-equipped upon the outbreak of war in 1939 and its final closure was delayed until 1958.

The railway historian, S. C. Townroe, commented on an odd sequel to the reorganisation of workshops and the transfer of former London, Brighton & South Coast Railway locomotives needing repair to Ashford and Eastleigh. The receiving Works asked for the necessary drawings in order that the working parts could be repaired in accordance with the original design. Astonishingly, it was discovered that not only were many drawings missing, but, worse, few of the engines bore much resemblance, other than outwardly, to such drawings that did exist!

He also referred to the comparative cheapness of building a steam locomotive and its economy in spares. All cast iron, bronze, brass and white metal could be recovered and re-used and all spare parts could be made at Ashford and Eastleigh, at short notice if necessary. A thrifty but ingenious management arranged that spare parts were transported to and from depots by having them carried on the backs of tenders. The method was well organised, as the parts were changed over from engine to engine en route to their destination.

Maunsell had some reassuring news for Ashford at the 1931 Annual Foreman's Dinner. As a result of the reorganisation an extra 235 locomotives would be maintained at the Works. In addition they were now beginning the erection of ten 'U' class engines and these would be followed by another order for 15 'N' class. A decision was to be taken upon a further ten engines and would be announced in the March rolling-stock programme. As regards carriage work, there were 70 bogie vans to be finished and a number of other vehicles, including Isle of Wight stock, which needed alteration and repair.

Wagon building would continue on the basis of 50 open wagons per week for the next two years and it was expected that after that open wagon production would be on an annual basis of 2,000 for some years to come. As a further palliative, Maunsell stressed that it was still cheaper to build locomotives, carriages and wagons in the company's workshops rather than buy in from outside sources.

Despite the bleak economic situation, the Southern continued to build on its reputation for improved rolling stock. In addition to new locomotives, new carriages were being introduced, giving greater comfort to passengers. An example was carriage No.6666, the walls of its first class compartment being polished walnut with sycamore panelling and with upholstery in 'Salidin' tapestry. The third class boasted walls of polished mahogany with upholstery in red, black and orange moquette. The lavatories were equipped with hot and cold water.

Notwithstanding Maunsell's reassurances there were clearly continuing worries about the national economic situation and its effect upon the Company's finances. Wishing he had something more cheerful to say, Maunsell told the foremen that in the 48 weeks ending 30th November the receipts for the four railway companies showed a total decrease of £9,561,000.It was little wonder that the companies sought every possible means to economise. Even so, he hoped there would be no reduction in their existing programme of work.

Private Road owned by Southern Railway which lead from the railway station,

to the railway works.

One of the last remaining flats built in the mid 1800s for the employees of the new works.

Early picture of Newtown Green and pump!

New houses built in 1906 when Longhedge work closed and transferred to Ashford.

New school built at the same date to accomodate Longhedge children.

Bomb damage 1942.

Neglect damage 2006. Klondyke, a sorry sight now, but hopefully will be rejuvenated into Ashford Railway Museum.

Set of locomotive wheels built in 1904 by Harry Wainwright and given as a gift by Esmond Lewis Evans. The plinth built and donated by Henry Headley who built the modern houses in the renewal of Newtown.

The Wheel Shop (from Harry Elgars album)

Every works would have had one of these early mobile cranes.
Late 19th Century.

Late 19th and early 20th Century Stirling O Class. Rebuilt by Wainwright and better cab. One still exists on the Bluebell Railway.

D Class 737 designed by R. R. Surtees and built in Ashford 1901.
Now in the York Museum since 1960.
(Kind permission of the Coney family)

D Class 737 with Robert Surtees, grandson of R. R. Surtees, taken at York Museum 2004.
(Kind permission from Sadie)

Wainwright H Class. Bullied Q1 Austerity. Both have run on the Bluebell Line. (Kind permission of Brian Morrison)

Ashford station 1925 with Stirling F Class and the classic signal gantry, not to be seen today.
(Kind permission of Brian Morrison)

The Councillor, the Committee, supported by the residents celebrate the glorious victory in the long battle to renew and save historic Newtown, built in 1860 by the new railway company for the new work force. To the left of the wheels holding the flag is chairman and retired railwayman Alfred Downs, behind him the hard working committee members. To the right of the wheels Gordon is surrounded by excited young residents waiting for the fun to begin. Standing behind very close to the wheels is the youngest committee member Dave Robinson.

Steam traverser boiler shop.
(From Harry Elgars album)

Machine shop, belt driven by steam.
(From Harry Elgars album)

CI "BB" 34051 Churchill Funeral Train. Built at Ashford works 1931. Now in USA. Will be repatriated if 40,000 can be found for sea trip. (Kind permission of Wainwright Preservation Soc., Chislehurst)

Maunsell King Arthur N15 Class 4.60 NOE 765 "Sir Gareth". With continental boat train at Dover Marine c.1927. From the Wakeman Collection. One of these, from time to time runs on the main line passing through Ashford.

117

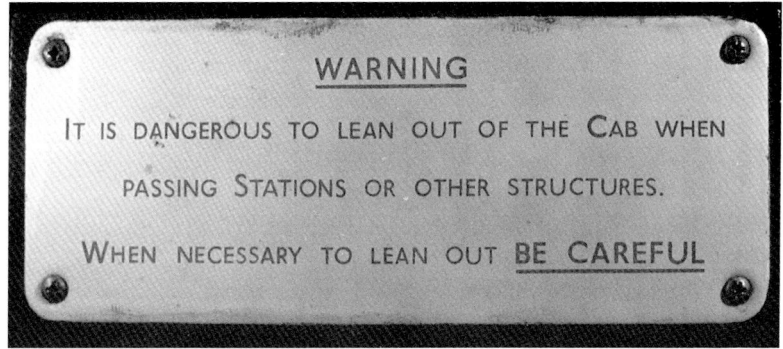

Cab warning plate installed in Ashford locomotives during the Maunsell era.

The striker/fuse of the last V1 (Doodle Bug) to fall on England during the War. It did not explode when it fell in the Works Yard alongside the old cooling pond near to Willesborough Crossing.

SE&CR station lamp made in the Tinsmith's Shop in Ashford Works at the beginning of the century. I have converted it for electric lighting but I still have the original oil wick fitting.

(above photographs kind permission Fred Imms)

My father's Railway Service Badge No. H17926. These badges, each with its unique number were issued to railway employees during the War.

Ashford works wagon plate 1952. I bought this at Carnforth where I found it in a very sorry and rusty state.

(above photographs kind permission Fred Imms)

119

Chapter Six

DIFFICULT TIMES

May his shadow never grow less,
May his boiler never grow rusty.
         The Engine Driver: Charles Dickens.

If the era could be difficult, even for many in employment, for others life was a severe trial. Jack Archer, son of a railwayman, recalls the difficult times facing his family: 'Life for the poor was always a great challenge. Being brought up between the two wars and experiencing the depression of the Thirties provided a hard down-to-earth training for the future. My father had served throughout the First World War and returned home to promises of 'A Land fit for Heroes to live in'. He left Folkestone in 1919 after demobilisation from the 11th Hussars, having obtained a job as a labourer in the Railway Works. His health had been broken by his wartime experiences and finally deteriorated to such an extent that he took to his bed. I recall seeing my mother and grandmother pooling their money to see if they had sufficient to send me to the Crown & Anchor for a tot of brandy to be given to father as a stimulant.'

'He died at the early age of 47 at our house in Albion Terrace, South Willesborough. My father lay in his coffin in our small front room to await burial. As a token of respect it was customary for all other residents in the street to pull curtains or blinds across their windows. We were taught that if we saw a funeral approaching we had to stand at the edge of the pavement, facing the road, with our cap held to our chest, heads bowed and in complete silence. A period of mourning was always observed by the family. My mother was granted a small allowance of two shillings a week, which had to be collected from the local Relieving Officer.'

'Our housing conditions left much to be desired. It was quite an experience to come downstairs during the night. The light that you carried, be it candle or oil lamp, would reveal cockroaches everywhere. Rats were in the copper flue and in the wood-boxed toilet. Somehow we kept the rest of the house clear. To obtain drinking water we had to carry a bucket to a tap installed five houses away in a back garden. This tap was for the use of several houses and it often froze up during the winter. Most houses had a rainwater butt, so there was always rainwater available.'

'Our landlord was a railwayman, and our rent had to be taken to his house every Monday, come rain or snow. We could never get repairs done. His only comment was: 'Where's the rent?'

'Once a week, mother would cover the kitchen table with old newspapers and we would be called to the table for 'de-lousing'. With a fine tooth-comb and holding our heads firmly over the newspapers, she would comb away. Any fleas falling on to the paper would be promptly crushed.'

'A frequent errand was to run to the butcher's shop for a pennyworth of pieces. A small joint of meat was indulged in only on rare occasions. We kept chickens and my grandfather bred rabbits, so at times they were an added dinner luxury. Although poor, we were honest and never went hungry. Every week my mother took in a small amount of washing to add to our income. Hop-picking, for our family, was a financial necessity. Every autumn we would be found in Batt's hop garden at Sevington, having left the house at 5.30am.'

'In happier days, before my father died, the family, plus grandparents and an uncle and aunt, used to hire a horse and open coach and set off on a trip to Dymchurch, getting out at every hill to help the poor old horse.'

'South Willesborough was well served with shops. The general store at the corner of Mead and Gladstone Roads had a butcher's department. Every market day cattle would be bought from Ashford and herded through New Town to the slaughterhouse. Pole-axing was the preferred method of killing, a rope being passed through the beast's nose, attached to a metal ring in the floor and all hands mustered to pull the beast's head down to await the descending pole-axe.'

'Opposite was a newspaper shop, which employed paper delivery boys. At five o'clock each morning they would set off on their rounds, some to as far afield as Hastingleigh.'

'Beattie & Armstrong's was a store that contained practically everything, and even provided a weekly tallyman to collect payments from the homes of local residents.'

'There were also vans, mostly horse-drawn, delivering bread, milk, coal and paraffin. Steam driven lorries delivered beer and ale to the public houses. Frogs Island (the nickname for South Willesborough), boasted three public houses – The Albion, The Bricklayers and The Crown & Anchor. There were 18 shops selling every commodity and a choice of two barbers, both railwaymen (Nigger Nixon and Strappey) operating from sheds in their gardens. Each charged tuppence for a short back and sides. The two Harolds – Thompson from Albion Terrace and Francis from

Canterbury Road each had a vegetable round and each a horse and cart.'

'There was a family who were woodmen and tree fellers supplying clothes line posts and props. Their house was so small that the mother would be seen cooking in the garden over a wood fire, the stove in the house being too small. Poor people, but honest and hard working.'

'During the nineteen twenties a local co-operative was opened in Cudworth Road. In addition to serving shop customers they offered a delivery service. I had a Saturday job, which involved helping the regular errand boy load a two-wheeled cart with cardboard cartons containing groceries for families in New Town. In the winter time there was a hurricane lamp hanging under the cart. Snow and ice was then the biggest problem. It was often 6.30pm by the time the afternoon round was completed. For this the payment was two shillings for the day.'

'Life was always enlivened by hawking characters. The ringing of a handbell and the loud call 'Any old rags, bottles or bones?' heralded the approach of Jimmy O'Keefe, a popular figure, sitting on the side of his cart with his old horse plodding unconcernedly along. There was Pope with his two-wheeled cart. If there had been a glut of sprats, his cart would be loaded to the limit. On another occasion, perhaps, very ripe bananas. Fred Down, who ran a shop in Cudworth Road, also provided vegetables. From the encampment at Willesborough Lees came Henry Club, with his call of 'Any old iron?' Most afternoons would see his old horse plodding along with Henry slumped on his seat, well oiled and fast asleep. The horse always got Henry home, but why he never fell off his seat is a mystery.'

'Residents who were not up early on a Sunday morning were often awakened by the calls of weekend traders: the hot rolls man with his cry of 'Fresh baked hot rolls', often followed by the watercress man calling 'Watercrease, watercrease, fresh green watercrease'. There was the shrimps and winkles man and a man riding a bicycle who, whilst balancing a large tray on his shoulder, called out 'Pease pudding and faggots'. The call of 'Knives and scissors to grind' came from a man riding his adapted bicycle with two emery wheels bolted on to the handlebars, which were belt-driven from the rear wheel. Charlie Keyte started the Island's first mobile library. Riding a bicycle, he towed a box on wheels around the houses, making a charge of two pence a book for one week.'

'During the summer months came the famous blue and white chequered boxes on wheels, pedalled by the Walls Ice Cream man with his slogan 'Stop me and buy one'. Finally there was always the annual visit by the Belgian onion boys, hawking their half-yard lengths of continental onions.'

'There was only one car owner on Frogs Island, although some ran motorcycle combinations, all British-made with large and roomy sidecars. The only other form of private transport locally was the horse and carriage of the boot and shoe repairer who had a shop in Gladstone road, which added a touch of quality to the neighbourhood.'

'One was never far from the harsh realities of life. There were several suicides from Crow Corner Bridge. In Mead Road there lived a family suffering from consumption. They were six or seven in number, all passing away in turn. One of the boys committed suicide by jumping off the bridge just as a train was approaching. There were also accidents. One Saturday morning the young daughter of Tom Hunt, the road sweeper, strayed onto the line and was hit by the Golden Arrow. The police and railway linesmen gathered her remains together and placed them in bags.'

'As ever, there were domestic problems. A young sailor from Albion Cottages had been home on leave from the Royal Navy. On returning to his ship he was accompanied to the railway station by his wife, who was unaware that he had a girl-friend who was already on the train and that was the last that his wife or family ever saw of him.'

'During the twenties and thirties one seldom saw a coloured man. It was a novelty then to see this man, possibly a Fijian, appear from time to time busking with his banjo. He was an unusual sight with his huge mop of frizzy hair and coloured clothes, walking along the middle of the road, singing and strumming away.'

'Life sometimes provided free entertainment. The Hunt offered a colourful and exciting gathering in front of the Crown and Anchor for 'stirrup cups' before starting off from Cock Martin's Field. Sometimes it was stag hunting, the stag having been brought along by the hunt: other times the meeting would be drag, with meat providing a scent for the hounds.'

'An event long remembered was Sir Alan Cobham's Flying Circus, which brightened up our lives when they gave their air display from the large field behind Sevington Church. An unscheduled occurrence was the appearance of a flight of RAF Bulldog fighters on a flight to Lympne airfield. Over Ashford they ran into a blizzard, cutting visibility to practically nil. One force-landed alongside Boys Hall, a second in the field in front of Sevington Stores and a third behind Sevington Church. What excitement for us boys!'

An amusing story from these times concerns a chance encounter near the Railway Works. From the level crossing footbridge around to the Works main gate, old railway sleepers formed a security fence alongside the footpath. One dark evening, a man walking along the path on his way home happened to pause for a while when, from the other side of the fence, a voice enquired 'Is that you Fred?' Quick as a flash he replied 'Yes', so the voice continued 'Coming over'. Reaching to the top of the fence, the so-called Fred found a large object wrapped in paper. Placing this under his coat he hurried on his way. On unwrapping the object when he arrived home he found himself in possession of a brand new copper kettle.

The Show

Many of Ashford's railway families had an agricultural background. The ancient family of Lancefield, who lived in a cottage at Willesborough, cheek-by-jowl with the Ashford to Folkestone railway line, were a typical example. For centuries, the family had lived in rural Crundale and moved into town when the railway arrived. During the 1890s, Mark Lancefield was invalided out of the Royal Horse Artillery in India, having suffered severely with cholera, and offered a position as smith in the Works. He later became a nightwatchman. His son, William, became a coachmaker and the Company allowed him to stay on at Ashford during the thirties' reorganisation because of his father's health problems. He was followed into the Works in turn by his sons, Albert and Mark, who both pursued the trades of fitter/turner. Albert recalls a highlight of his childhood years:

'Every August Penfold's Fair came to town. Actually it came to New Town, about half a mile from where we lived. It was carried by two steam traction engines – the first a large one with a canopy held up by four brass barley-twist posts, one at each corner. A real beauty of an engine. She pulled about seven or eight large long wagons, carrying all the parts driven by steam – the organ, the roundabouts, the swings and the small railway trains, all of which she powered herself on the Green. The second traction engine was a smaller one, which also pulled about seven wagons carrying the large tents, of which there were many, the lighting equipment and all other appliances`, which when assembled made a great show. It must have been one of the best in all England.'

'They used to come early on Thursday afternoon and everything was ready for Saturday morning, when the Fair started early and went on til late. It was a fascinating sight watching the two engines negotiate the bends in Boys Hall Road on the last stage of their journey, especially at Bo-Peep Corner, where dozens of children from the area gathered to watch from Court Lodge Meadow. Even the herd of milking cows used to stand and stare! We watched them come round the corner and get up extra steam to get over Crow Corner railway bridge, then sharp right into the rocky road, down to the water bridge and on to New Town. The driver of each engine turned the driving wheel furiously and slowed down almost to a stop to get round the corner, but get round they did.'

'The steam organ was the greatest attraction at the Fair, with its old tunes belching out all the time and its brass figures turning their heads and raising their arms in keeping with the tunes. It was something one could stand and watch for hours and keep in one's memory for ever.'

'There were swings, roundabouts, a big wheel and all manner of games one could have a go at, like coconut shies, and ringing a bell with a big hammer, or rather, not ringing it! We shot at moving targets for a halfpenny a time, watched the clown doing his stunts and telling his yarns and heard the gypsy fortune-teller in her tent with a magic ball – and very believable she was, too. A Punch and Judy Show was provided for the young ones and donkey rides at the bottom end of the Green.'

'There were shops selling all sorts of sweets and drinks. It was a day for gob-stoppers, sherbet dabs, aniseed balls, liquorice-all-sorts, mixed toffees, ice cream, bottles of Bing and ginger beer. These had a marble in the neck to save getting too big a mouthful and losing some of it.'

'For all the allotment holders and gardeners there was a huge tent opposite the Alfred Arms, where during the afternoon the New Town Flower and Vegetable Show was held. Everything that was growable was entered, and there was a concert by the Railway Works Brass Band, and as dusk descended there were fireworks of every description for about an hour.'

'We used to go home about ten o'clock but could hear the revelry going on til midnight. A day to remember every year.'

The Depression

By the thirties, the old fashioned, paternal attitude of the Railway Company towards its employees was fading fast. The 1923 amalgamation which spelled the end of the small companies seemed to have diminished the sense of responsibility that existed in earlier days. New Town's houses remained reasonably well maintained, but the Green, previously the pride of the Company and the envy of folks in other parts of the town, was suffering from neglect. Abandoned by the sportsmen, it steadily deteriorated into an area of unkempt grass and bare patches, which in turn became muddy pools in wet weather. The once neat white fencing fell into decay and potholes littered the surrounding road. How different from years gone by, when a well-kept Green provided the ground for New Town Cricket Club, whose members tended it every evening by rolling and mowing.

Life at New Town has been vividly portrayed by Frederick Imm, who came to Ashford from Lancing in 1930. On 1st January, his father was told to report for work in the Ashford wagon shop. With the country plunged into severe industrial depression and no other jobs available, a refusal was out of the question. The Company always made a board and lodging allowance to those who had to move, and in April the railwayman and his wife and young son were given an allowance for one week and a free travel pass in order to find a house. The offer by the Company of a tenancy at New Town was accepted, and so in due course a Pickford's horse drawn cart brought a furniture container to their Lancing home, and then made its way to the local railway station to await a goods train.

Their new home at 121 New Town had four rooms, an outside toilet, a coal bunker and a small garden. In the very small kitchen-cum-living room there was a coal-fired kitchen range, a laundry copper and a kitchen sink. Water was laid on but there was no gas or electricity for cooking or lighting. During the summer, when it was too hot to have a fire in the range, tenants had to rely upon a paraffin primus stove. Paraffin lamps were used for lighting downstairs and candles upstairs. The railway owned gas works had been adjacent to New Town for eighty years but a supply was still not connected to all the houses, and it was only after a strongly supported petition in 1931 that electricity was connected for lighting. The only bath facility for tenants was the Railway Bath House, which made a charge of 4d.

The initial rent for the Imms was 4/6d and this increased to 7/6d when they moved into a more modern house near the Hastings line. It was not possible to be in arrears with the rent because it was deducted from the tenants' wages. Painting and decorating was included in the rental charge and was carried out as was considered necessary by the Works Estate Department. Wallpapering was the tenants' responsibility.

Employment on the railway service carried few perks apart from railway fares at a quarter of the regular price, but useful scrap wood could be bought very cheaply and there was plenty to be had. A load of wood piled high on a two-wheeled hand truck took five men to push up the road from the Hastings line bridge and cost 1/0s. Larger loads delivered from the Works cost 3/0s. Pensioners were supplied with wood cut for them in 6" lengths.

Lodges, as back garden sheds were known at Ashford, cluttered up the small back garden spaces all over New Town. There were lodges of all kinds, new and old, large and small, some very well built and others a botch-up and often in a very dilapidated state. The lodge could be used as workshop, fuel store, vegetable store, garden shed and, on occasion, as a bathroom.

Fred Imm recalled that if someone employed in the wagon shops wanted wood for a lodge, there was no problem. A wagon maker would carefully remove end boards from a covered wagon and put the selected wood aside, ready for the load to be made up. Anyone else in the Works with a similar need contacted a wagon maker friend. There was nothing shady, there was always plenty of scrap wood to choose from: sole bars, cross ties, buffer beams and end pillars. Door handles, nuts and bolts were salvaged and old guard's van windows put aside. Nails, screws, paint, brushes and wagon roofing felt could be bought at discounted prices. To make a lodge watertight, only a few coats of gas tar were needed and this could be obtained at the Company's Gas Works, where 6d. would buy enough to fill a bucket or tin bath.

Both wood and coal deliveries were brought along the access lanes between the terraces of houses. During the summer months, householders stocked up with a ton of coal at reduced prices. The coalman brought his supplies round on a horse-drawn, four-wheeled flat wagon, so there was always the chance of a free bucket of manure to be picked up for the allotment garden.

The Imm family decided to have the convenience of a bath in their lodge. The foundation was first made up of solid oak sole bars. When the building work was finished, an old carpet was placed over the rough floorboards and a chair and a galvanised tin bath were installed, together with a Valour paraffin heater. Water had to be heated in the kitchen copper and then carried out in buckets. For lighting, a hurricane lamp gave valiant service.

The great industrial depression was at its peak in 1931 and brought to the fore those qualities of human kindness often most evident at times of stress and difficulty. This was very much the case on New Town. The atmosphere of mutual help resulted in bringing together the families of the Brighton and Lancing men with those of Ashford. The smaller families were very responsive to the needs of those with large families to clothe and feed. A communal kitty was arranged, into which were paid small but vital contributions, and this from men whose own income had been much depleted.

Grocery parcels were bought and given to the hard-pressed, together with surplus vegetables from the allotments. Children's clothes were turned out and put to good use. One former Lancing wagon maker who lived on New Town with his wife and family of seven young children made sure that the family footwear was in good order. He turned his hand to boot repairing. Boots were the usual form of footwear for workmen's children, only the better off could afford shoes. A sympathetic foreman in the Works gave him a gate pass to take out short lengths of scrap machine-drive belting, which he used when repairing the soles of his children's boots.

During the difficult times, the allotments were the salvation of many of the men with almost every householder on New Town having one. The allotments saved the sanity and preserved the dignity of the men. Not only did they have the satisfaction of producing essential food for the family while on short time, they also needed an outlet for the energy that they would normally have expended on their heavy factory work.

This was also a time when many grandparents played a fulfilling role by providing much needed support for the families. Shopping in Ashford market also helped those on tight budgets. One could buy eggs, fresh fruit and vegetables at the market auction more cheaply than in local shops.

With so many skills required in the works, it is no surprise that these found an outlet in the men's home life. Among Fred Imm's neighbours, a Mr. Shorter exercised his skills as a woodworker, taking orders for such small items as tables, kitchen chairs, table lamps and garden barrows. He was also the village 'saw-doctor'. Some of the men who worked in the locomotive shop possessed their own lathes, which they kept in their lodges. Here it was not unusual to find an enthusiast building a working replica of one of the main-line expresses. Even teenage boys demonstrated their talent by building themselves a bicycle from the bits and pieces they had salvaged from various sources. Pocket money did not stretch to £3.19s.6d. for a new one, but having built the bike for next to nothing, an enterprising lad would often sell it for 10 shillings and then build himself another.

Gardening represented the most absorbing interest for New Town's railwaymen but there were many indoor pastimes as well. Card games were in fashion for adults and board games for children. Many were the proud possessors of a gramophone but during the early 1930s only a few owned a wireless set, although three men had built their own. Outside the home the Alfred Arms, the Ashford Working Men's Club in Station Road and the Locomotive public house were popular venues for company as well as for liquid refreshment.

For the greater part of the first hundred years there were no paid holidays for railway workers, even the bank holidays were, in practice, a lock-out. Despite this, the extra opportunity for a day at the seaside for the men and their families was something to look forward to. The Kentish resorts were all within easy reach with the railwaymen's privilege fare, Dungeness being a special attraction. Here was an exceptionally good location for sea fishing in really deep water. Beside being an enjoyable and relaxing sport there was always the added attraction of hoping to take home a good catch to help feed the family.

Surrounding Dungeness lighthouse were a cluster of old coaches that had been pensioned off for use as weekend and holiday homes. Originally sold to railwaymen for £5, they were shunted down on a Saturday when a group of friends could assist the new owner by removing the carriage from its wheels and, by means of rollers, move it from the siding to its final resting place on the beachy headland.

Young Fred Imm listened open-mouthed as he heard about the annual Fair, which had been held for years on New Town Green. To his surprise, the Fair, set up over the August Bank Holiday, was the biggest he had ever seen. To young Fred, the whole of Ashford seemed to be there with the regulars of the Alfred Arms being crowded out of their favourite corners by the thirsty fair-goers. But the centre of attraction was a very large marquee, in which was held the annual show of flowers, fruit and vegetables, organised by the newly named Southern Railway Garden Committee, previously known as the New Town Gardeners' Society. Entries in 1931 were a record totalling 581.The wealth of flowers beggared description and included multicoloured bouquets and nosegays of wild flowers. One prize-winner was the proud owner of a yellow ridge cucumber, which, apart from its colouring, looked more like a vegetable marrow.

To Fred Imm, the railway scene around Ashford was always of great interest. There were the Moguls, as well as a variety of 4-4-0 and 0-6-0 tender engines and a wide range of 'tanks'. Wainwright's 4-4-0 'L' class engines had been relieved of some of their earlier, more demanding work and one of them often performed station pilot duty. An 'L' class which was fitted with a snifting valve was a give-away – it sniffed as the regulator was opened. An 'L' class with a Maunsell wide chimney was also easy to pick out, it had a much more throaty sound. As the boat trains pulled away from a stop on the down line, the exhaust beat of the engine could be heard all over Newtown, assuming the wind was in the right direction.

'Schools' class engines had a nasty habit of slipping when pulling a heavy train out of the station. The roar of their three cylinder exhaust beat together with the noise of the four driving wheels slipping on the rails, all mixed with the rattling of a motion which thundered out, letting everyone know that a 'Schools' class was at work. A Lord Nelson could easily be recognised by the soft eight exhaust beats per revolution of its driving wheels. They rarely succumbed to wheel slip.

On a still night the clonk, clonk of coupling rods with well-worn crank pin bushes on an 'N' class Mogul could be heard as it hauled a heavily laden coal train from the Kentish coalfields into the goods yard. The clanging of shunting and the shrill of engine whistles went on throughout the day and night. To add to the 'railway symphony', before the beginning of each shift at the Works, the main gate clock tower bell rang out, and at starting time the steam hooter screamed out across the houses. With the railway and the Works on two sides of its triangular shape, New Town lay at the very heart of railway activity.

Fred Imm's Working Life

Fred Imm recalls: 'In August 1930, at the age of 14, I left school and went into the Works. At that time only a very limited number of reasonably secure jobs were available for school leavers. A job 'inside', as it was known, as shop lad or office boy was considered one of the few plums available. Being a railwayman's son I was lucky and landed a job in the machine shop. I had to work Monday to Friday, 7.30 in the morning until 5pm and from 7.30 to mid-day on Saturdays. During the week we were allowed one hour for lunch. My pay was 5s a week, which would rise annually to £1 by age 20. Piecework made possible up to 40% additional earnings.'

'My father's take-home pay as a craftsman rarely exceeded £3 per week so I was expected to contribute 4s. towards my keep at home, leaving just 1s. for pocket money. A visit to the cinema cost 4d., 2d. could buy 2oz. of sweets and an occasional ice cream cost 1d. Inflation between the wars was virtually nil. Regular brands of cigarettes stayed at ten for 6d. Woodbines, Park drive and Players Weights were all five for 2d. Mars, Fry's Chocolate Cream, Crunchie Bars and Aero were all tuppence each.'

'Some years previously a kiosk had been set up just outside the main gate and was still a thriving enterprise, selling newspapers, cigarettes, tobacco and vespers. It was particularly busy on Friday evenings and Saturday morning after the men had picked up their weekly pay packet. Weekend supplies of cigarettes and tobacco were bought and settlements were made for what had been chalked up 'on the slate' during the preceding week.'

'An income of 5 shillings left no room for lost time so it was only on very rare occasions that I was caught running full tilt to beat the five minute warning bell that rang out from the gatehouse tower. Harry Ottaway, the timekeeper, knew the regular late starters and had no sympathy for them. He was, however, prepared to help out a normally punctual starter who might be just that little bit too far behind in spite of a last-minute dash for the gate. Before dropping the shutters as the 7.30 hooter sounded, Harry looked out of his office window and threw out the brass check on to the shelf, ready to be picked up by the out of breath sprinter!'

'In 1931, Harry Crowe and I were first year shop lads in the machine shop and I came close to being the only one. Harry was working on the nut tapper when the sleeve of his jacket caught in the pin which held one of the four collets on to the vertical rotating shaft. He was stripped naked – every stitch of clothing was torn off, except for his boots and tie. He was saved from certain death just as he was being twisted up into the worm gears of the machine. The man working at the adjacent tapper dived at the two-inch driving belt coming down from the counter shafting and tore it off with his bare hands. Harry suffered only minor bruises and slight shock. His rescuer had severe lacerations on both hands but after hospital treatment he was back at work next day. He just could not afford to take time off.'

'Steam drives had been replaced by electric motors for the line shafting in the shop but most of the old line and countershafting was still in use with a forest of belting to the machines. The electricity grid system was still in its infancy and the problem of handling peak loading had not been mastered. Often, early on a winter morning, there was a supply failure, which shut down the whole factory and put the place in darkness for 20 minutes or so. Lighting in the shops was provided by electric carbon-arc lamps. These gave a good light but required frequent adjustment and replacement of the carbon rods. To gain access to the arc lamps, 'Sparks' the electrician had to use the overhead crane as a working platform, causing a hold-up of work up and down the shop. In dark corners and for close work on machines, lighting was supplemented by candles.'

'On cold, frosty mornings, candles and heaters made from oily waste used to take some of the chill out of the various hand controls. Such mornings were a busy time for 'Strappy' the belt man, as cold belts were stiff and had a nasty habit of breaking as soon as the machine had to take a load.'

'It was normal practice to start up machines a minute or so after official starting time and leave them running light to warm up. For the next ten minutes the men would hang about, having an unofficial smoke, yarning, picking the winners for the day, warming their overalls in the blacksmith's shop or just idling.'

'At twenty minutes to eight, the cry of 'High up' was passed into the shop by the lookout, indicating that Phil Butcher, the assistant foreman was on his way across the yard. As he walked smartly up the shop in his suit and best bowler hat, everyone at least looked as if they were working. There was an interval of five minutes, during which Mr. Butcher changed into his smock coat and working bowler. At a quarter to eight the next 'High up' entered the shop. Ernest Burden, the junior foreman, did not conform to the standard headgear of the older foremen – he wore a trilby. By ten minutes to eight, when the senior foreman, Lewis Lewis (Lew-Lew) arrived there was yet another shout of 'High up', however by then most people had really got down to work.'

'Unofficial breaks were taken about 9 o'clock. A sharp lookout was kept to make sure there were no foremen about. Foremen were generally tactful and had a cup of tea in their office at the same time. In the unlikely event of foreman or a stranger appearing, the warning shout of 'High up' was passed down the shop.'

'The blacksmith's shop was conveniently situated alongside the machine shop. It was useful to make friends with a blacksmith so that a hearth was available on which to make toast or boil a billy can. At washing up time, it was the shop lad's job to go to the blacksmith's shop for a bucket of hot water, provided by a piece of red hot scrap being dropped into the bucket.'

'During the winter, heating in the shops was very primitive, with only a few open coke fire braziers known as 'The Devils'. The fires were started up each morning by a labourer with a shovelful of burning coke. When fires were made up with coke, which was usually wet, the factory was filled with thick choking smoke and fine ash, much to the annoyance of the overhead crane drivers. At the end of the working day the fires were doused with used washing up water, resulting in clouds of ash being deposited on machines, overhead shafting, counter shafting and ledges. Cleanliness left much to be desired.'

'As in so many factories in the thirties, there was a no-smoking rule but most men in the Works were regular smokers and found ways of getting round the ban. A few were able to make an excuse for going to a remote corner of the Works yard for some reason or other, but the regular venue for a 'crafty smoke' was the latrines. These were all very similar, with a long unroofed urinal stand, opposite which were a line of sit-down toilets with no doors. Smokers had to appear 'needy' and sit with their trousers down whilst they had their 'drag', at the same time hoping that the foreman would not need to come in.'

'Others who risked having a smoke in the workshop relied on the regular lookout for a warning shout, should the foreman come into sight. Snuff taking was a habit indulged in by a number of workmen. However, there were those whose movements were restricted and who were wary of being seen by a foreman anywhere about the shop but at their own place of work. Harry (Dasher) was on an auto gang under Jack Skee and would not risk being seen having a smoke. However, he was satisfied by having a regular pinch of snuff – he was a client of a snuff dispenser. A labourer and a grinding-wheel trimmer had jobs which allowed them to move around freely with their snuff-box. They had customers scattered about the workshop who paid tuppence a week for a regular pinch a couple of times each morning and afternoon. It was perhaps just coincidence that the best swept part of the shop floor was where the labourer had most of his regulars and that the best-trimmed grinding-wheels were those nearest the regulars of the wheel-trimmer.'

'Pipe puffing Erne Copeland was an old soldier who had seen service in the 1914-18 war. His job was rather monotonous, but I think he was glad to be alive after his war-time experiences and contented with his lot. He always appeared to be busy but in fact worked at a very easy pace. He operated an old wall drill that had been installed when the Works were built in 1847 and since returning from the war had not taken a single day off.

'Erne was a likeable chap, one of those people who gets on well with everybody. He had a snuff box and provided some half dozen addicts with a morning and afternoon pinch whilst they 'happened' to be passing his way. For this service, Erne collected his weekly tuppence from each customer, a lot of inside information and free snuff for himself. Although having no children of his own, he understood how to deal with teenage boys in the machine shop. He was able to chat quietly about the problems and evils of the world and philosophise in a way that boys could listen to and understand.'

'Jack Skee was the exception to the rule about the time that one should start work and for that matter he was the exception to all rules, custom and practice, official or otherwise. He was a Scot and deplored time wasting. Time was money to him. Jack disregarded the no smoking rule. He could take a 'drag' at an oily home-rolled ciggy behind his machines while they were still running and earning money for him with the foremen keeping conveniently out of his way. His gang had its own gas ring on which they could make a Welsh rarebit and have a brew-up, no need to waste time in the blacksmith's shop. Jack did not deny himself or his gang the creature comforts provided priority was at all times directed towards keeping the automatic machines going and earning money. Eating 9am lunch and having a cup of tea was accepted by Jack, provided the machines were kept at it for the full working day. They were started up on time and they finished on time. There was no washing up, just a rub over with a machine cleaning rag, soaked in paraffin.'

'Most of the men in the Works were members of either the NUR or AEU and many let it be known that they were committed Socialists. Jack was an AEU member, he was also a committed Socialist – but with a difference. He believed that wealth had to be worked for in any political system. Compared with the others in the shop, Jack was probably a better trade unionist. When a new job came forward which had not been priced, he would be conscientious in making an efficient set up for it, but would not let the foreman force him to accept what he considered to be an unfair price. He worked hard and said that he deserved his piecework. His attitude about sharing wealth was that those who were skilled should feel that they had an obligation to teach those who were not.'

'Working on the autos was certainly hard on clothing and footwear. A few of the boys of my age had an aversion to the still popular but old fashioned custom of wearing an 'Oxford' working shirt with only a front collar stud. From the start I made up my mind to wear a collar and tie, however it was not long before the original colour and pattern of the tie was unrecognisable. My oil soaked cap provided waterproof headgear, but the oil was not so kind to my boots. The stitching soon became saturated and in no time gave way. To counter the problem of replacement costs, my mother hit on the idea that I should wear hob-nail boots.'

'Many years previously the Kent Education Committee had taken over responsibility for the Railway Mechanics Institute from the South Eastern & Chatham. This provided technical education for employees. By the thirties, the Southern Railway had only partially come to terms with the fact that they were going to be left behind if they did not take a greater interest in such matters. Having granted the far-sighted concessions for half-day release to the Technical Institute, with pay increases for examination success, there was no other evidence of any encouragement for Company employees.'

'Disappointment about lack of training opportunities wasn't uncommon. There was no training workshop or formal training programme in any of the shops. Fitter and erection apprentices picked up their skills as they went along. They, at least, were helped by the craftsmen with whom they were working. In the machine shop, boys were left to work on their own initiative. It was very much a case of 'suck it and see'.'

'I soon found out that the attitude of the Company wasn't the only problem. Union restrictive practices exercised by a few difficult individuals in the machine shop didn't help. But this didn't apply to all shop personnel – some were most helpful and understanding.'

'Early in 1931, industrial depression was at an all-time peak and unemployment was widespread, with little help available to those who found themselves without a job. Ashford Works suffered a severe shortage of work, there were lay-offs and short time working, with most of the workforce suffering a drastic cut back in the working week. In many shops the cut back was to either four or three days per week. In the wagon shop, where my father worked, it was three days on alternate weeks. Every aspect of work was affected. In the old rolling mill, in which boiler plates had been rolled in the early days of the Works, there was a mass of material stacked up, including castings for obsolete locomotives. A fortune in scrap was lying about but in the days of depression there was no market for it.'

'It had been the done thing for a long time past at Ashford Works for employees to secure the future of their sons by putting their names down for a job 'inside'. They took this so seriously that a boy's name was often entered and accepted soon after birth. This tradition resulted in a long list of apprentices being available to the Company. The unskilled jobs left over were for 'outsiders', and the Lancing and Brighton men found all too soon that as far as jobs were concerned they were regarded as 'outsiders'.'

'There were some who were privileged. To become an apprentice, boys leaving grammar school paid a premium of £60, students or public school boys paid £365 a year. Next in line were sons of foremen or other privileged employees. Last came the shop lads, who had been at work since they were fourteen. A small number were selected as apprentice boilermakers, turners, patternmakers, foundrymen, blacksmiths, coppersmiths, tinsmiths and electricians.'

'For 1d. per week a boy was allowed to join the Railway Institute and its Engineering, Literary and Debating Society. This originated in the early days of Ashford Works when technical education of railway workers was its genuine aim. Although the building at New Town still provided a reading and quiet games room, debates and up-to-date reading material were things of the past. The Society's main function now was to organise visits to other engineering works with a railway connection, and an occasional brewery. With Saturday morning working, visits were restricted to Saturday afternoons. All trips were by rail with free passes provided. A welcome Works trip was to the Southern Railway Orphanage at Woking, to which workers were encouraged to make a weekly contribution of 1d. The Southern Railway had inherited the orphanage from the London & South Western Railway and full credit must be given for the way in which this institution was run and maintained.'

Changing Times

A general reorganisation of production space at Ashford followed the arrival of wagon makers from Lancing and fitters and erectors from Brighton. Technical innovations in the locomotive shops were almost non-existent however, and there was no change from the traditional system of one gang being responsible for the complete overhaul of one locomotive. One much-regretted departure from South Eastern days concerned engines which were no longer given an immaculate finish in a clean, centrally-heated paint shop.

The period saw considerable changes in the wagon department, both in design and production. The assembly of new, steel-framed wagons was concentrated in the Klondyke sheds. Steel wagon frames were either riveted or electric welded in one of the original wagon shops in the main Works area. This arrangement meant that frames had to be wheeled out almost as far as Ashford main line station and then shunted back to the assembly shop at Klondyke, where they were clad with woodwork on a semi-mass-production basis. Wagon design and construction was moving forward but overall production techniques were not keeping pace.

Wagon repair work was carried out in the Kimberley shops, where a dwindling number of craftsmen were the only ones able to undertake the repair of the older, wooden frame wagons. The construction and repair of the new steel wagon stock demanded relatively little of the old craftsmen's skills.

By 1932 the old four-road running shed in the main Works complex alongside the machine shop had been demolished and the site cleared. The increasing number of larger steam locomotives coming into service had led to the construction of a new ten-road shed between the Canterbury and Folkestone lines together with a 65 foot turntable. One of the first big engine sheds in this country to be built of concrete, its allocation of some 60 engines was a considerable increase for Ashford. It was here that checks were run on wheels, axle-boxes, cylinders, valves and controls, leaving a major overhaul with a complete dismantling of the locomotive to the main Works.

The feeling of hopelessness in 1932 was reflected by Maunsell who felt it difficult to express an opinion on the question of unemployment at the Ashford Works, having regard to the economic situation throughout the world. He hoped that those engaged in trying to solve the problems facing industry would succeed in inducing international confidence and restore prosperity.

Matters had improved by 1934, which led Maunsell to say that taking into consideration the depression through which the country was passing, he thought that, with orders for 25 locomotives outstanding, the prospects for Ashford Works were quite satisfactory. Ten of these orders were for the 'W' class goods engine. It had been intended that they would be erected at Eastleigh, but that works was now fully committed with work on the 'Schools' class and so the order was transferred to Ashford. Some might have felt that this was poetic justice – Ashford having lost a 'W' class order to Eastleigh on 1930.

The production of 2,376 wagons was required for the coming year and, curiously, in view of the previous workshop reorganisation, Ashford had secured an order for 25 corridor third-class carriages. Maunsell did not think the Works had much to complain about. Within twelve months, the position had changed dramatically. There were no further orders for locomotives and wagon orders only amounted to 1,400.

At that year's Dinner, Maunsell spoke on the advantages and disadvantages of streamlining locomotives, the matter still being in the experimental stage. He revealed that some time previously he had made models with differently shaped ends and careful experiments were carried out in wind tunnels at the National Physical Laboratory. It was found that alteration of the vehicle ends only effected a negligible saving in power, compared with what could be saved if the underpart of the vehicle was completely screened. Unfortunately, heating then occurred in bearings and other parts denied free circulation of air. It had been found that no advantage was obtained from streamlining until speeds of over 60 mph were attained. Given the speed restrictions from which the Southern suffered, right across its network, Maunsell's lack of enthusiasm can be understood.

Fred Imm was keenly aware of the wind of change blowing over Ashford during the thirties: 'There was wireless in the home and American talking films and newsreels at the cinema were influencing the outlook and attitudes of both the young and older generations. Air travel, the motor car and the road haulage industry were competing on an ever-increasing scale with railways. Boat trains were carrying fewer first class passengers, while Imperial Airways, flying over Kent to Paris, took an ever larger share of this lucrative traffic.'

'Young people especially were looking through a new window onto the world. Commerce and industry, including railways, were facing new challenges. There was the steady advance of technology and mass production, with the attendant economic pressures and changing attitudes. Railway locomotive workshops remained unchanged. There were rumblings about wage levels and stories were told of high wages in the United States, where it was said that a railway ticket collector earned the equivalent of £100 per week.'

'In Britain there was no annual round of pay demands and wage talks. Wages and prices had been stable for some years. For those who had a job, the regular pay packet, small though it was, was more important than continual arguments about more money. If one wanted a higher wage, it was either work harder and earn more piecework, move to another job nearer to London where wages were higher or find another job with more responsibility, none of which were easy.'

Fred Imm decided to move on. Having long been eager for a job in the drawing office but with no prospect of his hopes being fulfilled, he secured just such a position with a private company in Stafford.

Maunsell had mixed news for the Foremen's Association Dinner in 1936. The next year's locomotive programme was rather thin because of the continuing change to electrification. This had been demonstrated by the ordering and subsequent cancellation of a new 2-6-2 to meet the perceived need for a powerful medium-sized tank engine. Ashford would have erected ten of these general purpose locomotives but unfortunately this greatly anticipated work would not now materialise. Otherwise, there was a very healthy order book. 100 passenger luggage vans, 50 bogie passenger vans and 50 guards' vans were added to orders already in hand for 650 open ten-ton goods wagons, 500 twelve-ton covered goods wagons, 750 open ten-ton goods, 450 twelve-ton covered goods, 50 twelve-ton container tank wagons, 24 forty-ton bogie flats and 9 twenty-ton mineral wagons. A truly prestigious programme.

That the foremen's efforts during what had been a difficult period were appreciated was shown by management's offer of a trip to Southampton Docks to look over the transatlantic liner, Queen Mary.

The gathering little realised that this would be the last time that Maunsell would address their annual dinner. His health had been failing for some time and so, at the age of 69, in June 1937, he submitted his resignation, although it would be September before he finally departed.

He had selected a fine team to support him when first appointed and it had held together, very little changed, since then. He had earned a deserved loyalty from all levels of railwaymen throughout the Company, making regular visits to his Works, posing questions to his managers on matters of design, manufacture and repair. One manager likened it to fielding in the slips when Don Bradman was batting. Apprentices in particular enjoyed his interest and support. His prime purpose had been to introduce a new breed of locomotive to Southern lines and in this he succeeded brilliantly. Of all his designs, his masterpiece was the 4-4-0 'Schools' class. Little wonder that a member of staff wrote: 'After he had gone we felt it was the end.'

Bulleid Takes Over

The Southern Railway's new Chief Mechanical Engineer, O.V.S.Bulleid, represented a break with convention as far as Ashford was concerned. Ever since the coming of the railway, 'The Chief' had lived in the town, but Bulleid decided otherwise, opting to live in Surrey at Box Hill. A very different personality from his predecessor, he came to the Southern having been personal assistant to Sir Nigel Gresley, of the London & North Eastern Railway. A great steam enthusiast with innovative ideas, he would justify his place among the giants of locomotive design. It seemed to have become a tradition for every new Locomotive Engineer to produce a critical report on the state of the locomotive stock and Bulleid was no exception, in urging a modernisation programme. Even the locomotive and carriage livery was changed, from a rather sober green to a startling malachite green.

The wind of change continued to blow in 1937. It was not only the relationship between the Railway Company and its employees that was changing but also that between the Company and the town. The year saw the severance of a long standing connection with the community of South Ashford. In 1867, the Anglican church of Christchurch had been built with funds greatly swelled by South Eastern shareholders and provided with an annual grant of £100 towards its upkeep and maintenance. Now this was to be discontinued.

A further sign of change that year occurred when the Southern Railway produced its first diesel-electric shunters. Construction of the framing, cab and bodywork was undertaken at Ashford, but the high content of bought-in components was clearly seen as a threat to the steam locomotive workshops. The shunters were typical 0-6-0 design and having been partially completed were then hauled to the English Electric Works at Preston to be fitted with their 350hp power units. During the coming war they would be commandeered by the War Office and render sterling service, serving a number of long-range gun positions and other military installations around the Kent Coast.

Third rail electrics were already operating over the London to Brighton route and plans for the extension of electric traction to other parts of the system were well under way, albeit slow off the mark. Generally, Ashford Works had only indirect involvement with electric traction. Many small items were produced in the machine shops, although not easily recognisable as being related to any particular part of the electric units. One item of heavy machining that was new to Ashford in the thirties was electric traction motor axles. The journals of these axles took quite a hammering caused by the high rate of acceleration and in consequence required frequent returning. One big lathe had a steady flow of these axles to deal with. Other types of new work trickled into the shops but there seemed to be no great upheaval to the pattern of traditional working practices and routines in the locomotive shops.

Welcome news at this time was the decision to restore all economy cuts that had been imposed during the depression of 1931. In addition, for the first time railwaymen were to have paid holidays and there were to be improved rates of pay for some of the lower paid men. There was to be no short time working, which had been restricting the working week to less than five days.

The happy tradition of celebrating Royal events was continued with the arranging of a Coronation tea party for all children living on New Town. Transferred from the Green to the old wagon shop because of poor weather, the 230 children present were welcomed into a gaily decorated hall with disused railway wagons flanking the laden tables and flags and bunting hanging from iron girders and trailing over railway trucks and spare parts of carriages.

Accidents

A more sombre side of life in the Works was provided by the many accidents that occurred. Sometimes they happened because of a lack of safety measures, sometimes from carelessness, often from bad luck. Fitters regularly featured among the unfortunate. A lost eye caused by a chip 'flying' from a hammer; a crushed toe from a press machine mishap; a lost leg when a locomotive unexpectedly moved. More grievously, a fitter losing his life when a shunted wagon ran over his stomach. A fitter erector from Newtown suffered a shocking injury one Saturday morning when working on a locomotive which was being lowered onto its wheeled frame. Two cranes were run over a pit for what was, at the best of times, a delicate operation. The fitter was sitting on the edge of the pit, his legs dangling over, when the clutch on one of the cranes failed and the locomotive came crashing down, severing both his legs. Both Maunsell and Pearson, the Works Manager, were on their regular Saturday rounds at the time, and they rushed to the spot. Incredibly, the man survived, was fitted up with artificial legs and later took his place in the brass shop.

Many trades were at risk and a lost finger or thumb was not exceptional. Much more serious was an incident on a Friday afternoon when a big steam travelling crane, carrying over five tons of timber, toppled over whilst being worked in the carriage sidings at Kimberley. Its driver, Harry Collyer, was killed, all the bones in his skull and jaw being fractured and his body badly crushed. The subsequent inquest, held at the Victoria Hotel in Beaver Road, revealed a frightening lack of management. The crane, which was designed to carry a load of only two tons, was heavily overloaded. Cole, the chief locomotive foreman, when asked if it was fair to put a fitter's labourer in charge of a crane, and leave him to decide whether the weight was within its safety limit, replied: 'Gibson borrowed the crane and he took responsibility.' Gibson, the yard foreman, said the crane gang did not belong to him and he could not take responsibility. He had thought it was a ten ton crane but was of the opinion that: 'the crane driver should have exercised his own judgement.'

No prosecutions were proceeded with. The coroner commented on the fact that nobody seemed to be responsible for the overloading and hoped that in future the responsibility for determining loads would be clearly defined.

Accidents around the Works were not confined to its own men but could also involve footplatemen. Astride the double turnout junction from the Ramsgate branch line to the running shed was a footbridge to enable staff walking between the station and the shed to cross the running lines in safety. It was largely ignored by all and sundry, since a quick nip across the tracks was preferable to the climb of twenty-odd steps up and over the bridge and down the other side, especially if it was getting perilously close to booking-on time.

And so it was with this certain young fireman one foggy morning. Sadly there was one hurried and misjudged step taken just as the signalman in 'E' box set the road and pulled off the 'boards' for a down train to Ramsgate. The fireman's foot was sufficiently far from the tip of the points blade so as not to prevent them from closing completely, yet close enough to trap his foot securely when the fateful lever was heaved over.

Fog prevented the signalman in his box less than 100 yards away from seeing his terrible predicament and also blanketed his desperate shouts for help. The final seconds of anguish can only be imagined as he first heard the approaching locomotive, then saw it looming out of the fog, knowing that as he threw himself sideways nothing could prevent those flanged steel wheels from crushing his lower leg to sever his foot.

His career cut short, he later became a foreman cleaner, always walking with a pronounced limp, having been fitted with a false foot.

The Company had ensured that ambulance services were well organised in the Works. In every shop there was a trained member of St. John's Ambulance Brigade, part of a 120-strong team, who were able to provide emergency treatment and dressings for minor injuries. They, in turn, were backed up by a specially equipped Ambulance Room, with a full-time attendant.

In earlier times, badly injured men would be taken to the Ashford Cottage Hospital by means of a hand-wheeled litter, now a motor ambulance could be summoned from St. John's Town Brigade and the unfortunate man rushed to the new Ashford Hospital.

As early as 1936, a time of political tension in Europe, Ashford's M.P., William Spens, had warned about the international situation. At a smoking concert in the Crown & Anchor at South Willesborough he declared that Ashford, as an important railway junction, would be a centre for air attack in the event of war. He did not contemplate war: 'As things are at the moment, this country is in a position of greater independence that we have been for a long time. We are in a position to localise any trouble if it comes along at any time in the future. I don't want you to think we are going to be involved in a war, but no-one can say for certain. Several big countries are jealous of our Empire and prestige; Germany and Japan both want something. The Government, in its preparations for defence, is relying upon the co-operation of the people. They must make elementary preparations in case of attack. Especially is this the case in Ashford.'

'You must remember that here in Ashford you have the most important railway junction in the south of England. It would be a perfectly legitimate act of war to wipe out this railway. By reason of its position between London and the Channel ports it would be an important objective to attack. If Ashford is selected as a target we must make certain that risk and damage is as small as possible.'

The following year, the general managers of the various railways were in discussion with the Government about the enormous operational problems that could be expected to arise, should there be a major conflict. In 1938, with the European crisis deepening, the Government made clear that, as with the previous war, it would take control of the four main-line companies, under the Defence of the Realm Act.

Plans were made on a national basis for dealing with the expected bomb damage, with equipment, permanent way materials and mobile cranes being based at key points. Protection against gas-warfare was a prime consideration. Gas cleansing centres were built, breakdown trains for gas decontamination were specially equipped and thousands of oilskin suits were issued for protection against the effects of mustard gas. Arrangements were quickly hurried forward, resulting in one in every ten railwaymen being trained in Air Raid Precaution schemes.

Chapter Seven

ASHFORD AT WAR

*The time will come, when thou will lift thine eyes
To watch a long-drawn battle in the skies,
While aged peasants, too amazed for words,
Stare at the flying fleets of wond'rous birds.*
                                    Thomas Gray (1737)

With the mounting crisis, war preparations became increasingly evident. In April 1939, the Government introduced conscription, and in Ashford the first of the young railwaymen were called to the colours. An appeal for voluntary helpers resulted in local people joining the Civil Defence services and becoming air-raid wardens, fire-watchers, first-aid workers, firemen and aircraft spotters. Gas masks were issued and if anyone had a spare room, instructions were given on how to make it gas proof.

The war crisis reached its climax over the weekend of 1st/3rd September. Hitler's invasion of Poland triggered a mass evacuation of children from British cities to the countryside. Ashford had been designated as 'safe' and so became a reception area for children from London, who arrived by train, each with a name label, a gas mask and a bag with their belongings. New Town School served as the local reception centre from where they were allocated a billet.

From midnight on 31st August, the railways had come under the control of the Government appointed Railway Executive Committee. The next day the Home Secretary issued an emergency order requiring all lights at stations and railway yards to be of low intensity, greenish blue in colour and screened from above, as a precaution against air-raids.

At 9am on Sunday 3rd September, Britain sent an ultimatum to Germany calling for an undertaking that they would withdraw their troops from Poland. Everyone who could was huddled by their radio set, when at 11.15 they heard the Prime Minister, Neville Chamberlain, utter in his thin reedy voice, the fateful words: '....I have to tell you now that no such undertaking has been received and that, consequently, this country is at war with Germany.' Almost immediately the air-raid sirens began to wail, causing alarm and apprehension. Fortunately it was a false alarm, but it was just the first of 2,881 alerts which would sound in Ashford before the war was over.

An air-raid precaution immediately and strictly enforced was the 'blackout'. Many inhabitants were provided with Anderson shelters – thick corrugated steel structures that were partly sunk into the ground, and most latticed their windows with adhesive tape as a precaution against flying glass. Construction of public shelters proceeded apace and included one on New Town Green.

Realising that this country would be subject to aerial bombardment, management gave serious thought to the protection of Ashford Works and its workforce. Shop roofs were camouflaged and windows blacked out to allow 24 hour working. Importantly, air-raid shelters were scattered everywhere, some underground but most above ground, either brick blockhouses or old engine smoke-boxes, surrounded by sandbags. Wagons were removed from their wheels, filled with ashes and placed around the yards so that men caught in the open could crouch behind them. Everyone could reach shelter, however rudimentary, within one minute. In addition, the main office was shored up with heavy timbers and the telephone exchange, now manned night and day, had the added protection of large steel shutters over the windows, which were to be closed in the event of a raid.

The Works air-raid defence services were independent of the town. Four fire stations were established, the main one being close to the clock tower and three others strategically placed around the Works. Eight full time firemen were supplemented by 15 auxiliaries, all under the able command of Walter Clark.

As in the First World War, heavy military traffic began flowing through Ashford carrying troops, stores and munitions to the British Expeditionary Force in France, while in the opposite direction trains had to cope with thousands of soldiers returning home on leave. To add to the difficulties, the winter of 1939/40 was the coldest in living memory, with even the sea freezing off Folkestone and Dungeness. In these appalling conditions, military activity virtually ceased on the Western Front. During the seven months of what became known as 'the phoney war', evacuees drifted back to their homes in London, but the period of quiet was deceptive. On 9th April, Hitler launched an invasion of Denmark and Norway, quickly followed by a blitzkrieg against Holland, Belgium, Luxembourg and France. With German Panzer divisions sweeping across France to the Channel ports, war was getting dangerously close to home.

Meanwhile, the Government again acknowledged the potential of railway workshops to meet the needs of the armed forces, and orders were received at Ashford from the War Office, Admiralty, Air Ministry and

Ministry of Supply, as well as a number of armament manufacturers. An early order for eighteen Army mobile workshop units was speedily completed and sent to France but like much other equipment, was lost in the retreat to Dunkirk. Each unit consisted of a main workshop van fully equipped with machine tools and three covered wagons for a generator, welding apparatus and spare parts.

In May 1940 Anthony Eden, as Secretary of State for War spoke on a BBC Home service programme about the threat of attack by German parachute troops. He called upon men between the ages of 17 and 65 to join a new defence force, to be known as the Local Defence Volunteers. Men were to continue with their normal occupation and not receive service pay but would have a uniform and be armed. The following August, their name changed to the Home Guard, which removed the wag's name for the force – Look, Duck and Vanish!

Ashford Works Home Guard, designated 1st Southern Railway Company, was one of the first to be formed in the country. Under its commander, Bob Bolton, it was responsible for the defence of the Works and the Railway Station. Local regular army units provided instructors and the men were soon engaged in intensive training, which introduced them to musketry, fieldwork and arms drill. Armed at first with little more than sticks, the 50 volunteers welcomed the issue of Canadian Long Ross rifles, although they first had the laborious task of removing the thick grease in which they had been stored since the first world war. Later, in addition to three Vickers heavy machine guns, they acquired a Northover Projector for launching phosphorus grenades, a cumbersome weapon, not at all accurate beyond 150 yards.

A leading member of the Battle Platoon was welder and fitter, Corporal Percy Russell, who later told how they challenged the army to a contest on the firing range, which the railwaymen won – but the army had its revenge. A company that was bivouacked in Godinton Park was ordered to 'capture' Ashford's railway station in an exercise, with the Home Guard defending. Percy Russell was on duty at the sandbagged 'E' signal box in what was a night time operation. The army attacked using troops with blackened faces in the middle of a snowstorm, and emerged the victors.

Concern was now expressed at the exposure of the Southern's coastal running sheds to enemy action. As a result, the Company decided to close those at Dover, Folkestone and Ramsgate and move their locomotives inland. Ashford became 'home' to 150 engines and the centre from which all emergencies had to be dealt with, but to avoid a dangerous concentration of motive power, engines were dispersed into various sidings in the district.

A task in which Ashford's railwaymen took much pride was the making of armour plating for 12 armoured trains. Each train consisted of an LNER

2-4-2 tank engine running push-pull with two supply wagons and a 20 ton armoured truck at each end, equipped with two Bren machine guns and a six-pounder Hotchkiss cannon. Their duties were to patrol the line, to protect railway workers engaged on permanent way repairs and if necessary, to form a defence point for troops. Given the threat of invasion, they were kept continuously in steam. 24 such trains operated in various parts of the country, all of them manned by independent units of the Free Polish Army. An unusual feature was the high percentage of officers to other ranks, cause by the preponderance of officers and professionals who had arrived in Britain from Poland. Usually a Sergeant Major and two cooks were the only 'other ranks' in the thirty-man crew. In Ashford, the unit's headquarters were in a former garden nursery building in Elwick Road, near the railway station, and its soldiers were billeted in private houses around the town.

Another wartime task for the Works involved a train from the 15 inch gauge Romney, Hythe and Dymchurch Railway. One of the Company's little 4-8-2 locomotives was positioned between two bogie hopper wagons, which Ashford's men then covered with armour plating. Equipped with two Lewis guns and a Boys anti-tank rifle, it became Britain's smallest armoured train. Although its full potential was never put to the test, the crew claimed the destruction of at least one enemy aircraft.

As an anti-invasion measure, Ashford's railwaymen were also called upon to fill two 21 ton Southern Railway coal wagons with concrete, following which they were parked at Sandling junction. Two tank engines were kept standing by in steam, and in the event of an enemy landing, they were under orders to shunt the wagons into Sandling and Shakespeare tunnels. A special mechanism was fitted to cause the wagons to collapse, thus blocking the line and impeding enemy movement. A round-the-clock guard was maintained for the duration of the emergency by footplatemen working a three-shift system.

Anti-invasion activity was widespread and intruded upon the lives of everyone. Home Guard and Civil Defence duties absorbed what time men had for leisure, which was little enough after working overtime. Visits to southern and eastern coastal districts became a thing of the past for most people when a land strip ten miles deep was placed out-of-bounds other than for visits to very near relatives or for reasons of business. No visitors were allowed on seafronts where gun-emplacements, concrete pill-boxes and barbed wire entanglements had replaced tea parlours, ice cream stalls and the Punch & Judy shows. Defences were also in place all around the town, with road blocks on all main roads. Many bridges were mined, anti-tank blocks were set up and open meadow land strewn with obstructions such as posts and old cars and carts, as a precaution against airborne landings.

At the end of May, troop trains from Dover, Folkestone, Ramsgate and Margate were rolling past the Works in a steady procession bringing back the army that had been rescued from the channel ports and the Dunkirk beaches. Responding to this national emergency, rolling stock from the Great Western, LMS and LNER poured in adding to that of the Southern, with many drivers, firemen and guards working up to 24 hours at a stretch. Never before had Britain's railways faced such a challenge. Single line working was introduced between Ashford and Hothfield, the down line being used as siding capable of berthing 17 locomotives with their 183 coaches at any one time, before they went forward, either to the Kent coast or the port of Newhaven and the piers of Eastbourne and Brighton.

Many of the returning trains had a local signal stop, giving the local community an opportunity to offer refreshments. Heavily overloaded trains straddled a 'stile' crossing at Crowbridge Road in South Willesborough, which gave access to the line. The local Civil Defence team led the way, ably supported by housewives. The local milkman provided milk churns filled with water, the landlord of the Albion Tavern offered beer and many provided tea and gave cigarettes. The troops, anxious to allay the anxieties of loved ones, handed over letters for posting. For nine long days the community rallied, even the children helping where possible and often receiving badges, buttons and French francs as souvenirs. There were similar scenes to the west of the town, where townsfolk rushed to Bailey's Crossing with food and water.

Over 400 trainloads of troops passed through the town, with most of the soldiers in a begrimed state and without rifles or adequate clothing. Worst of all were the ambulance trains carrying men, often with shocking wounds. In a pitiful condition, many had lost an arm or a leg, some had been blinded. To those who witnessed their plight it was a heart-rending scene. Despite a series of bitter and hard-fought rearguard actions, an exhausted, dirty and ragged British Army had been driven out of France, and many of the soldiers wondered what their reception would be. To their surprise they were treated as heroes and cheered, feted and given comfort all along the line, and not just the English soldiers but also French, Belgian, Dutch and even some Poles.

Ralph Neat, Motive Power Superintendent, was both surprised and greatly relieved when his only son, then serving in the Sherwood Foresters, managed to throw a hastily scribbled note addressed to his father when passing through Ashford on one of the last of many troop trains.

Feelings of overwhelming relief swept the country when it was realised that the Army had been saved, but Winston Churchill now gave warning to the nation: 'The Battle of France is over…..The Battle of Britain is about to begin.' Ashford, only 36 miles from enemy occupied France, was now in the front line.

The Battle of Britain

The war began in earnest for the Works on 17th July 1940 when, without any warning from the air-raid sirens, a high flying lone raider dropped 11 high explosive bombs. In the Works, the men heard a whistling noise and the cry went up 'They're bombs!' as they dived for cover. Newly apprenticed Bob Barham was perched on top of a locomotive boiler when his mate nonchalantly remarked there was a plane overhead and its engines seemed to be falling off. Realising they were bombs, Bob jumped the ten feet to the ground and lay flat, watching with horror as the stick of bombs exploded, one hitting a building only 200 yards away, sending up a column of smoke and debris.

Two of the bombs exploded in the Works, hitting both the erecting and the tin smith's shops, injuring several workmen, but the greatest damage was to the railwaymen's homes at New Town. This was the first but not the last time that New Town would bear the brunt of attacks aimed at the Works. Bombs had straddled the Green, reducing houses and flats to rubble. In one flat, Esther Birt, her son Jack and baby Woodcock were all killed. The fronts of three houses were blown out, chimney pieces had crashed through the slated roofs, floors of upstairs rooms were left hanging at perilous angles and furniture was strewn about the debris.

An eye-witness said: 'I was only 20 or 30 yards away when the flats were struck. I fell off my bicycle and threw myself flat on the road against a fence. My mouth was full of dirt after the explosion, which left a black cloud hanging over the ruins.' ARP workers were soon on the scene, and doctors, ambulance workers, police, firemen, air-raid wardens, special constables and rescue workers all worked to clear the debris and give aid to the 15 people who had been injured.

During 1940, German bombers appeared to regard New Town as a legitimate military target. The reason for this may have been revealed in one of the news broadcasts regularly beamed to Britain by the German authorities. The broadcaster was the traitor, William Joyce, who was promptly nicknamed 'Lord Haw Haw.' Opening a programme in his usual sardonic style, with his nasal voice proclaiming 'Jairmany calling – Jairmany calling', he was reported as saying: 'Yesterday the Luftwaffe was active over many parts of southern England – The New Town Barracks at Ashford were bombed.'

Although the Battle of Britain began officially on 10th July the first four weeks were devoted almost entirely to repelling German attacks on coastal shipping. Tuesday 13th August was named 'Eagle Day' by the Luftwaffe for the beginning of their assault upon mainland Britain, with a declared intention of 'wiping the RAF from the sky.' From this day and for many weeks to come Kent would echo to the roar of aircraft engines, the thump of cannon fire and the crackle of machine guns. Despite German triumphalism it quickly became evident that the battle would not be easily won, the ferocious fighting on the 15th, with its heavy German losses, earning it the name of 'Black Thursday.'

On the 17th the sky over Ashford was the scene of a determined defence with the RAF using a tactic requiring both courage and nerves of steel. One of the finest of 'The Few,' Squadron Leader Michael Crossley led his Hurricanes of 32 Squadron in a head-on attack on fifty Dornier 215s and Junkers 88s with their screen of Messerschmitt 110s, at a closing speed of over 400 mph. Crossley quickly despatched a Junkers and sent a Me110 limping away. German pilots, in their perspex nosed bombers feared and hated these head-on attacks in which they were horribly exposed and which inevitably broke up their formations.

Until the end of the battle, the airspace directly above Ashford provided an arena for some of the fiercest 'dog-fights' and witnessed more fighting than any other town in Kent with the exception of Dover. Despite this intensive conflict in the skies above the Works continued to operate with a full workforce. Weekends no longer provided a respite – even Sunday was just another working day. For the railwaymen it was work as usual while from above came the sounds of battle, as the RAF and the Luftwaffe fought with unyielding ferocity.

During the early days, workers were often in air raid shelters for hours while German planes passed overhead. Frank Mercer, newly apprenticed, recalled: 'I remember one day, we had been in the shelter nearly all morning. 12 o'clock dinner time arrived and we were hungry, so some of us got on our bicycles and rode home. Having eaten, we came back to sit in the shelter until the 'All Clear' sounded. Of course, this could not go on – production suffered badly and there were plenty of locomotives coming into the Works that had been shot up by enemy machine-gun fire and which urgently needed attention.'

Given the Works' hazardous situation and the constant red alerts, there was a risk of an enforced shut down. Thus was born a system of 'spotters', with a team of railwaymen located on the roof of the Old Bath House at New Town. Trained in aircraft recognition, their warnings of 'Immediate Danger' gave the workforce a chance to get to shelter and also enabled everyone to continue normal working during periods of red alert. The 'spotters' worked a shift system, but still had to carry out their usual working day duties.

Shortly after 1pm on the hot afternoon of Sunday 18th August, an extraordinary incident occurred just south of Ashford on one of the hardest fought days of the Battle. Hurricanes of 56 Squadron, patrolling at 20,000 feet, literally massacred a group of five twin-engined Messerschmitt 110s. The British pilots spotted the aircraft approaching from the south and immediately went into line astern formation. Realising the danger, the enemy planes formed themselves into a tight defensive circle but to no avail. The Hurricanes attacked and sent them all spinning down, one after another. None of their crews bailed out.

Another notable encounter was witnessed in the skies above just before seven o'clock on the evening of the 29th. Richard Hillary, whose name would always epitomise the courage of 'The Few', arrived over Ashford with Spitfires of 603 Squadron at the same time as two dozen Messerschmitt 109s. Hillary at once opened fire, sending an opponent down in flames. The remainder of the German fighters fled back to France. It was the grim fortune of war that saw Hillary's own plane go down in flames six days later during a 'dog-fight' over Kent. He suffered the most horrific burns, which required months of plastic surgery by Sir Archibald McIndoe at his East Grinstead Hospital.

The following day the Germans showed they had forgotten nothing from the previous war. Railway lines had played a useful role as an aid to navigation then, and time and again would do so again in this conflict. The line through Ashford and across Kent pointed like an arrow towards London. At 6pm a large force of bombers swept in from the coast, passed over Ashford and headed for the capital. Within the force was a group of Junker 88s, Germany's most effective bomber. Breaking away to follow the Redhill line, they then turned to deliver a crippling attack on the RAF base at Biggin Hill with their 1000lb bombs. During the afternoon of the next day the Junkers returned, flying low over Ashford and on up the line, delivering another stunning attack upon Biggin Hill, wreaking enormous havoc and causing heavy casualties. It was these raids that many years later were to feature in the film 'Battle of Britain'.

Lone raiders were often a problem and on both 1st and 13th September high explosive and incendiary bombs were dropped on Ashford, causing damage to the railway and houses. The raid on the 1st was the town's first night raid. The time was shortly before midnight and two raiders were prowling about overhead. Suddenly one was caught in the beams of the searchlights and anti-aircraft guns opened up. Meanwhile the other plane, whilst remaining in the darkness, dropped a high explosive bomb and incendiaries, causing damage to the Kimberley Works.

During one raid, Frank Mercer recalls he was trapped inside a locomotive as he was cutting out the bronze bush that the steam rod moves in. His body became so overheated in the confined space he was unable to wriggle out between two narrowly spaced bars. The 'Immediate Danger' warning had sounded, but Frank was forced to stay put. When he finally managed to emerge, the bombs had been dropped and the raider was gone.

The defences were placed under huge pressure on 2nd September when multiple attacks were made, aimed particularly at Kent's airfields. As early as 7am 140 bombers and fighters came in over the coast at the commencement of what would prove to be a very lively day. An hour later Squadron Leader 'Ginger' Lacey, one of the RAFs highest scoring pilots went into battle above Ashford leading his Hurricanes of 501 Squadron (motto: Fear no man.) Sighting fifty Dornier 215s escorted by fifty Messerschmitt 109s, he was quickly on the tail of a red-cowled 109 which succumbed to a five-second burst from his eight Browning machine guns. Following this up he attacked a Dornier which, breaking from its formation, with smoke pouring from one of its engines, rapidly lost height.

Another attack developed about noon, with 250 enemy planes being intercepted by more than 70 Spitfires and Hurricanes. Keeping up the pressure at 5 o'clock, yet another armada of bombers and fighters swept in. On this occasion, ten squadrons of Spitfires and Hurricanes were present to challenge the intruders and a colossal dog-fight developed over Ashford, providing a noisy backdrop for the workforce as they changed shifts.

Polish pilots had acquired a fearsome reputation which was now brilliantly displayed by fighter ace Flying Officer Stanislaw Skalski. Having only joined 501 Squadron on August 30th he now achieved his fourth victory by sending two Messerschmitts spinning down over the town. In the countryside around Ashford the crashed remains of British and German aircraft provided ample evidence of the days fighting.

The raids seemed interminable and were made more unnerving by the heavy throb of the bombers' engines. During one raid the drone of aircraft seemed to make the very ground tremble as people gazed skyward at the huge fleets of enemy aircraft passing over towards London. A small boy shouted: 'Blimey! Look, there's hundreds of 'em!'

The threat of invasion, which had been present ever since the fall of France, now appeared about to become a reality. Heavy enemy air attacks had been delivered against south-east England throughout the first week of September and RAF reconnaissance had revealed increased military activity in the Pas-de-Calais. Barges and small craft were pouring down the canals towards Belgian and Dutch coastal waters, where yet more shipping was assembling. Within the past six weeks, hundreds of barges together with steamers, tugs and trawlers had filled ports and harbours from the Scheldt to Cherbourg, enough to move at least 60,000 men. Dive-bombers were being concentrated at airfields near the coast, other large bomber reinforcements were arriving and huge guns were being positioned for long-range bombardment. Intercepted radio messages all confirmed the German preparations.

Troops were to be seen actively training on the beaches and practising embarkation from the French ports. Of the 41 divisions assembled for the invasion, two spearhead divisions were planned to land between Folkestone and Dungeness while an airborne division was to seize Lympne airfield.

Apprehension was further raised when a fishing vessel, escorted by two German minesweepers, crept in and landed four spies in two separate dinghies at West Hythe and Dungeness, who, upon capture, revealed their understanding that invasion was imminent. Now on Friday 6th September, a huge German convoy of 60 vessels was seen moving down into the Straits of Dover. A meteorological report gave news of very favourable weather conditions for a channel crossing that weekend. That night, the Admiralty ordered all cruisers, destroyers and patrol craft to be kept at immediate notice and the Royal Air Force was placed on alert.

On the afternoon of the 7th, with large shipping movements off Calais continuing, Luftwaffe Chief Reichmarschall Herman Goering launched the most massive air armada ever seen. Over one thousand bombers and fighters swept across the English coast between Dover and Beachy Head. A British fighter pilot said: 'As far as you could see there was nothing but German aircraft coming in, wave after wave.' One of the bomber formations was estimated as 20 miles long, with a horde of fighters above. The RAF tore into the raiders although outnumbered by ten to one. Hundreds more enemy bombers passed over Ashford in the early evening to give London yet another heavy pounding. The build up of activity was enough to persuade the Chiefs of Staff who were meeting in Downing Street that evening. At 8.07pm, convinced that an invasion was close at hand, Home Forces HQ issued the code word 'Cromwell': All troops to battle stations.

A full scale evacuation, particularly of children, was put into effect immediately, Ashford people being told: 'If you don't leave now you will have to stay put.' Special trains were placed in service, as quietly and methodically hundreds of people passed through the railway station, heading for safer areas in the Midlands. Districts around the Works were denuded of youngsters, a mere handful remaining at New Town. Many families suffered the agony of separation as, throughout the week, trainload upon trainload of women and children pulled out of the station. Even the rail journey was a hazard, with the constant danger of being bombed.

Friday 13th could well have lived up to its reputation when the town had a brush with disaster. The weather was miserable, making fighter interception difficult. Taking full advantage of these flying conditions, lone raiders wandered about over south-east England, causing the 'Alert' warning to be in operation for most of the day. At 10.30 that morning, a German bomber emerged from heavy cloud cover and laid a stick of 11 high explosive and 50 incendiary bombs along the line near the railway station, hitting an office on the down platform. Standing just a little way away on the up platform was a train full of evacuees, ready to leave the town. A truly miraculous near miss.

Ashford's railwaymen would have been intrigued had they known that Winston Churchill had passed by their Works at this time, on the main coastline. The Prime Minister had been disturbed by an Admiralty paper on the 11th, concerning the security of guns along the Kentish coast and in his usual forthright way resolved on an immediate inspection. The very next day he left Holborn Viaduct station for Shorncliffe, together with top-ranking army and navy commanders. He then proceeded to examine the 9.2 inch railway guns and all other coastal guns and shore defences, from Dungeness to Ramsgate, in order to satisfy himself about the suitability of defence arrangements.

Sunday 15th September dawned and heralded a hot summer day. By 11.30 the sirens had wailed their warning and everyone prepared themselves for another onslaught, but the sheer scale of the fighting that was about to erupt in the skies above took everyone by surprise. Massed formations of the Luftwaffe crossed the Kent coast between Hythe and Dungeness, the heavy droning and number of the big black bombers seeming to overwhelm watchers on the ground. But on this 'day of days' the Germans were going to have to admit their failure to defeat the Royal Air Force.

Following advance radar warnings, 12 squadrons of Spitfires and Hurricanes were put up between Ashford and Canterbury to meet the raiders head-on. Another 11 squadrons were brought in to form a reception committee over South London. They hurled themselves against the enemy, the skies becoming a swirling mass of fighters and bombers, the contorted vapour trails, the constant sound of gunfire and the sight of stricken aircraft trailing oily smoke and falling to earth, all bearing witness to the fierce fighting in progress.

Despite suffering heavy losses, at 2.30 that afternoon the Germans were back with another throw of the dice, pitching their huge bomber fleets against Britain's defences. Again the skies over Ashford seemed to darken as the great aerial armadas passed overhead, but again the Luftwaffe were surprised by the numbers of the ever-vigilant Spitfires and Hurricanes which, with heroic determination, decimated their ranks.

At the height of the battle over Ashford, a local man watched a group of six Spitfires attack a group of eleven Dorniers: 'It was the most thrilling sight I have ever seen. The Dorniers came along in perfect formation, high in the air. It looked as if they would get away to their base. Suddenly the Spitfires appeared on their left flank and a terrific fight began. One Dornier was turned away from the group, a Spitfire's machine guns roared and a few seconds later, the German dived, spun and crashed into the ground. None of its crew bailed out. As the other Spitfires attacked, the rest of the Dorniers broke formation and sped for home.'

This was not the only occasion on that historic day when the nerve of German pilots broke. The resistance of the RAF had been too great, the Luftwaffe losses too high. Everyone sensed a great victory had been won, delivering a hard blow to the myth of German invincibility.

On the 16th, the railway residents of Newtown again paid the penalty for living in the shadow of the Works. Early that sunny evening a twin-engined Heinkel bomber circled leisurely over Ashford for nearly half an hour. It began its final approach flying very low and at full throttle, the black cross and Nazi insignia clearly visible on its fuselage and tail. As it came over the top of the church, several rifle shots were fired at it. There followed a series of terrific explosions as its 500lb bombs fell on New Town. Three of the 'Dutch Gable' houses overlooking the Green were totally wrecked. In one of them, retired railwayman William Raffe and his wife Mary were killed. 54 year old Henry Drury and 16 year old ARP messenger Donald Byrne were injured and died later. A row of houses nearby was shattered by blast and about 20 others looked as though they had been struck by a typhoon. Doors and windows were blown in, ceilings were down and the framework of houses torn and twisted.

With youthful impetuosity, railworker Vic Packman had taken a large telescope with him as he ran to the shelter. He said: 'I lined him up as he approached Newtown for the fourth time. I saw his bomb doors open and four bombs drop out – taking the telescope away from my eye I realised that they were coming my way and got under cover.'

As the plane flew away it scattered 60 incendiary bombs across Newtown and neighbouring South Willesborough. The raid left seven people seriously injured. Nurses and first aid workers attended minor injuries, wardens cleared houses of residents near an unexploded bomb, rescue squads tackled the job of finding victims amidst the wreckage, ambulances lined up to take the injured away and Newtown school was made ready to accommodate those who had lost their homes.

While the rescue work was going on there was a huge explosion from the direction of the allotments as the unexploded bomb went up, throwing debris in all directions. It prompted a comment from one of the rescuers: 'It's only the time bomb', typifying the reaction of the railway tenants, who gave little sign of fear, only deep concern for the injured.

The Alfred Arms suffered considerable damage, with practically all its windows blown in, but the landlord cleared up, proclaimed 'Business as usual' and things were soon in full swing with a pianist playing popular tunes in the club room.

Despite the courage of the British pilots the result of an engagement did not always favour the RAF. On the 17th a squadron of Hurricanes from 501 Squadron was on patrol high over Ashford. Unknown to them they had been seen by elements of the German III/Jg26. Their squadron leader, Oberleutnant Gerhard Schopfel, protected by an umbrella of Messerschmitt 109s, stalked and attacked the unsuspecting Hurricanes, shooting down four within two minutes, one of the pilots being killed. 'Ginger' Lacey's

Hurricane went down in flames but he was able to bale out and land uninjured. Unaware of the drama being enacted overhead, the railwaymen below worked on by artificial light in their blacked-out sheds.

Many suffered a disturbed night during the early hours of the 21st when a raider dropped two parachute-borne landmines at Kennington and Godinton, causing blasts so violent that scarcely any house in those areas escaped damage. Equally short and sharp was a raid five days later when bombs were delivered to the centre of the town near the Ashford West railway goods yards. The Co-operative Bakery, which backed onto the yards, was hit and houses were demolished in East Street and Regents Place, causing the deaths of seven people.

Having suffered such heavy losses with their slower bombers, the Germans now changed to mounting a series of wide-ranging raids with their faster Ju88s and bomb-carrying Me110s. During the afternoon of 27th September, Spitfires of 66 Squadron on patrol near Ashford ran into a formation of Ju88s with a protective cover of Me109s. 'A' flight led by Squadron Leader Rupert Leigh hit the 88s and when the 109s dived down to protect them, Pilot Officer Bobby Oxspring and his 'B' flight fell upon the 109s resulting in a vicious dog-fight which spread across the sky. In fast-hitting raids that day, which ranged from Dover to Portland, there were heavy losses on both sides.

October saw more action and the fighting on the 6th was vividly described by a local journalist: 'In the morning a terrific battle was fought over Kent as the German planes tried to force our defences and reach London. The air battle reached its fiercest between Maidstone and the coast. The sky was alive with twisting, darting machines from which came the roar of machine guns and the popping of cannons. Now and then a plane hurtled to the ground with some of the crew, who had escaped by parachute, drifting across the battle area. Ignoring the danger from falling bullets and cartridge cases, people at Ashford collected at vantage points in the streets to watch the drama overhead.' Even more dangerous was the shrapnel from exploding anti-aircraft shells when fighters were not around. During the afternoon there was more drama when a group of Messerschmitt 110 raiders flew over the district, scattering their bombs. Five high explosive bombs and twelve incendiaries found their target along the Hastings line causing damage to railway rolling stock in the Works sidings.

The railway once more played a navigational role in an aerial battle later that month, when Bobby Oxspring was patrolling with 66 Squadron over mid-Kent at 31,000 feet. Operations control directed them towards an incoming squadron of Messerschmitt 109s and, taking advantage of their superior height, Oxspring and his co-pilots were able to 'bounce' the enemy – 'We carefully chose our individual targets. My speed advantage was so great that I had to throttle back to keep behind mine. After my first burst he dived, and we belted on downhill. His heading directly followed the Tonbridge to Ashford railway line, which I suppose pointed his way home. Around 12,000 feet he pulled out and started to climb, which enabled me to shorten the range and let him have another dose. I fired a couple more bursts before my windscreen iced up and I lost sight of him when he was down at tree level. Later that evening it was satisfying to be told that he (Feldwebel Rungen) had crash-landed in a field six miles east of Ashford (Hastingleigh).' Shortly after this encounter, Oxspring learned that he had been awarded the DFC.

New Town again suffered because of its vulnerable situation on a cloudy 28th October, when during the late afternoon a large formation of enemy bombers was passing overhead on its way to London. Whether it was the thought of the reception they were bound to receive from Spitfires and Hurricanes or the sight of a tempting target below in the form of a railway works will never be known. Whatever the reason, seven bombers suddenly peeled off and swooped down in a most unexpected attack. They unleashed their bombs, causing only slight damage to the Works but spreading destruction across New Town and South Willesborough. Several houses opposite the school were demolished but fortunately there were no fatal casualties, although ten were injured. It would be a day to remember however, for two elderly ladies - 90 year old Mrs Rose Parker and her 70 year old daughter, Miss Celia Parker. Both were trapped in the debris. Rose Parker was rescued quite quickly by a member of the Fire Brigade, who burrowed his way through bricks and mortar, but her daughter was buried much more deeply although she could talk to her rescuers as they worked their way towards her. It was not until five hours later that she was released.

Superstition dies hard. Vapour trails in the sky were commonplace that summer. One railwayman came home for his dinner declaring that a stationary trail circle in the sky would be used that afternoon by the Germans to aim through in order to bomb the Gas Works.

31st October 1940 is officially recognised as the last day of the Battle of Britain and the threat of invasion had now passed, but it was certainly not the end of the German aerial assault. The blitz on London was mounting to a peak, and night after night throughout that long winter and following spring the heavy drone of bombers was heard over Ashford as the Luftwaffe made a desperate attempt to destroy British defiance

The air-raid warnings were highly disruptive of sleep. Families rose from their beds and either sped to an outside Anderson Shelter or, putting warmth before safety, sheltered in their favoured spot, which was usually under the kitchen table or in the cupboard under the stairs. The tension was heightened when, the sirens having sounded, the distinctive throb of bomber engines was heard. Searchlight beams stabbed the darkness, seeking to locate the raiders and once they were overhead, Ashford's two heavy anti-aircraft batteries swung into action with their guns booming and the sound of their explosive shells crashing across the sky.

A raid warning signal which would forever remain in the memory of all who heard it was the sound from the town's gasworks hooter. Its heavy baleful note, deeper even than a foghorn, and full of menace, was enough to chill the heart and create a fearful apprehension.

Although the German's main objective was London, there still remained the danger of bombs being dropped on other targets. In addition to the night-time bombing, enemy activity continued during daylight hours to the extent that more high explosive bombs were dropped upon the district during the gloomy month of November than any month other than the previous September.

Despite the constant threat to life and limb, day-to-day activities continued, the Railway Works never ceasing production. In the event of telephonic communications being destroyed and services disrupted by bombing, Southern trains would still have operated. Fourteen emergency radio stations assisted by six mobile road units were set up across the system, ready at all times to transmit and receive train control instructions. Locally, a radio station was built in readiness at Hothfield Halt.

By the year's end Ashford had received 558 air raid warnings. 100 high explosive bombs had been dropped on the town and another 483 on the adjoining rural area, together with 1,517 incendiary bombs. However, the most extraordinary scene lay in the surrounding countryside within a ten-mile radius of Ashford. It still bore the marks of the huge battle that had been fought out overhead and was littered with the crashed remains of over 100 German and British aircraft.

Christmas arrived and with it, so far as Ashford was concerned, relief from enemy air attack. Railway families had a choice of entertainment: a 'Good Cause' dance at the Corn Exchange led by the Embassy Band, admission two shillings, or a visit to the Odeon, which was showing a comedy – Eddie Cantor in 'Forty Little Mothers'. Because of wartime conditions the cinema was permitted to open on Christmas Day. Alternatively, the enjoyment of a day at home could be increased with a bottle of port or sherry from the local wine store at 5s. and 5s. 6d. respectively.

The railwaymen's local Co-operative Store boasted: 'There'll always be an England and there'll always be a Co-op.' On a more serious note, everyday life had been transformed following the commencement of rationing. Food controls had been introduced since the beginning of the year: 4oz. bacon, 4oz. butter, 12oz. sugar per person per week, and extended in stages to include virtually everything in the kitchen cupboard with the exception of bread. Now a stringent cut was made to the weekly meat ration to only one shillings-worth, and imported fruit such as grapes, apricots, grapefruit and bananas became a thing of the past, freeing up shipping space for essential goods. The 'pleasure' of Spam and dried eggs was still some way off. Petrol was only available to essential users, clothing would be rationed within six months and the rationing of coal was forecast. Warnings were issued that identity cards and gas masks should be carried at all times and that the traffic 'black-out' on roads and railways must be strictly maintained.

British humour prevailed – Householder: 'I don't understand why you want to raise my rent because the house next door has been bombed?' Landlord: 'Ah, my dear sir – you must realise that your house is now detached!' In fact, with the constant danger from bombing, property prices sank to a very low level. A railwayman tenant in Ashford's Christchurch Road was told he had a new landlord after his house changed hands for £200.

Strangely, because of the war, the Works now had a very tidy appearance. Over the entire Southern Railway system a salvage drive was in full swing and odd corners of shops that had been closed for years now yielded up much needed material. Never had the Works had such a clean-up. All the scrap that young Frederick Imm had seen lying about during the depression years of the thirties was now put to good use. Hundreds of tons of old rails and chairs were collected, along with pipes, girders and boilers and the entire contents of the old rolling mill.

Tradition continued to be observed. On the Friday before Christmas, O.V.S. Bulleid presented long service gold medals to five railwaymen, each with 51 years of continuous service to the Company. They were wagon-makers Ernest Weller, Ernest Leggett, James Hole, Basil Noble and Henry Crux, a turner.

Wartime Achievements

After the bombing of October 1940, although the town suffered, the Works itself enjoyed nearly two years of freedom from enemy attack. The man in charge of civil defence in Ashford was Major Ronald St. John Cole. By the time of the Munich crisis in 1938 he had already planned the town's defences. Now, becoming concerned at the damage to property around the district as a result of night bombing, Major Cole, in conjunction with the Intelligence authorities, decided to set up a decoy to deceive enemy pilots who were searching for the railway works. On the North Downs above Brabourne, an elaborate but simply operated system of electric lights and fires was installed. At first, four civilians were sent out there by taxi and connected to Civil Defence Headquarters in Ashford by a 'hot line' and told to switch on the decoy when German bombers were in the vicinity. After a while it was found that the men had been guilty of breaching security by talking about their work with friends and neighbours, so men from the RAF were drafted in to take over. Major Cole claimed that the ruse worked quite well, as the imitation Works was bombed several times.

Major Cole faced further problems when the town's Civil Defence headquarters moved to an old factory near the railway station in Victoria Road. Being in such a vulnerable area, the basement offices were reinforced and it was decided to create an extra escape route. An underground tunnel was constructed with the aid of sewer pipes, but in practice drill it was found to be very tiring, having to crawl along it on hands and knees. The ingenious solution was a four-wheeled trolley attached to pulley ropes, so that defence workers could be hauled out, one at a time.

Ashford and the railway would play their part in another deception later in the war, when captured German spy Dietrich Schmidt turned double agent and agreed to pass back false information. Prior to D-Day, a friend was invented as a clerk at Ashford Railway Station, who gave him details of the movement of troops, supplies and armour, in preparation for an invasion in the Pas-de-Calais area. The German spy-masters at Abwehr HQ in Hamburg were suitably deceived.

The following year saw the appearance in the Works of Europe's largest railway gun – the giant 18 inch World War I howitzer, HMG Boche Buster, which could throw a massive shell, 2,500lb in weight and six feet in length, a distance of 12? miles. Normally based at Elham, this 250 ton monster had a complement of 80 men. There were three other giant rail-mounted guns, all requiring the maintenance facilities of Ashford Works. These were the 13.5 inch guns originally made for the 'Iron Duke' class of battleships during the First World War. Named HMG Peacemaker, HMG Scene Shifter and HMG Gladiator, they were moved to firing spurs along the coast to attack German shipping in the Channel.

The arrival of the first gun was dramatic. An air-raid alert sounded just as a fierce thunderstorm swept the district. Through the deepening gloom, with lightning flashing and thunder booming, the gun's huge, rain-lashed, grey shape moved silently along a Works rail spur towards its destination alongside the light machine shop.

Invasion defences were beefed up in May 1941 following the arrival in Kent of Lieutenant General Bernard Montgomery. He immediately decided that Ashford would be one of a series of 'hedgehog' towns – strongly defended tank-proof fortresses. His orders were: 'There will be no withdrawal under any circumstances – Ashford will hold out to the last against all attacks.' On 19th May, Monty arrived in the town to confirm plans for its resistance, and defence works began the next day. Within two months, an outer perimeter of wire obstacle 4? miles long had been thrown up, the greater length of the River Stour deepened, explosive charges laid, flame throwing equipment installed, extra mines laid and an inner perimeter of anti-tank defences three miles long constructed. Around the town were 50 road blocks, five rail blocks, 32 machine-gun positions and numerous anti-tank gun emplacements. In the event of invasion the railway was to be ready to evacuate all civilians not required for essential services. Everyone else, together with the garrison of 2,000 soldiers, would remain sealed off within the fortress.

In the Works, an urgent conversion programme was carried through on 26 heavy 9.2 inch guns. Manufactured in 1916, the guns, now in mobile rail form, were to be stationed at key points as part of the defence of south-eastern England. Locally, railway sidings at Coningbrook, Kingsnorth, Hothfield, Sevington and Sellindge provided an operating base, motive power usually being provided by pairs of 0-6-0 locomotives. In addition, two mobile 12 inch guns stood by at Ruckinge and Sellindge.

Bulleid's new 'Merchant Navy' class locomotive had been revealed to the public the previous March. Work during wartime on this 4-6-2 Pacific was shared between the Southern's three workshops, with Brighton responsible for much of the design work and Eastleigh its construction. However, pressure of work resulted in the preparation of the main framing being passed to Ashford. The task of building the tenders for many of these and most of the subsequent 'West Country' and 'Battle of Britain' classes also fell to Ashford, where modern welding equipment, together with the latest techniques, were available. Constructed of thick steel plates, they featured cabs equipped with cupboards for tools and clothing. Special coal doors prevented dust spreading onto the footplate while two conveniently placed water-filling holes removed the chore of the fireman having to climb to the top of the six-wheeled tender, which had a water-tank capacity of 5,000 gallons and carried five tons of coal.

Fifteen months later on 4th June, the Ashford men saw the full result of their labours when a sleek black locomotive, No.35006, slid into a Works siding. It was the sixth engine in its series and was to receive the name 'Peninsular and Oriental Steam Navigation Company'. In accordance with tradition there was a full turn-out of top brass and the ceremony was enlivened by the presence of the Works Band. Colonel Gore-Brown (Southern deputy chairman) paid tribute to the courage and enterprise of the men and women who had helped build the locomotive, which he said would take its full share of hauling heavy trains of war freight.

His reference to the war was apt, seeing that Ashford had been bombed the previous night and Canterbury had experienced its second night of blitz. Little wonder that some expressed surprise at such a ceremony taking place in such a risky situation but there was a general British attitude of 'business as usual' and the pre-planned affair would have been seen as an act of defiance. The war-time atmosphere was heightened with the line-up of contingents of the Southern Railway Home Guard and Works fire-fighters. The locomotive's nameplate was unveiled by Sir William Currie (Chairman and Managing Director of the P&O), watched by Bulleid.

Another innovation for Ashford in 1941 was the design and production of an electric locomotive, claimed to be the most ingenious ever developed, the joint design of Bulleid and Raworth (Southern's electrical engineer). Bulleid's influence was clear from the smooth, box-like body, finished in grey livery with white stripes. The massive underframe was mounted on two six-wheel bogies, resulting in a locomotive weighing 99 tons, able to haul 750-ton passenger trains and 1,000-ton goods trains at 75 miles per hour. A pantograph was fitted to enable working in goods yards where there was no third rail. This first machine, designated CC1, with English Electric 1,470 hp engines, was followed by a second, two years later, and a third in 1948.

During the early months of the war Bulleid had foreseen a developing shortage of locomotives, and so in August 1940 he made a recommendation to the Board urging construction of 40 goods engines. The need was for a locomotive that would cope with the Southern's varied network of inclines and curves and run tender first when required without loss of performance. Bulleid succeeded brilliantly in his objective, creating an engine that proved to be the most powerful 0-6-0 in the country.

Although the Board moved speedily in granting authorisation, there was some delay, caused by the Ministry of Transport. Thus it was the next year before all necessary materials could be assembled and 1942 before the completed locomotives were revealed to their startled crews. Bulleid had decided that the largest possible boilers were needed and planned to provide the largest firebox that could be safely accommodated. In providing this size boiler and firebox, and in order to keep the weight down, the most dramatic and unconventional economies had to be made. As with his Pacifics, he used electric welding for the boiler, avoiding the need for weighty rivets. But what stunned traditionalists was the discarding of anything considered to be an unnecessary frill, including running plates and wheel splashers. The result was an engine of revolutionary and controversial appearance. The livery was a plain wartime black, the Company name appearing across the tender and its number painted on buffer beams and cab sides.

Fears were expressed by enginemen concerning braking power and the stability of the tender when running in reverse at speed. In order to calm those fears, Bulleid arranged for a dramatic demonstration by climbing up onto the tender for a fast run, tender first, from Ashford to Maidstone. At a point when a speed of 65 mph had been reached, Bulleid called for the engine to stop, and this was followed by a smooth braking. Nothing more was heard of 'the problem'. Despite the initial reaction to their slab sides and unfinished and stark appearance, Bulleid's austerity 'Q1' class turned in a superb performance. 20 were built at Ashford and a further 20 at the Brighton works, numbered C1 to C40.

War is the cause of many changes, but the one that would have caused the old pioneers greatest amazement was the introduction of women into the Works. 30 first came into the workshops at the beginning of 1941, working eight-hour shifts, night and day, with half an hour for meals. They were soon playing a full part in the life of the factory, demonstrating their skills in a way previously unheard of, and operating a wide range of machines such as multiple drills, capstan lathes, milling machines and radial drills. A supervisor at the time said: 'The machinery frightened the life out of most of them at first, but they did work well.'

Visitors passing through the various workshops saw them in their blue boiler suits working at practically every kind of job. In one shop they operated electric butt welders for boiler tubes, in the wagon shop they could be seen working at the smiths' fires, handling their tongs with ease and throwing red hot rivets to their mates for riveting parts of wagons and vans. The jobs of flame-cutter, welder, steam hammer driver, motor truck driver and painter were taken in their stride. On an official visit the local M.P., William Spens, discovered his former parlourmaid hard at work at a bench and watched fascinated as he saw Dorothy Stanford Beale, previously a servant at Olantigh House, wield a blacksmith's hammer. At the peak of their contribution, 422 women were in the workshops and 23 on clerical, inspection and quality control jobs.

A feature of wartime life was the need for long hours to be performed by the entire workforce. Shift-working and extended overtime was the norm and the women were not excused this. A Works outpost was the New Town Baths, where on the lower floor women workers, supervised by Miss Bertha King, were engaged in upholstery repairs, their lives being enlivened by the regular arrival of troops from camps in the district who came by the lorry-load to take advantage of the Baths' washing facilities.

Women were also needed to staff the Works canteen that had been opened following the outbreak of war, serving hot mid-day meals. Most of the Royal Train shed had been converted for this purpose and it was memorable for the occasions when the BBC broadcast one of its 'Workers' Playtime' programmes. Guests included George Robey, Charlie Chester and Norman Wisdom, with the musical accompaniment of Ashford's Southern Railway Band. There was also entertainment entirely home-brewed called 'Works Wonders'. In addition to the Works Band, the Potter Hills dance band performed with regular vocalists such as Ernie Cuttress and Norman Turner, often accompanied by George Lancaster on piano together with other local support.

In a morale boosting visit, Squadron Leader Roderick Learoyd, who lived locally at Littlestone, appeared on one occasion. On the night of 12th August, 1940, he had flown with a five-strong Handley Page Hampden bomber formation in a raid on the heavily defended aqueduct of the

Dortmund-Ems canal. In order to make certain that the target was hit, a low-level attack was planned. One by one the Hampdens went in with the moon reflecting clearly in the water of the canal. The first and fourth bombers defied the fierce reaction of the German gunners and bombed successfully, although suffering heavy damage to their aircraft. The second and third paid the price for their courage, both being shot down in flames before they could complete their bombing run.

In the fifth aircraft, Learoyd made his approach flying down the canal at only 150 feet above its surface, knowing the odds against survival and having to run the gauntlet of rows of anti-aircraft guns lining the banks. The German defences were now more than ready as they threw up an enormous flak barrage, but although caught in the glare of searchlights, Learoyd pressed home his attack. So low was his aircraft that the Germans were now firing at point-blank range. Machine gun bullets spattered the underside of the plane, pom-pom shells hit the starboard wing alongside the engine and the hydraulic system was shot away, leaking oil everywhere. Despite the intensity of the opposition Learoyd held steady and with absolute precision released his bombs, which slammed into the aqueduct, blasting a hole that released tons of water, draining that section of the canal. As he flew away, pursued by tracer shells, the damage caused to his aircraft became very apparent. He found that, in addition to his other problems, neither the wing flaps nor the undercarriage indicators would work. Avoiding prowling German night fighters, he struggled home, wrestling with the controls and in this battered condition managed to keep the aircraft in flight until dawn, not wanting to risk the safety of his crew by attempting a night landing.

The result of the raid only became known when Learoyd was asked by the BBC to broadcast a description of the attack. In successfully breaching the aqueduct he had seriously delayed the movement of invasion barges from the Rhineland to the channel ports. The mission earned him the Victoria Cross and saw him acclaimed as one of the country's war heroes, the first member of Bomber Command to be so honoured.

Despite the war, life for apprentices continued much as usual. Frank Mercer, who entered the Works in 1940, recalls his 5? day week with pay starting at 8s. per week rising to 20s. in the fifth year. Apprentices were allowed three weeks holiday each year but without pay, nor was there pay for the Easter, Whitsun or August Bank Holidays. They were required to attend evening classes and discipline was tight, bad conduct or poor timekeeping, either at work or in classes, was not tolerated and could result in being dismissed.

Frank Mercer started in the fitting shop and found apprentices were given dirty or monotonous jobs, such as wire-brushing 'black valves' which left him covered in dust, or 'draw filing' new connecting rods to remove defective marks and then to make them shine like silver. Another laborious task was to push in large side-rod bushes using only a hand pump, until one's arms ached. At the time, nothing was thought of having to fill water and steam locks with asbestos packing or string, sometimes using the now infamous blue asbestos.

It was usually the lot of the apprentices to work on the older lathes, which had very few safety devices. There was no safety guard and to start the lathe a drive belt was pushed into position with a piece of wood. Fitting and turning was found to be interesting but became boring after doing the same work for weeks on end. More interesting were the erecting and boiler shops, although here the work was much heavier and much more dangerous.

Frank Mercer decided to join Ashford's Air Training Corps, which met in the then unused Newtown School. With the dangers from enemy air attack, he decided that if he was going to die he would rather it was in uniform and so he volunteered for service with the Royal Air Force.

Of all the wartime achievements in the Works, perhaps highest honours go to the wagon shop towards the end of 1941. By now Russia had been invaded and that country's need for equipment and supplies of all kinds was dire. Despite Britain's own predicament, full support had been promised by Winston Churchill for what would now be a combined Allied effort against Hitler. Ashford Works received a desperately urgent order for 1,000 13-ton open freight wagons and immediately rose to the challenge with an upsurge of great determination. The enthusiastic fervour was further encouraged by a profusion of Russian flags that decorated the shop, accompanied by patriotic slogans chalked up on the walls. If any man faltered he was urged on by his workmates with cries of 'Come on! Old Joe (Stalin) wants that one.' The entire shop workforce worked double shifts night and day, producing double the usual output in each shift. The job was completed in less than ten weeks despite 76 air raid warnings, which the workforce ignored. 130 men, 19 boys and 22 women averaged 67 hours a week in this quite extraordinary effort.

Upon completion, the wagons were sent in batches of ten to the Middle East, each wagon containing 792 parts and each part stencilled with letters and numbers to correspond with photographs, sent on ahead to assist with assembly. The whole consignment was shipped in crates built specially for the purpose. Colonel Llewellin, Parliamentary Secretary to the Ministry of War Transport, came down to Ashford to celebrate the completion of the order, driving the last nail into the last packing case with an American hammer to symbolise the unity of the now three Allied Nations.

On arrival at their destination, the parts assembly system devised at Ashford worked with incredible success. Wagons were erected at the rate of one every 45 minutes by a unit that had no workshop facilities, few trained artisans and no wagon builders. It was 20 working weeks to the day from the beginning of work at Ashford till that on which the last wagon was assembled and put into service 12,000 route miles away. As a result, Britain was able to send urgently needed war supplies by way of the Persian Gulf to Russia.

In Ashford there was little time to relax. At the beginning of December another urgent order was received, this time for 600 12-ton open freight wagons. These were to be equipped with screw couplings and the French type of Westinghouse brakes and also to be shipped overseas. Work began on 4th December and on the last day of the year the order was complete. An average completion rate of a little over 22 wagons a day.

The Locomotive Works

Situated at the very heart of the Works stood the main office, a building dating back to 1847. Here were to be found the leading hierarchy in the form of the Works Manager, Chief Clerk and Chief Draughtsman. Running down the centre of this Victorian edifice was a long stone corridor from which a stone staircase embellished with a cast-iron balustrade led to the accounts offices. Staff were divided into two groups, the cost accountants and the wages section. Wages clerks sat on high stools at long sloping desks while the costing section enjoyed large polished desks, which boasted shining brass rails supporting heavy ledgers.

Some arrangements, although rudimentary, were of long standing. Internal Company mail was taken to the railway station for despatch to various locations. Other mail was left at the town's sorting office in Elwick Road. Every evening, without fail, rain or shine, the 'messenger' mounted his bicycle and, weighed down by leather bags slung over his shoulders, made his way along Newtown Road with the Works post.

An outside man, whose normal employment was that of milkman, brought in the cash for the wages each week. As a secondary occupation he ran an old Austin taxi and the money was ferried on its back seat from a bank in Ashford to the Works. Security was minimal, although fortunately the milkman was a very large man who always carried a truncheon, and he was always accompanied by a Works clerk. The cash was subsequently packed into buff wage packets and stacked in wooden boxes ready for distribution to the various foremen's offices every Friday afternoon.

Given the laid-back ways of the British, there was some amusement when units of the US Army, having arrived in the district, needed to withdraw money from the bank. An officer and an NCO arrived by car together with a lorryborne squad of 12 steel-helmeted soldiers armed with rifles, to guard the cash.

The drawing office, much depleted since earlier days, was serviced by a small but dedicated staff who worked at long desks, supporting a row of drawing boards which ran down the centre of the room. Beneath were sets of drawers containing numerous numbered drawings in current use. The main drawing store, located away from the office, was home to scores of thick blueprints. Layer upon layer of racks provided storage for the plans, each wrapped around a strong wooden pole. Other drawings, on either tracing paper or linen cloth, were kept in heavily lidded circular metal containers and stored in an old carriage. This had been lined out with asbestos giving some protection from any fire resulting from an air raid.

The heavy machine shop was noted for its variety of machines, both large and small. Drilling machines, shapers, millers, slotters, grinders and lathes crowded the workshop floor, mostly run by a dated line shaft system from high up on the walls. Powered by a large electric motor at one end of the shafting, power was transmitted by means of flat leather belts to individual machines, which dealt with a range of components including pistons, coupling rods, axle boxes and buffers. Standing prominently among this veritable array was a huge and very old machine for slotting locomotive frames. The effect of war was apparent here as elsewhere, with the men now performing the unusual task of producing gun-turrets for Churchill tanks, despite the difficulty of working by artificial light in the blackened-out workshop.

Adjacent to the machine shop was the fitting shop, into which finished components were subsequently moved. Work was shared by a number of gangs. The motion gang, who refurbished valve-gear parts; the reverser gang, who overhauled both steam and air-assisted reversers and rebuilt piston valve assemblies; and the cylinder and coupling rod gang: all responsible, among others, for particular areas of locomotive repair.

The light machine shop produced its fair share of noise as girls worked hard at their machines, turning out a whole variety of steel pins, bushes, studs and boiler fittings, together with replacement boiler stays, which were made in their thousands. In addition to normal railway work, the shop was now also responsible for producing parts for Sunderland Flying Boats and Typhoon and Tempest fighter aircraft, as well as burster bomb rings and shell caps. The shop's equipment included all the well known names in British-made machines of the day, such as Ward Capstan and Herbert & Gridley, together with some of World War One origin, previously acquired from Woolwich Arsenal. There was perhaps an element of poetic justice in that amongst the machines were some German Pittler lathes, now working for the Allied war effort.

Later in the war the shop was dominated by two huge, room-sized auto-production lathes, which came to Ashford from the United States under the war time lease-lend arrangements. Known locally as the 'Conos', they were impressive machines, although extremely noisy when their eight spindles were hard at work. As protection against bomb blast, these expensive machines were covered over by a strong metal roof and surrounded by sandbags, reducing the possibility of any interruption to their high rate of output.

Associated with the light machine shop was the bogie shop, located on the works boundary near the Willesborough gate. Much of the work taking place here was regarded as 'hush-hush'. In addition to maintenance work on the Army's railway guns, the men were called upon to use their skills to produce a whole range of war equipment. Forty-three 3.7 inch Howitzers arrived, all needing to be fitted with new carriages, converting them from their previous horse-drawn form to a motorised role, with pneumatic tyred wheels and fitted with armoured screens. With an Allied invasion of Europe in prospect an order was received for 75 tank-ramp bogie wagons, and an already full workload was increased when the Works was asked to convert 40 American freight cars to breakdown trains and supply a number of mobile workshops for the United States Army.

The smiths' shop was not for the faint-hearted. Coke fires could be seen burning on both sides of the building with each smith and his mate bent over their work in careful concentration, every forging needing the attention of a sharp eye and a skilled hand. The white heat of the furnace, the incessant thump of the power-hammers and the clang of hammers on anvils all combined to create an indescribable bedlam. The spring makers also 'lived' here, manufacturing and repairing engine and wagon springs. Metal heated in the furnaces was shaped whilst still hot and put in a 'buckle' with a steel pin through the centre.

Close-by was the forge, which operated under the watchful eye of the smith's shop foreman. This really was the Ashford Works' version of 'Dante's Inferno'. Permanently dark and scorchingly hot from the heat of its coal-fired furnaces, billets of steel were brought up to white heat. Two large steam hammers then forged the steel into heavy parts such as coupling and connecting rods, each weighing as much as a quarter of a ton. The whole of Willesborough and Newtown knew when the hammers were at work, their thumping shaking every house in the district.

Another place to be avoided by those with an aversion to noise was the boiler shop. Once inside the clamour was deafening, the ceaseless noise continually rising and falling. Pneumatic rivet guns worked ceaselessly alongside pneumatic drills tapping holes for firebox stays. Almost all the boilermakers were completely deaf, having worked so long without the protection of ear plugs.

A great 500-ton press stood in the area known as the flanging yard, together with a coal-fired plate furnace, and it was here that hot, thick plates were formed to become firebox or boiler plates. Outside, beneath a 25-ton semi-Goliath girder crane, were lines of boilers, either awaiting their turn for repair or having been repaired, ready to return to active service. Making for easy movement, a transverser ran between the shops and on to the boilers outside, enabling both them and the tenders to be moved from bay to bay.

The main erecting shop was a long building on the north side of the Works, alongside the main line. As in other shops, the men maintained a prodigious output to meet the demands of war. Here one could see the unorthodox Bulleid Q1s taking shape alongside a much larger and more conventional locomotive. During the war, the Southern had been directed by the Ministry of War Transport to build a batch of 14 engines based on the standard LMS '8F' 2-8-0 design. This was a powerful class of engine designed by Sir William Stanier and chosen at the outbreak of hostilities as a standard locomotive suitable for large scale production. Those built at Ashford were used on the Home Front, but many others were sent to the Middle East and saw service in Iran and in the Western Desert campaign.

Other engines were being repaired, either as part of normal maintenance or as a result of enemy action. There could also be the sight of an engine headed for the scrapyard, although not very often during the wartime period.

Overhead, large electric cranes ran on trackways the length of three of the four bays, the longest running from the tender shop through to the fitting and heavy machine shops. At 1206 feet in length this was believed to be the longest continuous crane runway in England. Locomotives and tenders were lifted from their wheels and deposited on huge timber baulks over the maintenance pits. Working in cramped conditions, men had to fit a range of components, working only by the light of candles, which were wedged for support into large steel nuts. Sometimes they had the luxury of a low voltage headlamp.

At the far end of the erecting shop, locomotives coming in for repair first passed to the stripping pits, where parts were removed for cleaning and renovation. Caked in grease and dirt, they were moved on to the 'Bosh', a large steel cabinet positioned over a pit filled with a steam-heated caustic soda solution. From this cauldron arose a truly sickening smell, making a nauseating job even more odious. Being a member of the stripping gang was a filthy job and during the summer months, heat added to the men's discomfort. The uniform for the job was not the usual pair of overalls but a strong, stiff canvas jacket and trousers.

Another fascinating range of machines could be found in the locomotive wheel shop. Here was located a wheel press for removing or replacing wheel discs on their axles; a wheel lathe for machining the correct tyre profile simultaneously on two wheels which had already been pressed onto an axle; a journal lathe for re-machining and burnishing the axles' bearing surfaces; and a quartering rig to ensure that driving wheels on the same axle were at 90 degrees to one another. In its gas-fired tyre furnace, new steel tyres were heated and expanded to allow wheel centres to be dropped into them. As the tyre cooled, it shrunk firmly on the wheel centre.

Smaller shops included the white metal shop where axle-boxes and main and big-end bearings were re-metalled and given a new lease of life; where coppersmiths prepared pipework for locomotives and their tenders; and where millwrights were responsible for carrying out statutory inspections of the many cranes and chains and much of the machinery.

At this time, and until the late nineteen fifties, wagon underframes were all riveted. This was the task of shop 40, known to everyone as 'the madhouse'. Components and raw materials went in at one end of the shop and completed wagons emerged from the other. The noise was unbelievable, with girls and lads first heating rivets on portable coke fires and then tossing them, red hot, across the floor. If ever a quart was produced from a pint pot, it was here, with over 100 wagons being produced every week.

Boiler tubes were repaired in the tube shop. Fed into long machines, they clattered between rollers for descaling, the constant rattling being a continual assault upon the ears, rivalling shop 40.

A hazard of a different nature presented itself in the welding shop. Numerous bays were screened off with canvas or sacking to contain the vivid blue flash of ultraviolet light, so dangerous to unprotected eyes. The welders wore goggles, but for anyone who was careless or unwary an uncomfortable night was in prospect, when they awoke in the early hours with eyes that felt as though they were full of sand. Remembering the raids by the Luftwaffe, it was with grim satisfaction that the welders turned to their wartime task of constructing large numbers of bomb trolleys for the RAF.

A separate building housed the trimmers shop, where the women operated industrial sewing machines, making the canvas suits for the men in the stripping pits. Their wartime tasks included the repair of bell tents for the army, which Mrs. Elsie Wood ruefully recalled as 'really hard work'. The men were responsible for reupholstering chairs and settees from station waiting rooms and cushions from any guard's brake van presently in the Works for overhaul.

Amidst the pandemonium in so many parts of the Works, there were one or two oases of tranquillity – one was the pattern shop, where men went quietly about their trade, producing wooden patterns. These enabled the moulders in the brass foundry to create a sand moulding into which molten metal was poured for the making of brass or aluminium castings.

Another quiet spot was the power house, where three stand-by electric generating sets stood ready for use as a precaution against a failure in the grid power supply putting vital equipment at risk. The Works power supply was taken from the National Grid at 6,600 volts and then transformed and converted to 400 volts DC. This process took place in the adjacent substation, where the presence of mercury arc rectifiers was only betrayed by a soft hum and accompanying blue flashes, rather reminiscent of the classic horror films of the day.

Adjacent to the canteen were two laboratories, one known as the Physical Lab and the other as the Chemical Lab. The Physical Lab was responsible for examining metallurgical components that had failed in service, conducting routine testing of purchased materials and engaging in research into engineering problems and welding techniques. Much of the credit for the department's reputation was due to the faultless work of its head, Basil Byrne. Its wartime duties now included checking aircraft parts and other military material. The Chemical Lab tested water each day for all motive power depots in the South Eastern division. Impurities or hardscale having been identified, a chemical treatment was prescribed. There was a constant flow of 'runners' with their little Works-manufactured metal cans, to and from these outside depots. In addition the lab was also responsible for oil and paint testing and that of any foodstuff damaged in transit.

A job that was unglamorous but nevertheless essential was the work of the shunters. Several puffed and clanked their way around the Works every day moving engines not in steam or wagons both loaded and empty. Working in conjunction with them was the yard gang, whose chore it was to unload wagons by hand every day, regardless of the weather. Hard and laborious work. The gang included one man who spent his whole time coupling and uncoupling the wagons.

Such was the Locomotive Works during the darkest days of the war.

More Bombs

An unexpected air attack on Ashford occurred in 1942. The savage blitz on Canterbury had taken place in the early hours of 1st June. Two nights later the raiders returned to the city but for whatever reason, some found themselves over the Ashford district and unleashed 2,800 incendiary bombs over the town and the country areas. There were a large number of incidents, which were all dealt with by the Civil Defence services, but the most notable feature of the attack was the destruction of a bakery in North Street. Owned by the Alfred Joint Stock Bread and Flour Company, the enterprise had been founded in the years soon after the Railway Works had opened, with shares subscribed by the railway workers. From this humble beginning it had grown into the largest bakery in the district and its yellow and maroon vans, both horse-drawn and motorised, were a feature of local roads. Now a raging fire was sweeping through its bake-house to the despair of its workers and the consternation of its neighbours. Valiant work by Ashford's fire fighters failed to get the blaze under control and the next morning, passers-by were presented with the sad sight of a smouldering, smoking ruin. Fortunately all the horses were rescued from their stabling.

The war returned to the works on the morning of 30th September, when without any warning a Junkers 88 appeared out of the clouds, firing its machine guns. Swooping low, it skimmed the roofs of the Kimberley shops, its rear wheel carrying away the wire strung between the lamp posts as workmen scattered in all directions, urgently seeking shelter. A group of firemen who happened to be nearby dived into an air raid shelter with bullets literally throwing up concrete chippings at their heels.

One bomb exploded and demolished part of the sawmills. Thomas Young, the foreman, had taken shelter under a stack of timber in the yard when one bomb, which fortunately did not explode, just bounced past him and went on down one of the concrete paths. In the wagon shop a man saw a bomb bouncing straight at him, when it erratically bounced back again, to the relief of the man, who 'legged it' behind a pile of timber.

Walter Clark, the fire captain, had thrown himself to the ground and was unhurt. Another workman had taken refuge in an old railway carriage. Upon looking in to see if he was all right, Walter found him sitting placidly eating a piece of cake.

As the bomber flew back into the clouds it continued to blaze away with its guns, leaving five people injured. The anti-aircraft guns surrounding the town went into action as the raider flew down the line towards the coast with bits falling off it and leaving a trail of smoke. It is believed to have gone down into the sea off Hythe.

One month later the Works' luck ran out. The south of England had experienced raids by sneak raiders throughout the week, carried out under cover of low clouds. On 26th October a Dornier bomber was plainly seen through breaks in the cloud as it circled Ashford before dropping its bombs. The first bomb hit the factory of the Ashford Underwear Company, leaving a great crater. A young girl died and four others were injured.

More serious was the effect of the second bomb, which struck the Works, damaging the heavy and light machine shops and the brass shop. Because of the suddenness of the attack, many had not taken shelter. The bomb crashed down in the yard of the old running shed, collapsing the wall of a building and killing eight, some dying immediately, others the following day. Mrs. Celey Lloyd, George Sweetman, William Dray, Robert Blair, Charles Holdstock, Jack Blake, Jack Terry and Harold Woodgate were all killed and twelve other workers were injured.

Jack Blake's wife, Mary, had been looking out of the window of their South Ashford home just as the German bomber came through the clouds for its bombing run. She watched spellbound as she saw its bombs fall, little realising that her husband was about to meet his death, leaving her widowed with a two-month baby and a two year old child.

Just a few minutes before the attack, 24 year old Celey Lloyd, recently married to her fiancé in the Royal Corps of Signals, had been showing her wedding photos to work colleague Violet Nixon. They had gone their separate ways moments before the bomb exploded.

Peter Mercer had started work only two months previously as an office boy in the erecting shop office. He recalled how his colleague, Cliff Kenward, was always looking out of the window, saying 'I'll bet they'll be over today'. Today he was right. Outside the shop a group of locomotives awaiting repair were seriously damaged. Peter Mercer's thoughts were that they looked like giant water cans with water pouring from their tenders. Fortunately a train on the Folkestone line, that had been held at the signals and that may well have been the target, escaped damage. A few hours later a second Dornier passed over, machine gunning the area, but there were no casualties.

There was to be an unhappy echo of the raid in the summer of 1947, when the decapitated body of a young woman was found on the railway line at Bailey's Crossing. Evidence was given at the inquest that 24 year old Elsie Brunger, daughter of railwayman S. A. Caspell, had been severely injured in the 1942 raid. Having left a note indicating severe depression, she had taken her own life.

Four weeks later, the Germans again tried their luck, but ended up getting more than they bargained for. On Friday, 27th November, two Focke-Wulf 190s roared in at low level, sweeping over the Works with their guns blazing the whole time. George Barnes, a fireman on an 'N' class locomotive, working at the coal stage, fell victim to the bullets and four other railwaymen were wounded.

The raiders decided to return to France by following the Romney Marsh branch line. Nearing Lydd, they bore down on the 3.18pm train, which had just left the station, full of troops and ATS girls going on leave. Attacking it with cannon and machine gun fire, the locomotive boiler was hit and exploded, but its flying debris struck one of the planes, causing the pilot to lose control and crash.

The fireman, Dan Hills of Ashford, suffered from shock and scalds, but the engine driver, Charlie Gilbert, also of Ashford, had a miraculous escape. He said: 'I'm lucky to be here. I don't know what happened and I don't remember the explosion, but I can remember finding myself on the footplate and struggling to get up. I saw that my engine boiler had exploded and where I had been standing I could have walked through. The chimney was gone, the boiler plates blown outwards and the side tanks collapsed. I was smothered with dirt and dust, my eyes, ears and mouth full of it. My head is still sore. Some of the passengers, none of whom were injured, came along and shook me by the hand and said: 'Good for you, mate, you brought it down.' The pilot was found dead in a field ditch 100 yards away and bits of the plane were strewn over a radius of half a mile.

Charlie Gilbert was later interviewed on the radio programme 'In Town Tonight' and recounted his experience to an appreciative nation, having been introduced to listeners by music from Ashford's Southern Railway Band.

Heading Ashford! Heading Ashford!

The town fell victim to an attack by German raiders in February 1943, when four Fock-Wulfe 190s swept in over Ashford at roof top height from the Romney Marsh direction with guns blazing. Their bombs caused severe damage both in the town and at Kennington, resulting in seven deaths and 25 injured. One bomb landed near the railway station and bounced across to St. John's Lane before exploding. On this occasion the Works escaped, but worse was to follow. On 9th March a German reconnaissance plane, flying at 25,000 feet and emitting tell-tale vapour trails but well beyond the reach of the town's two heavy anti-aircraft batteries, took photographs of remarkable clarity. They covered Ashford and the surrounding five miles, showing in great detail the Railway Works, the Royal Ordnance Depot and other industrial sites.

The incident was clearly of great concern to the authorities because the Army promptly moved extra defences into the Works and along the line. A carriage was put down the sand road next to the running shed and became their headquarters. An Oerlikon cannon was mounted on an empty truck against the stops on the coal stage road. Double Bren guns in emplacements of old railway sleepers and sandbags were installed on the roof of the stores, on the coal stage bank, at the Willesborough Gate and on the footbridge by 'E' signals cabin. Platforms were erected on the far side of Newtown and at the Kimberley wagon works for twin Vickers guns. Similarly a gun platform was erected above the railway station for yet another twin Vickers.

Along the Maidstone branch line, the Army mounted a twin Oerlikon cannon on the footbridge leading to Bailey's Fields and a Lewis gun on the bridge at Godinton Road. All this added to the ring of Bofers guns that surrounded the town. Little wonder that there were feelings of apprehension among the workforce.

The German reconnaissance photographs would be of great importance at a Luftwaffe briefing later that month. During the winter months a special attack squadron, equipped with the latest Focke-Wulf 190A-4 fighter-bombers had arrived at an airfield in the Pas-de-Calais. Designated Gruppe 1 of Schnellkampfgeschwader 10 (Fast Bomber Wing 10) of Luftflotte 3, these powerful aircraft were equipped with 20mm cannon and machine guns and could carry a 1100 lb bomb. The squadron was lead by the notorious Oberleutnant Paul Keller, known in the Luftwaffe as 'Bombenkeller' and highly skilled in low-level attacks.

Wednesday 24th March dawned as a warm, sunny and spring-like day. Business in the market town was proceeding normally and in the works, employees were working at their routine tasks. Unknown to Ashford, a squadron of Focke-Wulfs had taken off from their base at St. Omer and was heading across the Channel. The flying time from Nazi-occupied Europe to Ashford was only seven minutes. Skimming the waves in close formation, the enemy intruders crossed the coast, but were forced to gain height in order to cross the Aldington ridge. Batteries of ack-ack guns sprang into action, their heavy barrage causing the low-flying planes to break formation. The time was just 10am. Unknowingly the town and the Works were seconds from an appalling disaster.

On the roof of the Bath House at Newtown two railwaymen, Joe Knowler and young Fred Smith, were just commencing their four-hour 'spotters' shift. Their alertness paid off – they spotted the bombers flying in directly out of the sun from the Mersham direction. Head-on and flying low they swarmed in around Colliers Hill just three miles away. As they came into view, travelling at around 350 miles per hour, the spotters realised they were Focke-Wulf 190s. Joe Knowler hit the button, sounding the 'immediate danger' in the Works. The warning signal gave the workforce just 20 seconds to get to shelter and, although not all of them made it, extraordinarily most did. How many lives were saved by the spotters' warning can only be surmised, but certainly without the warning the numbers of casualties would have been hugely increased.

An eye-witness to the day's event was young Robert Barham, who recalls: 'My apprenticeship had just been completed but I was still temporarily employed as a supernumerary fitter. I had been given the job of facing-up an axle-box bearing to its journal out in the open at the east end of the running shed. Who could have wished for a better deal on such a grand morning, away from the gloomy interior of the blacked-out shed? I had been back to the fitters' shop to sharpen up a couple of scrapers on the old grindstone and was making my way back towards the big double doors and the sunshine when the Loco Works 'immediate danger' sirens began their high-pitched scream. When that happened it meant only one thing – drop everything and get to shelter.'

'As I ran out through the doors towards the air raid shelters, all hell broke loose! Green and yellow streaks flashing by on all sides – Christ! Tracer shells! Stuttering roar of aircraft cannon guns; aircraft engines loud – getting louder. Bloody hell – five of the bastards head on, very low, big radial engines, FW190s, a big black bomb dropping from the belly of one. It all happened in seconds, yet in slow motion as I flung myself to the ground. Heavy explosions, the ground kicks me in the stomach, engine noise deafening as the FW 190s sweep over at rooftop height. They're gone and I get up and race for the nearest shelter because I can hear more of the sods coming. There's a great clattering of feet as many others join me surging down the shelter steps.'

'More cannon gunning, a crescendo of noise as the second wave sweeps over; another lot of bombs and sand trickles down from the shelter roof. Ack-ack firing back now. The rattle of light machine guns and the slower bark of a Bofors. In the background the belated mournful wail of the public air raid warning sirens. Yet a third wave comes in, their bombs further away.'

'It seems to be over now, but as we begin to file out towards the shelter steps, a voice, strained and urgent: 'Bob Bowes, are you there? For Christ's sake come quickly, there's terrible injuries.'

'As I emerged from the shelter I was shocked to see a great pall of black smoke rising above the shed roof – God, that one must have been bloody close. It was closer than I thought. People were running. I joined them and later wished I hadn't. 'E' class loco 1515 had been standing at the coal stage prior to taking its turn over the disposal pit, having just worked a stopping passenger train down from Tonbridge. A 1100 lb bomb had hit the right hand side of the boiler just below the steam dome. It had torn open a riveted seam, entered the boiler and twisted the fire-tubes to resemble the rifling in a gun barrel before bursting through the tube-plate into the firebox, striking the foundation ring below the fire door, which unfortunately for the poor fireman still on the footplate, was open. The bomb then turned through 180 degrees to emerge some 20 yards in front of the engine, where its delayed-action fuse caused it to detonate a few seconds later, leaving a crater 30 feet across and 15 feet deep.'

'The blast caught the 55 ton loco, pushing it over sideways to lean drunkenly against the coal stage with its side-framing ripped vertically upwards. A second bomb failed to explode. The driver, apparently not seriously hurt, was lying near the edge of the crater and urged those who came to help him to see to his fireman first, as he was trapped on the footplate.'

'His fireman was indeed trapped, under nearly two tons of coal. The boiler, with several hundred gallons of water and steam under pressure had literally exploded, all of the water converting instantly into steam at nearly twice the temperature of boiling water. Some escaped through the hole made by the bomb. The rest came out with terrible force through the firedoor, searing the flesh of the fireman from his waist up. Notwithstanding this agonising injury, he struggled to the gangway between the engine and tender, which he had reached at the moment when the bomb exploded. Fragments of the bomb caused further horrendous abdominal and leg injuries, flinging him backwards across the footplate to be buried by coal cascading off the tender as the engine tilted.'

'When we reached him he was conscious and screaming in his agony. As he was being stretchered to the ambulance his cries of; 'God, dear God, please let me die', haunted my dreams for weeks. Mercifully, heavily sedated with morphine, he succumbed to his injuries some three hours later.' By the time our first-aiders returned to the driver, he too had died. Although having no outward signs of injury, the blast had caused fatal damage to his lungs.'

'Not surprisingly, everything not in the immediate vicinity had been blotted from my mind. Now, with time to think more clearly, the full impact of what had happened began to dawn on me. I realised with horror that one-third of the 600 foot long erecting shop had virtually gone. Only the girders and stanchions supporting the overhead cranes remained.'

Of the bombs which fell on the Works the greatest number of casualties was caused by a bomb which, travelling almost horizontally, skidded off the wheel shop roof and penetrated the end wall of the erecting shop, where it shot along for another 100 feet before its delayed action fuse set it off a few feet above the ground. The destruction was immense. 80-ton locomotives were flung around like toys, the casualty list was long.

Fred Wade was working in the erecting shop as a fitter when the raid warning sounded. Climbing from the working pit underneath a locomotive he ran towards the large doors, heading for an air raid shelter. As he ran he saw a plane firing its guns, its tracer bullets spraying the doorway. He dived against the shop wall for protection just as a bomb crashed through. Part of the wall hit him on the head, rendering him unconscious. Later, the bomb having exploded, he made his way to the Willesborough Gate, where he was helped by a blacksmith from the rolling mill, put on a stretcher and taken to the casualty centre in the old kiln. From there he was taken to the Willesborough Hospital in a makeshift ambulance. The locomotive on which he had been working was one of those that had been blown across the shop. He had a badly cut head and shrapnel in his arms, legs and body. It was nine months before he returned to work.

Jimmy Keene was also in the erecting shop that day. Deciding that there was no time to get to shelter, he dived into one of the pits, emerging afterwards covered from head to foot in mud and oil. His prompt action had saved his life.

During the previous two weeks a group of men had been discussing the merits of various places to shelter in the event of a sudden air raid. Arthur Ward pointed to a pit, above which was a locomotive with an axle-box under repair. 'That's the safest place', said Arthur, but when the air raid came the 1100 lb bomb which bounced into the shop exploded as it hit the locomotive, lifting it up into the air. As it crashed down into the pit Arthur Ward was struck by its buffer beam and now lay dying in his hiding place.

One engine being 'wheeled' at the time was high in the air, slung between two overhead cranes. There was no time for the crane drivers to either lower the loco or to take cover themselves, with the result that one was injured by the exploding bomb.

Thirteen engines were damaged and for three days nothing could move in or out of the Works. Erecting shop working was halted for some weeks and it was months before things returned to normal.

Vic Packman booked on at the running shed as usual at six o'clock that morning and attended to his regular duties. At ten o'clock he called to his friend, Jack Tabrett: 'Come and have a cup of tea. The stage can wait for five minutes.' As they sat down they heard the local air raid siren sounding the 'alert' which changed within seconds to the 'immediate danger' signal. Vic recalls the most terrifying moment of his life: 'We ran out and as we broke clear of the shed we could see them coming. Jack shouted; 'Quick! Under the coal stage!' I said; 'No, come back!' and dived under a Dean's goods engine. I saw six of them pass over the erecting shop, no more than a house high. The Bren-gunner on the running shop tower actually had to depress his gun downwards, they were so low. The next moment I seemed to be turning over backwards in a big cloud of boiling smoke and something passed over me. As the dust settled I could see that poor old Jack had been hit, so two of us went to his aid. I removed his clog, which was full of blood.'

'At that point an Army officer came up to me and asked: 'Where were you?' I said: 'Under the front of this engine'. He took my hand and said: 'Well it wasn't your turn this time.' What I had seen pass over my head turned out to be a bomb and its fin now lay inches from where I had crouched. It had hit the engine on its smoke box, tearing the Westernhouse pump off. It ricocheted onto the tank of an 'H' class loco, skipped over a coal stack and finally exploded in the long pit, killing Jack Brown. He was another victim of blast-damaged lungs and his body was found under the pit's ashes. A veteran of the First World War, Jack was the father of twelve children, the youngest only nine months old.'

Percy Russell was working just outside the boiler shop and saw a bomb leave one of the aircraft. He rushed into a nearby fire-box, which was serving as a shelter, and was looking through a slit in the box when a bomb bounced off the boiler shop roof and exploded about 100 feet away. His eyes were so affected by the blast and dust he thought he had been blinded. When he finally emerged he was confronted with a blazing gas main and on looking up saw the body of Seman Beale draped over a wrecked gantry crane.

Adjacent to the shop was a tall pile of steel plates. Clem Cork, a chargeman, decided to shelter inside the pile, but the effect of the bomb-blast was to cause the steel plates to close up and Clem was crushed to death. 'Tibby' Fox ran to shelter but was caught by blast as he reached its entrance, while a high explosive blast also blew away Bob Salmons. The drawing store in which all the Works blueprints were kept was wrecked by a bomb which exploded 50 feet away, destroying much of its contents. There was some consolation that, at the outbreak of war, all this information had been photographed and stored away from Ashford. Consolation, too, for storeman Henry Clover, who was away from the store at the time.

Not so fortunate were Harry Andrews in the boiler shop, Ernest Morris, an apprentice and two of the women war workers, Lydia Roberts and Eleanor Court, who all now lay dead.

In the town, for the first and only time during the war, the siren 'alert' changed to 'immediate danger' in mid-warning. A few seconds more and with the sirens still sounding their warning blasts, the planes roared in at roof height. Bombs were exploding as cannon shells and machine-gun bullets were ripping through the streets and into the buildings. There was no time to take shelter. Most of the population was caught in their homes, at their place of work or in the street. One moment all was peaceful, the next moment they were overwhelmed with danger.

The heavy ack-ack fire that had broken up the bombers' formation caused them to approach the town in three waves on different alignments. This undoubtedly saved the Railway Works from destruction but as a consequence the town suffered from the fury of the Focke-Wulfs as they dropped their bombs indiscriminately.

The crash and roar of exploding bombs was matched by the reverberating booms from Ashford's anti-aircraft batteries. The town was surrounded by a ring of Bofors guns to provide defence against enemy aircraft. An enormous explosion ripped through the sky over Godinton Road as the British gunners found their target and one of the bombers, with its bomb still on board, blew up. The result was to cause extensive damage to many buildings in the area, both from the result of blast and from pieces of the plane falling to earth.

The burning torso of the pilot, which proved to be that of Keller, leader of the squadron, was thrown from the plane and landed, with its decapitated head, in a playing field between Western Avenue and Norwood Gardens. Other parts of the body landed on a small-holding near Bailey's Crossing, owned by a George Janes, and were devoured by pigs that he was rearing. Another bomber fell victim to the defences when it was intercepted by an RAF Channel Squadron and was shot down on its way back to its base in France.

Robert Barham again takes up the story from the Railway Works: 'My attention was drawn towards the town. Near its centre a very large fire raged; even from a mile away great leaping flames could be seen through the heavy pall of dense black smoke. What had happened at home? Fortunately, the bus service, which started right outside the running shed, was still operating. On the journey it became obvious that damage was widespread. In the High Street a fire engine was pumping from a hydrant with twin hose lines snaking away up Castle Street. New Rents was blocked with rubble with a big gap where once stood shops. A police Special said: 'You can't go up there, sir, there's heavy damage and casualties.'

'Using an alternative route I found Milton road, thickly strewn with roof tiles, slates, brick rubble and shattered glass. I was shocked to see the roofless ruin that was our home. Roof timbers and rafters bare of slates, window glass blown in and the remains of the curtains hanging in shreds. Worse was to meet my eyes as I walked inside. Ceilings had collapsed and everything was covered with plaster and thick choking dust. The front door had been blasted off its hinges and lay halfway up the stairs. An inside wall was split open from top to bottom. My mother told me how she had just managed to fling herself into our Anderson shelter, which protected her from the blast and concussion from some of the closer explosions. When she emerged she thought the whole place was on fire – everything was red. But the red colour was pulverised brick dust from nearby houses, which had received a direct hit. Across the road a neighbour's son, Sonny Heath, sat on his front doorstep. A cannon shell had shattered his right arm and it was hanging by sinews and skin from his elbow. Whole families had been wiped out, one a few doors away from my grandparents' house.'

Robert Barham's experience was being repeated all over the town, with railwaymen returning to their homes to find them wrecked, or worse. Buildings in Dover Place were demolished, whilst in Star Road a bomb wrecked many houses. One resident had just entered her Anderson shelter when her house collapsed. Another said: 'It sounded as if we were being dive-bombed – the explosion from the bombs was terrible.' A direct hit demolished seven houses near the Alfred Joint Stocks burnt-out bakery in Hardinge Road and every house in the neighbourhood was damaged. Two little girls escaped from a wrecked building with their pet dog but a mother and child in another house were later found dead. Houses in Milton Road were hit, killing three people.

The worst damage was to be found in the New Street area. Three bombs exploded almost simultaneously, one destroying Heddles clothing store in New Rents whilst another hit Haywards' Garage in New Street. The garage and the cars stored there were wrecked and a huge fire started which raged all day. The blast from the bombs flattened many of the lath and plaster houses in New Street. The road was completely blocked and the area took on the appearance of a village street on a Flanders battlefield.

Some of the worst scenes were in evidence at the Stanhay Agricultural Works, which was located between Godinton Road and the railway. It was over this Works that the Focke-Wulf blew up. Whether the pilot was saving his missile for what he may have thought was a railway workshop will never be known, but he caused carnage, nevertheless. Michael Harris, son of railway worker Sydney Harris, had a harrowing experience: 'We were not allowed to take shelter until the 'immediate danger' siren sounded, but today there was no time to do so – I just threw myself on the floor. Cannon shells from enemy planes blew holes the size of footballs through the wall. One hit my mate in the chest as he was standing in the doorway, killing him instantly.'

'There was a tremendous explosion as the plane blew up and all the roof disappeared. I got up and went into the baler shop and found a woman lying there, spectacles still on her nose but very dead. In the yard another woman was in a terrible state and hysterical – she died later. A few feet away was another dead woman alongside Ginger Johnson, who had both legs blown off. He was fully conscious and as I knelt down he looked at me and said: 'Is it bad, John? I can't feel my legs.' What do you say to a work mate when both his legs are three feet away? I looked for another mate and eventually saw his two boots sticking out from under the baler. My search was over.

Trixie Godden, a 17 year old, never forgot the horror. 'There was pandemonium, with people killed and injured. I saw a girl running in front of me, and her head was blown off. A colleague had his jaw blown away – he would need grafting operations for years to come.' Worst of all for Trixie, she had arrived that morning hand-in-hand with her sweetheart, Sammy Milton, and now Sammy too was dead.

A sad postscript concerned the case of Ginger Johnson's son, Bramwell. Only 13 at the time, he never came to terms with his father's sudden and savage death. He went into shock and spent his life in mental hospitals.

The town quickly became aware of a 'miracle' that centred on the Beaver Road Junior School. Over 300 children between the ages of eight and eleven years were present, a large proportion from railway families. Alerted to the coming raid, the girls' classes immediately rose from their desks, and taking a book with them, went quietly but swiftly to their underground air raid shelters just across the road. They were followed by the boys, who filed into their blockhouse shelter in the playground. As the last child went to safety, the school received a direct hit from a bomb which had first bounced across the railway station yard and ricocheted through the Victoria public house.

A shaken teacher said: 'We were in the shelter, heard planes, and then heard the most frightful crash.' Young Bob Surtees described the noise of the bomber as 'like a train roaring through a tunnel'. He recalled that the school bell was blown up into the air and landed on their shelter with an almighty thump. When the children emerged, covered in dust, they were confronted with a scene of the utmost havoc – ruined buildings, debris, textbooks and school equipment all scattered about.

News of the school bombing soon reached the Railway Works, arousing dread and consternation amongst the children's fathers and relatives. Leaving their workshops a flood of men poured out of the Works and along the Newtown Road. Fresh in their minds was the massacre of 38 children in a south London school only two months before by the same squadron of bombers. As they ran, overcome with anguish and dreadful anxiety, tears poured down their work-begrimed faces. Arriving at the scene of devastation, they tore frantically at the wreckage in an effort to find anyone trapped in the debris. There was universal and overwhelming relief when it became clear that there had been no casualties.

Previous to the raid, some parents had objected to their children being continually taken to the shelters upon receiving a first alert, believing they were suffering a loss of education. Many had become rather blasé at the sound of the sirens, only reacting when the 'immediate danger' alert sounded. Now they were grateful for the insistence of the girls' school head, Miss Adams. Praise was lavished upon the Railway Works spotters, whose alertness had not only saved the lives of many railwaymen, but whose danger siren was said to have been heard by Mr. White, the boys' school head who quickly got his pupils to safety.

Seven fires were left burning in the town and 25 fire engines were ordered in from outside to reinforce the efforts of local rescue workers. Rescue work continued in the town for the rest of the day and then by floodlight. Buildings had been wrecked, hundreds of houses damaged, roofs stripped of slates, window panes shattered and walls cracked.

The valiant work of the Civil Defence was supported by Army units, the Home Guard and the police. The W.V.S. and the Salvation Army brought food and hot drinks. Black smoke, mainly from the inferno that was Hayward's Garage, covered the town and the air was full of dust. There was feverish activity during the next few days as squads of workmen strove to make premises safe and weatherproof. Windows were boarded up and large tarpaulins, to cover the gaping roofs, were in great demand. The devastation was all too apparent – piles of rubble lay where once there had been buildings.

The casualty list from the raid was dreadful: 50 killed, 77 seriously injured and 79 slightly injured. This was the highest death toll from a single air raid on any town in Kent throughout the entire war. Despite the death and destruction, people in the town and at the Railway Works turned up for work as usual.

On Monday afternoon, 29th March, there was a mass burial in Ashford's Bybrook Cemetery for most of the victims. Coffins covered by the Union Jack were borne to the Cemetery on open Army and Civil Defence trucks. A Guard of Honour was provided by the military and the Bishop of Dover attended with local clergy. A full military band was present and buglers from the Home Guard sounded Last Post and Reveille. The service came to an end. The war continued.

(See Appendix 1. Air attack on Ashford)

Last Shots

Perhaps the most astonishing feature of the war was the determination of the people to live as normal a life as possible, even though they were under threat of enemy action at all times. On Easter Monday, only five weeks after the devastating air attack, railwaymen staged a fete for their 'Front Line Kids' on New Town Green. The varied attractions included children's races and a football match between the Newtown Ramblers and an Army XI, which resulted in a win for the home side. Despite the difficulties of food rationing, a tea party was provided and a great day was brought to an end with community singing to the strains of an impromptu 'Alfredo Armsico's' band.

For some weeks during the winter of 1943/1944, the Luftwaffe had been planning a new night bombing offensive against Britain with London as a prime target. A force of over 300 bombers had been assembled in Northern France for an operation codenamed 'Steinbock', with the intention of exacting retribution on the British, whose airforce had been causing such devastation to German cities. The attack was launched on 21st January, the main body of aircraft crossing the coast between Folkestone and Hastings, setting air?raid sirens wailing in Ashford and anti-aircraft guns pounding. This night was to be the fore-runner of 31 more raids, seventeen of them against London. In the early attacks the raiders made their exit from the capital down the Thames estuary, but an alternative route brought them in over West Sussex at 13,000 feet, allowing them to make a high speed descending withdrawal from London, down the rail corridor across Kent in the direction of Dungeness.

Shortly after 10.30pm on the evening of 24th February, a drama was enacted holding watchers in the town and in the Works spellbound. Ashford's anti-aircraft defences opened up, the gunfire being described by witnesses as the fiercest of the war – ten times heavier than during the 1940 blitz. Clusters of rockets from a chandelier gun were fired and at one time the scene resembled a Brock's benefit night. Making 'strange noises' a Dornier 217 bomber flew across the town while the guns barked venomously and the sky blazed with searchlights.

On its flight across Kent, successive beams had formed a cone and the plane caught in the centre twisted and turned, trying every device to try and escape the fatal glare, but the searchlights held on relentlessly. Seemingly from nowhere, a Mosquito night fighter appeared, signalling by means of a little red light for the gunners to cease fire. Travelling at high speed with 'a vicious hum as of an angry bee' the Mosquito poured two bursts of cannon fire into the bomber.

Streaks of yellow and billows of smoke issued forth as the Dornier burst into flames. Watchers in the street cheered as it dived into the ground with the exultant gunners yelling 'Got him!' Three airmen successfully bailed out, but the fourth perished. Flung against the tailplane, his legs were severed and he bled to death on the way down. The plane crashed near the Railway Works sewerage farm, a short distance from the Kimberley Works, creating a brilliant white glow that lit up the area. Thomas Young, the sawmill foreman, was one of the first on the scene and, along with many other railwaymen, collected a memento from the wreckage.

After the war, the Luftwaffe pilot, Werner Spiering, told his story: 'My unit had to make a mission to London. It was a hard task because there were many night fighters and anti-aircraft guns. The route to London was without incident but on the way back my plane was caught by searchlights and it was impossible to get out of them. Then it didn't last long – my plane was hit by high explosives. The cabin was badly damaged and the foot steerage was broken. My navigator jumped out immediately, he was wounded. I tried to get the plane over the Channel but the right engine stopped over Ashford and then the plane went down topsy-turvy. My gunner and I had much luck getting out of the plane; we came free and the parachute brought us safely to earth. Not so lucky was our radio operator. The officer of the police station at Ashford told me the radio operator was badly wounded and lost so much blood that he died in the air coming down. I think he is buried in Ashford but I have no verification. His name was Matin Vogel.

'I came down near the house of Mr. Town. It was very dark and I couldn't see anything. Only the voice of Mr. Town I heard and he was very quickly at that spot where I dropped. He took me in his house and I must say that the treatment I got there was very good and correct. His wife bandaged round my hand because it was bleeding. Then he called the police station and I think it was Ashford where I stayed the first night of my imprisonment.'

The Germans suffered huge losses as a result of these raids, nicknamed the 'Baby Blitz', and they petered out during April and May after attacks on provincial targets. The failure of 'Steinbock' brought to a virtual end the manned-bomber attacks on Britain.

The Dornier was not the first nor would it be the last of the many German and Allied planes that crashed in the huge area of open countryside south of the railway works that stretched away towards the parishes of Kingsnorth and Mersham. Two Messerschmitt 109s and two Spitfires came to grief during the Battle of Britain. The first German fighter was forced to land near Finn Farm by a Hurricane of 46 Squadron late in the afternoon of

2nd September 1940, having suffered damage to its fuselage and petrol tank. A local farmer captured the pilot as he walked away. The two Spitfires crashed on the 4th and 6th of that month and were followed by the second Me 109 four weeks later on 5th October.

The railway children from South Willesborough were always keen to acquire pieces of perspex for modelling or bullets and cannon shells which were broken open for their gunpowder. Most boys had a 'museum' at home, conataining pieces of aircraft and shrapnel. Thus it was that when an Me 109 crashed near Andrews' Farm, young Bob Sayer and Bob Surtees were quickly on the spot and watched as the pilot clambered from his plane. Remembering that he had failed to turn off his electronically controlled guns, he returned to the cockpit while wagging a warning finger at the children, pointing to the firing button and saying 'Nein, nein.' Bob Sayer was then astonished when the pilot then gave him his Nazi embellished dagger as a memento.

Another Me109 crashed between the Folkestone railway line and Waterbrook Farm. Peter Foley, still a schoolboy, watched the scene from Crow Bridge. Six members of the local Home Guard advanced across the field with bayonets fixed to meet the German pilot who came towards them, hands held aloft, while a local farmhand walked behind him, prodding him liberally with a pitchfork.

Many of the girls were as adventurous as the boys. They also sought perspex, but for making rings rather than model planes. Pamela Barnes, now Mrs. Elston, ran out to a Messerschmitt 109 which she had seen crash near the Hastings branch line and was on the scene so quickly that she saw the pilot burning his papers.

A Spitfire that had been on a sortie over Northern France ran short of fuel, forcing the pilot to make a forced landing between Captain's Wood and Cheeseman's Green, joining another that had crashed a few days previously. The military soon appeared and the plane was heavily guarded against souvenir hunters. This Spitfire was destined to have an honourable future in the years ahead as part of the Battle of Britain Memorial Flight.

After the Americans entered the war, their planes were often seen flying on bombing missions into France and Germany. On one occasion during the summer of 1944, a stricken Flying Fortress passed over as the crew was forced to bale out. They landed south of the Works, and although some were wounded, they successfully made the drop. One was so badly hurt he was helped by another crew member. Clinging to each other and using the same parachute, they came down fast and unfortunately landed on the roof of one of the Kimberley sheds.

There was alarm on the morning of 20th June, when a Liberator heavy bomber returning from a mission came in low from the east, trailing smoke. Clipping an electric pylon near Roberts' Farm, it belly-flopped close by

Royds Road at South Willesborough. The crew spilled out as the plane broke up into sections. A garbled message to the Civil Defence services caused fears of heavy civilian casualties and one rescue vehicle crashed into the parapet of the Albion Bridge as its crew rushed to the spot. Happily all was well, with the airmen being taken into the homes of local residents and given cups of tea. Members of the U.S. Air Force were soon at the scene but not before the local children had a field day collecting ammunition, which was scattered everywhere. Peter Foley recalls the highly respected local policeman, Constable Campion, calling at the children's homes saying: 'We know you've got bullets and shells. Hand them over and we'll say no more about it.' The ammunition was duly handed over, although one suspects some were thinking: 'We know where we can get some more.' An area of fascination was the advanced landing ground set up across the fields at Kingsnorth, as part of the preparation for the invasion of Europe. This was one of a group of five such landing grounds in the surrounding district. Three squadrons of Spitfires arrived on 1st July 1943, followed by other Spitfires and Hurricanes which used the ground until the following October. Preparations were made during the subsequent winter months for three squadrons of Thunderbolts of the United States Tactical Airforce who arrived on 4th April, remaining until 17th July. A side effect was that the American airmen became a regular source of cigarettes and chewing gum.

There were two more incidents during the summer of 1944 before the curtain fell on this war-scarred area. A Spitfire, having been repaired at the landing ground, took off for a test flight and promptly nose-dived into the ground at Bilham Farm, with tragic results for the pilot. Finally, a Mustang fighter of the Royal Canadian Air Force, whilst on patrol, shot through the cloud for reasons unknown and plunged into the ground near the Hastings branch line with the unfortunate pilot still aboard.

Back in the Works, March 1944 saw the last of the L.M.S. '8F' 2-8-0 locomotives completed, bringing to an end new steam locomotive construction at Ashford. Few realised that No.8674 would be the last steam engine to be built in the Works, however this was not the last that Ashford would see of this class of locomotive. 50 such locomotives had been loaned by the War Department to help the Southern during the busy build-up period leading to the Allied invasion of Europe. Their having rendered valiant service, the Works now had to carry out hasty inspections and repairs to prepare them for military service on the Continent. Following the clearance of enemy forces from France and Belgium, they could be towed to Dover for shipment across the Channel.

Despite the pressures of war, the Southern Railway continued to find time to recognise the efforts of long-serving railwaymen. Bulleid came to the Works to present diplomas for 50 years service to a number of Ashfordians, with the promise that after the war they would also receive their gold medals. Those honoured were William Barnes, 67, tuber; Alfred Goldsmith, 65, chargeman erector; Wilfred Mortley, 64, chargeman wagon-maker; Ernest Stickells, 72, labourer and Frederick Ward, 712, carpenter.

D-Day dawned on 6th June and with it thoughts that, with the Luftwaffe engaged on the Russian front, in Italy and now in France, the risk of bombardment from the air would now diminish. It was not to be. A new danger now materialised in the skies above Ashford and the Works. Hitler's secret weapon, the V1 (quickly dubbed 'Doodle Bug' by the British) appeared to a crescendo of noise from all the guns in the district.

Robert Barham, who had remained in the Works throughout the war, was now a sergeant in the anti-aircraft unit of the Works Home Guard. Formed the previous July, this was one of the first such units in the country, and destined to become known as 'the Doodle Bug Boys'. They had received advance warning of the coming attack: 'Three days before the first sighting we were briefed under the greatest secrecy that in a few days an attack against this country would commence by "pilotless aircraft". They would, we were told, fly straight and level at 1000 to 3000 feet, and at a high speed, possibly up to 400 miles per hour, which turned out to be a remarkably accurate assessment.'

The first flying bomb crossed the Kentish coast at Dymchurch at seven minutes past 4 o'clock on the morning of 13th June, its speed, staccato barking noise and bright flaming tail, puzzling many. It was fortunate that RAF pilots at nearby Newchurch airfield had just received Britain's new superfighter, the Hawker Tempest V. Their high speed, combat manoeuvrability and accurate firepower gave them a superiority over all other piston engined aircraft at low altitude. The squadron's first success came quickly after a short but precise radar intercept, and the first V1 to be destroyed in daylight went down and exploded near Ashford. This was the first of 638 kills recorded by the squadron during the first 80 days of attacks which posed danger to all who lived or worked in the path of the missiles.

The new aerial offensive lasted until the end of August by which time British and Canadian troops had overrun the launching sites in the Pas de Calais. Throughout the period, the sheer weight of the attack made the normal use of the air raid alert signal difficult. Although the Works benefited from its 'spotters' warning system, work in the town and countryside often went on as usual. Whenever a V1 was heard approaching, people paused in case they should hear the engine cut out, whereupon during what seemed a particularly deep silence, they dived for cover to protect themselves from the coming explosion.

The flight paths of the flying bombs included routes directly over the Works and as each one flew over, the buildings shook with the vibration caused by their noisy jet engines, a nerve wracking situation for those below. The Works narrowly escaped damage at seven o'clock in the evening of 4th August. A flying bomb was being pursued by two Spitfires: it was on fire, its engine was labouring and it was clearly in trouble. A group of youths, members of the local Air Training Corps, were in Newtown Road, heading for Newtown School, where they held parades and received instruction. Watching this dangerous situation unfold, they realised they had to make up their minds where to take shelter – the pedestrian arch under the railway line or the bombed out ruins of the Beaver Road school. They chose the former, and had no sooner reached it than the V1 landed and exploded with an almighty bang near the school. Had they run that way, they would have added their number to the 24 injured – or worse.

Robert May, an apprentice at the Works tells how they were told to go to the shelters when the spotters' warning was given, but the lads wanted to see all the action that was going on outside. 'We went to the Bofers gun that was operated by the Works Home Guard and saw it firing at a flying bomb. It was going low over the Christchurch area and the sky around it was peppered with black dots of exploding ack-ack shells.'

'My next encounter was on 16th August. A lot of men at the Works came from Folkestone, Dover, Deal and Canterbury, so the evening trains were always full. On that evening I was standing in the carriage corridor on the side facing the Works when we saw a V1 coming in quite low above the main railway line. When it reached Willesborough we all thought it was going to pass over but as it got closer an RAF Meteor fighter suddenly appeared, slowed alongside the flying bomb and nudged its wing tip, causing it to go haywire. It coughed, spluttered and then there was silence as it dropped like a stone. A loud explosion followed as it hit a goods storage area near the station, and wrecked the 'E' Signal Box. There was heavy derailment in the sidings with many steam engines damaged. The man in the signal box had a lucky escape but nine other railwaymen were injured. Our train left for home – a little late.'

Fred Imm had returned to his parents' home at Newtown to see his father who lay critically ill, and recalled: 'Over Ashford and the surrounding countryside, fighter planes provided the defence against the V1. One day while I was watching a stream of bombs flying over, a twin-engined fighter appeared from above the Kimberley wagon shops. It fired its cannon and secured a direct hit on one of the invaders, which was coming straight towards me. There was a thunderous explosion as the V1 shattered into a mass of bits and pieces. The fighter banked and flew off with smoke pouring from its engines. I thought: 'The bloody thing has hit our fighter! But the plane accelerated and continued on its way. I then realised it was one of the new Gloster Meteor jets, an aircraft I had not previously seen.'

'Particularly spectacular was the sight of flying bombs passing over after dark. On what would otherwise have been a still moonlit night the flashing of their engines could be seen as soon as they flew in from the coast. Anti-aircraft shells bursting all around them lit up the night sky. Blast from some of the shell bursts blew more than the odd one or two off course and some were turned round and flew back across the Channel. When the gunners made a hit there was a huge flash of light as the V1 exploded.'

There were many acts of heroism on the part of the fighter pilots and on two occasions, Ashford would have suffered heavily but for their bravery. In each instance, a flying bomb was on fire and dropping towards the town when a fighter pilot, with complete disregard for his own safety, charged in practically head-on and blew it to pieces.

By the time the offensive had ended over 9,000 missiles had been launched with 2,444 brought down in the coastal and land area bounded by Ashford, Folkestone, Romney Marsh and the Weald. The president of the South Willesborough Women's Adult School, which was located only a little way from the Works wrote to the local newspaper; 'For the present relief from the assault of flying bombs, of which it has been stated that by far the greater number was shot down over the Ashford area, we should like to voice our gratitude to those who, under God, have saved us from so much. To the RAF, the AA gunners, the searchlight crews… we would be glad to tender our undying gratitude. May God bless and keep them all.'

Wartime conditions are notorious for being responsible for relaxed moral conduct. With large numbers of soldiers and airmen stationed in the district, Ashford was no exception. Long lines of carriages were regularly parked overnight on the embankment sidings above Newtown Road. With their unlocked doors and separate compartments they provided an ideal place for servicemen and girls to indulge their love-making. A Kentish Express midweekly edition appeared to display a mischievous streak when it took advantage of a court case to give front page billing to a misdemeanour in one of the carriages.

The carriages were cleaned every morning and no doubt there was often evidence of unauthorised nocturnal intruders. On this occasion, unfortunately for the culprit, an identity card had been left behind. Hauled before the local magistrate, the no doubt embarrassed girl was fined five shillings for illegal entry into Railway Company property.

More serious was a tragic case, which shocked the town in August 1944. Just after 7am. on the morning of the 23rd, George Marsh of Sydney Street was working a shunting engine over the Hastings Bridge when he saw something that looked to him like a body. Entering the field by the Black Path with his fireman, Arthur Tourney, they found the inert body of a young girl with her clothes bloodstained and disarranged. The police were immediately called and the corpse was removed to the Ashford Hospital mortuary.

The victim was Betty Green, the 15 year old daughter of a Newtown railwayman, who had clearly been raped and murdered. Evidence was given to the police that the girl had acquired a reputation and the previous evening had been seen in the company of two American servicemen. Police enquiries were concentrated on an American airbase a few miles from Ashford.

By an extraordinary quirk of fate, Betty's father, William Green, was in the nearby Smith's Arms that evening and saw two Americans getting rather drunk on strong bitter ale. He little realised, as he sauntered home along the Newtown Road just after 10.30pm, that his daughter lay dead on the other side of the fence. At an identity parade, William Green picked out a Corporal Clark and a Private Guerra as the men he had seen in the pub. A post-mortem examination provided evidence of an attack of unusual ferocity, with the victim having been manually strangled and with injuries to her body.

The two servicemen were placed under arrest and subsequently appeared before an American Court Martial, which was held in the Ashford Council Chamber in the High Street. They were charged with '....choking and strangling a female child under the age of 16, both aiding and abetting each other by holding and subduing the girl.' Evidence was given that they had left the Smith's Arms in Torrington Road shortly after 10 o'clock in a drunken state. Upon meeting the girl, they had overpowered her and taken her to a field known as the Old Cricket Ground, raped her and left her lying on the ground. Guerra described how they both went from one public house to another, drinking beer, gin and whisky. He said: 'The only thing I can say is I was drunk and did not know what I was doing. When I get drunk I lose my mind or something. I will not believe the girl is dead. If I knew I had killed the girl, I would have it on my nerves, but I haven't.'

Clark had elected to have a separate trial, which took place two weeks later. He admitted rape but denied murder. However, the evidence was against them. As a result of the struggle that Betty Green had put up, Guerra's scalp bore scratches and a clump of Clark's hair was found under the victim's fingernails.

Guerra's trial lasted for eight hours, the trial judges returning a verdict within 15 minutes. He was found guilty. Clark was similarly condemned at his trial, the President of the Court announcing that they were 'To be hanged by the neck until you are dead.'

The two men later received the services of Albert Pierrepoint , Britain's legendary public hangman, when he executed them at Shepton Mallet Prison.

In times of trouble there is usually a lighter side and old habits die hard, even in wartime. When the erecting shop roof was being repaired, large quantities of felting were being salvaged. Upon enquiry a railwayman was told that it was required 'for the war effort'. However, 'in accordance with tradition', some of the felting found its way to the top of an engine tender and was later dropped off along the line, adjacent to the railwayman's house.

The tale is also told of a workman who had been directed by the Ministry of Labour, using its powers of wartime regulations, to take up railway work. Deciding that the work was not to his liking, he went to the office of Jack Finch, the assistant works manager, demanding his release. Upon being told the office had not that authority, the workman replied that he could get his release if he 'sloshed' him and with the words 'take this then' struck the manager on the jaw. He certainly obtained his release, but only after the local court had sentenced him to one month's hard labour.

With Allied forces now sweeping across France and Belgium, Ashford and the Works at last gained a respite from enemy attacks. In September, the rigorous 'black-out' restrictions were eased and replaced with what came to be called a 'Dim-out'. Throughout the autumn and winter, everyone looked forward with anticipation to an Allied victory.

Towards the end of October, the Works Home Guard held their final parade. A stand-down concert was held for the men, their families and friends, with entertainment being provided by local performers and the Works Band. Major Bob Bolton, who had commanded throughout the emergency, thanked his company for their devotion to duty. Together with other Kent Home Guard units, the railwaymen attended a service in Canterbury Cathedral and were addressed by Lord Cornwallis. He recalled the never-ceasing watch of the Royal Navy, the courageous 'Few' of the Royal Air Force, the endless train-loads of troops taking the hard-pressed Army retreating from Dunkirk, and called upon everyone to remember the citizen army that arose in the South-east and was ready to fight on the beaches, in the fields and in the streets. His final salute to the Home Guard was:

> 'And had the Huns befouled our land,
> The story we should tell
> Was that 60,000 sons of Kent
> Had sent them back to hell.'

And so, after nearly six years, the war in Europe drew to a close. The last air raid alert sounded in Ashford on 25th March, 1945. On 8th May, Winston Churchill addressed the nation in his usual bulldog style and concluded: 'The German war is at an end. Advance Britannia. Long live the cause of freedom. God save the King.'

A two-day public holiday was declared and Ashford went en-fête. Bunting and flags quickly appeared on shops and houses throughout the town and in the evening there was dancing in the High Street, music being provided by the Southern Railway Works Band. After being hung from a gibbet outside the Corn Exchange, an effigy of Hitler was dragged through the streets and later burned, while the jubilant crowd sang 'Land of Hope and Glory'. The Parish Church, Council Chamber and windmill were floodlit and all public houses were given an extension to their opening hours until midnight.

Street parties were held in various parts of the town, with railway families joining in. A children's party was arranged on the Green at New Town and a victory party quickly organised at South Willesborough provided entertainment for 230 children. Celebrations in Upper Denmark Road attracted some 300 people who sang and danced in the street. One householder had a piano accompanied by drums out in his front garden and the festivities remained lively until one o'clock in the morning. On the following Sunday, after a thanksgiving service in a packed Parish Church, nearly 1,000 troops joined with Civil Defence units in a Victory Parade through the town.

Amidst the celebration, many who had suffered or lost loved ones must have had sober thoughts. In the air raids on Ashford and its rural district, 974 high explosive and 12,645 incendiary bombs had been dropped, killing 103 and injuring 407. 184 properties had been entirely destroyed and a further 11,750 were damaged. Given Ashford's position as a front-line town, the suffering and losses could have been far worse.

Peace finally arrived in Ashford with victory over Japan in August. Again the town was decorated, although the celebrations seemed rather more muted. A huge Fête was held in Victoria Park, but in the residential areas, railway families were very much to the fore. 200 children from the roads adjacent to Denmark Road were given a tea-party, and at a party held at the South Eastern Tavern in Torrington Road children were given beakers with their names and the flags of the Allied nations hand painted on them. Children were entertained in north Willesborough, but the star performance was put on by the South Willesborough community, in Mr. Glass's meadow, where 500 children were entertained with sports and tea, followed by an evening fireworks display.

For railwaymen looking back over the war years, the resilience of the steam locomotive was clearly shown. Of 190 Southern Railway engines damaged by attacks ranging from a direct hit to falling into a bomb crater or being shot up, only one was scrapped. The most severe damage was to the Wainwright 'E' class No.1515 in the 1943 raid on Ashford, the locomotive taking eight months to repair. 1,000 Southern wagons were destroyed but these were more than compensated for by the 13,900 wagons built in the Ashford Works during the war period.

Two months later, the town's victory celebrations concluded with a Thanksgiving Week. On show in various parts of the town were a number of armoured vehicles, including a Daimler armoured car in which rides were offered to the public. Mobile searchlight units gave a display from the

High Street, others illuminated the church and the windmill. Not unnaturally the railway had a prominent role in the week's proceedings with a band concert every day in the canteen and ENSA artistes providing entertainment on one occasion. On the final day, Miss Jean Batten, the famous airwoman, toured the workshops and later gave a rousing speech in the canteen, which was packed to capacity for a performance by the band of RAF Fighter Command.

O.V.S.Bulleid came down for a special visit to an exhibition of working model locomotives, mostly made by Works employees. An exhibit which demonstrated welding prompted him to say he was sure that nowhere else in the world were locomotive parts being welded as they were in Ashford and if everybody in Ashford knew of that skill , they would be extremely proud of the Works.

The week also saw a steady stream of railwaymen and townspeople heading for a floodlit display in the station yard. On display was one of Bulleid's West Country locomotives and his exciting new carriage, which the Southern was keen to introduce. Arriving from exhibitions at Waterloo and Victoria, the Company canvassed the opinions of visitors. Unsurprisingly, with such a beautiful product, the public reaction was overwhelmingly favourable. Such a carriage for normal public services had not been seen before on Southern rails, nor was it equalled during the following 50 years. This prototype corridor composite had compartments with hammock-sprung seating of deep green or red-brown moquette with space under for luggage and electrically heated foot-warming under-floor panels in addition to steam heating.

Each compartment was superbly fitted out, with polished wood veneers of medium walnut for first class and light mahogany in the 'Thirds'.. There were mirror-finished stainless steel corridor hand-rails, luggage rack brackets, ash-trays and door latches, and diffused overhead lighting, together with individual reading lights. In the corridor, illuminated signs guided passengers to either 'Firsts', 'Thirds' or toilets. Each of the First Class compartments seated six, and the Third Class eight. Sadly, these truly loved carriages were destined for a very short life and by 1966 most had followed the steam locomotives into redundancy. It was said that Bulleid's coaches were an expression of the Southern Railway's desire to give its customers as much comfort and spaciousness as it could afford and in this the Company was successful and deservedly popular.

The homes of Ashford railway families could be heard ringing with the shouts and laughter of Dutch children during the early weeks of 1946. With the war over, the local branch of the NUR felt there should be recognition of Dutch railwaymen who had responded to calls to help the Allies by 'going underground' and paralysing the railways when the Germans advanced on Antwerp. They were also very conscious of the appalling deprivation of the Dutch people prior to their liberation. So was born the idea of hosting 300 children of the Netherlands Railway employees in homes of British railwaymen across the South, 100 of whom were to come to Ashford.

Townsfolk poured out their hearts throughout the children's nine-week stay; local schools, churches and even neighbouring towns joining in. Local organisations provided entertainment, a highlight being a huge party, which was held in the Works canteen, with the inevitable presence of the Works Band. At the end of the visit there were many emotional scenes as the hosts bid farewell at the railway station, it being remarked on how much the children's health and strength had benefited during their time here, having endured so much suffering during the German occupation of their country.

With former railwaymen returning from the armed forces, the Works began to settle down to peacetime conditions although this was far from easy, with a frustraing shortage of raw materials. Nor was the men's home life as easy as they had hoped,with food, clothing, coal and petrol rationing continuing – even bread was rationed for the first time. Echoing the end of the previous war, returning servicemen were promised 'a brave new world' with better housing, a universal health service and a national insurance scheme giving protection 'From the Cradle to the Grave' without the need for means testing. No-one was prepared for the grim reality of the country's economic position.

In the first full year of peace, the Works order book included an urgent request from the London and North Eastern Railway for 1,500 sixteen-ton all-steel wagons. Ashford was also entrusted with the production of monster 40-ton wagons, which were to be used for re-balancing track. These had previously been obtained from specialist contractors. In addition, open goods wagons were coming off the production line at the rate of one every working hour.

The locomotive shops were heavily engaged during this difficult postwar period, coping with scores of engines which were in urgent need of major repairs, after their wartime battering. Other work included the manufacture of 60 complete tenders, together with main frames and other components for Bulleid's Pacifics, the production of coaching stock components and the overhaul of motor bogies for the Southern Electrics. There was plenty to do for a workforce which now numbered 2,400.

The difficulties of the times were emphasised by the Minister of Transport, George Barnes, when he visited in January 1947. His words recalled those used after the First World War: 'During the war a terrific load was thrown onto the railways – far heavier than they were designed for. The railways were very much like the infantry – when a rough job came along, they had to do it. Unlike some factories, which had a breathing space when the war ended, while they re-tooled for civilian production, the railway repair shops had no let-up. They had to get on with the job.'

The Minister's visit had followed his call to railway workshops, asking individuals to roll up their sleeves and make an extra effort – if necessary by working extra hours. He acknowledged that in view of the hours worked and the output achieved at Ashford, his appeal was not needed here.

By the year's end, the railway conditions were still far from normal. Official figures revealed a deficiency of 100,000 wagons to deal with coal, iron, steel and general merchandise. Everyone concerned was asked to clear wagons on the day they arrived. Men were asked to work at weekends and that situation was expected to last for some time. Ashford's men set the pace with the daily turn-round of wagons.

Townsfolk were soon made aware of one change in their lives. Before the war, at the end of morning and afternoon shifts, hundreds of men poured out of the Works on foot. Now hundreds streamed out on bicycles. A 'black river' of riders swept out from both the main and Willesborough gates, occupying the entire width of the road and travelling at a pace. Woe betide any foolhardy optimist who decided to attempt to travel against the 'tide'.

Wartime experiences were recalled with the awarding of honours to a number of railwaymen who received the British Empire Medal. Ralph Neat, Motive Power Superintendent, was in charge of all the locomotive power which had been concentrated at Ashford. Of his experiences he said: 'Few who travelled in the district at this period realised the almost insurmountable difficulties that daily confronted the staff when bombs destroyed locomotives and rolling stock and caused serious track derailments. We never had to cancel a single train – somehow we got through every time.'

William Goldup, District Inspector of the Permanent Way Department said he accepted the honour on behalf of other members of staff who rallied round during the war and by their loyal support and devotion to duty had succeeded in keeping the lines open. Often gangs had to work nearly 24 hours at a stretch to clear lines damaged by enemy action. During the Battle of Britain he was constantly called out to advise on the repair of a line resulting in no part of it being obstructed for more than two hours. His responsibilities included the gas decontamination train and the emergency train, which was always standing ready loaded with material for repairing bomb damage to any part of the railway.

William Goldup's remarkable railway service began when he joined the South Eastern & Chatham Company in 1906. During the First World War he had served with the R.N. Division, but was discharged with serious chest wounds in the 1918 retreat in France.

An award to Arthur Bushell gave much satisfaction to those who had worked with him during his 45 years of railway service. It recognised his war service as stationmaster at Ashford's important railway junction and in particular his work during the Dunkirk evacuation. Like many other senior men he had seen service in France during the First World War and he had received the Military Cross for bravery while serving with the Railway Operating Corps.

An honour which, in effect, recognised those who had laboured in the Works throughout the war, was that given to the highly respected Basil Noble, when he too received the British Empire Medal. His trade was that of coachbuilder and he had already received the Company's gold medal for his fifty years of service from 1889 to 1939. Despite his age he had continued to work throughout the war. A man with a deep social conscience, he had devoted himself to public affairs serving on the Kent County Council from 1919 - 31 and again in 1934 – 49. He was the Labour Party parliamentary candidate for the Ashford Division in three successive general elections from 1922 – 23 – 24 and for the Hastings seat in 1929. Active in educational affairs, a local magistrate and long serving chairman of the Railway Works Trade Union committee, he was described by the Kentish Express as; 'A courageous personality in Ashford's political and social life.'

Bygone ages seemed to produce 'characters' and the Works was no exception, indeed, old timers expressed the opinion that the place seemed to be a regular breeding ground for them. One character was very well known at the time. With a buttonless black jacket, tied in the middle with a piece of string, pin-striped trousers at 'half-mast' and a bowler hat of some vintage, he presented an unforgettable image. Curiously this extraordinary exterior concealed a brain of considerable ability and he had the reputation of being able to calculate complicated piece-work rates in his head faster than anyone else could with pen and paper. It was unfortunate that he always insisted on expressing his answers in the form of Roman numerals, which nobody else could understand. He possessed a cultured voice, which gave rise to rumours of an aristocratic background.

A true eccentric was the workman who, every lunch hour, would clamber on to any convenient wagon near the clocktower and proceed to deliver a sermon. His choice of words was anything but ecclesiastical and their ripeness left even hardened shopworkers stunned.

Chapter Eight

A FORLORN HOPE

*My engine now is cold and still,
No water does my boiler fill,
My coal affords its flame no more;
My days of usefulness are o'er.*

                                  Engine Driver's Epitaph

A milestone in the history of Ashford Works was reached on 6th October 1947, when its centenary was celebrated. To commemorate the occasion an exhibition was staged in the old Royal Train shed comprising relics of earlier years, including old prints, paintings, historic photographs and working models of locomotives which had been made by employees in their leisure hours. Crowds estimated at 8,000 took advantage of the occasion and poured into the Works during a week of celebrations. All the various departments were open to the visitors but it was the erecting shop, where all types of engines were undergoing repair, that excited most interest.

In the paint shop (cleared especially for the occasion) visitors were able to climb into the cab of the new Bulleid Pacific locomotive 21C155 Battle of Britain class 'Fighter Pilot'. Behind it a brand new Bulleid coach was on show. Both, of course, were resplendent in their Southern Railway livery.

Welcomed at the exhibition opening was Grenadier Guards war hero, Lord de L'Isle and Dudley, holder of the Victoria Cross, Henry Brooke, Deputy Chairman, Southern Railway and Lieutenant Colonel John Bell, Ashford Works manager together with directors and officials of the Company.

Lord de L'Isle said: 'Ashford Works is a very good example of the foresight and energy of the railway directors of 100 years ago. The railway system of Great Britain is a national institution and I am still young enough to be thrilled by the sight of Southern Railway expresses roaring through the countryside. The century upon which we are looking back today is probably the most important hundred years in British industrial history.

No-one can deny that the development of railways is important to our economic life, as it was not until the railway age that this nation made those great advances which have placed Britain in the lead of world affairs.'

'There is no railway system, and above all no railway management or railway staff, that can hold a candle to ours. Of all the people engaged in industry from top to bottom, none has a better record than the railways and no railway has a finer record than the Southern.' As regards the Southern's war record, Lord de L'Isle said: 'The great invasion of the coast of France would not have been possible without the Southern Railway.'

Henry Brooke commented upon coming changes: 'At the end of this year, the Southern Railway will pass under the control of the new Transport Commission and this may be the last appearance of the directors at Ashford Works. I want to thank all those who have worked here. We are truly grateful to you and feel certain that you will carry on into the future the traditions of the past.' The formalities concluded with O.V.S.Bulleid observing: 'I have no doubt that Ashford Works will still be here in 100 years' time.'

As part of the centenary celebrations the Works' sixth 'Workers' Playtime' programme was broadcast from the canteen on 16th October by the BBC Home Service. A large and appreciative audience was entertained by the nationally well-known stars, Jeanne de Casalis, Radcliffe and Ray, and Norman Evans.

Another piece of entertainment for Ashford was a visit from the 'Musical Railwayman'. Thirty-five years a signalman at Southborough, this great-grandfather became a professional entertainer when he retired, and was now booked for engagements nearly every night of the year. During the war he had given over 800 shows and broadcast three times, entertaining with the aid of a bicycle pump and a saw. Having first learned to play when serving with the Royal Engineers in France during the 1914-18 war, he still used the same pump, playing it by blowing through the valve and moving the plunger up and down.

Other talent was also on display. South Willesborough was notable for its Frogs Island Concert Party. It was formed during the time of the Battle of Britain by two wagon builders, Charlie Keyte Snr. and Harry Coxwell, supported by their wives. Stage entertainment was provided both locally and in the villages around and pantomimes such as Cinderella and Mother Goose were enacted, together with musical revues. The Concert Party had a huge following in this railway community and the devotion of its supporters created for it a reputation unequalled throughout the entire district. It eventually boasted its own band, which included Charlie Keyte, who had been in the Works Band during their winning performance at the Crystal Palace in 1908.

A remarkable worker at this time, known and highly regarded by the entire workforce, was Sid Doy. Sid was with the Grenadier Guards at the time of Dunkirk. During the vicious fighting he was blinded by an explosion and subsequently captured, spending the war in a German prisoner-of-war camp. Freed at the end of the war, Sid was taken into care by St. Dunstan's and trained to work a capstan lathe. The machine was pre-set and always carried a notice to the effect that under no circumstances should the machine's settings be interfered with. Sid had a reputation for his high production rate for boiler stays. Every day he caught a bus into the High Street from his home and arrangements were made to escort him to the Works every morning and back again at the end of his daily stint.

Evidence that changing times had not eliminated all the old quaint customs was shown by the experience of young Bernard Epps, who came into the Works just after the war. As a junior clerk in the accounts department, he always looked forward to collecting the gas money from Newtown tenants as an opportunity to be away from the office. Their gas was paid for by the insertion of a penny piece into a slot meter, which was always located in the coal lodge, making the task rather a dirty one. Bernard was accompanied by a senior clerk, together with a labourer, whose job it was to push a wheelbarrow holding the heavy coins. While the two clerks were offered, and often accepted, cups of tea on their round, the labourer was required to remain at the garden gate and stand guard over the leather holdall in the wheelbarrow with the collected coins.

During 1947 a national committee investigating the construction of locomotive sheds visited Ashford and produced an alarming report concerning the running shed. Ashford had been at the forefront of concrete construction when the shed was built in 1931. Unfortunately there was insufficient appreciation that maintenance was something that could not be neglected, as was often the case with traditional buildings. Bonding mastic had dried out, crumpled and had not been replaced. Moisture had penetrated and the concrete had become damaged, particularly as a result of frost during the winter months. Its condition worsened in the long and bleak winter of 1946/47, when Britain experienced an unparalleled freeze-up, with heavy snow and sub-zero temperatures, providing the coldest weather in recorded history.

So concerned were the officials at the decay and corrosion, their report ended up marked 'confidential'. Rejuvenation measures were undertaken but 'the writing was on the wall' as regards the shed's long term future. That the measures taken were insufficient was demonstrated during the severe gale of 1953 which caused severe damage to the shed, resulting in pieces of cement falling from the roof onto the locomotives below. The situation caused such a danger to the workforce that the foreman ordered them to abandon their work for the night. Problems were not only caused by weather conditions. If a King Arthur or a Schools class locomotive developed excessive steam pressure, its Rospop valves 'blew' resulting in a vertical burst of steam, which was always guaranteed to bring down a few cement slates.

Nationalisation of the country's railway system had been signalled since the election of a Labour government in 1945. All the Companies were unanimous in their hostility, but to no avail. The Transport Bill was passed by Parliament and the vesting date was set for January 1st, 1948. At midnight on New Year's Eve the Southern Railway became part of British Railways. It was perhaps a tribute to the quality of the Southern's management that their General Manager, Sir Eustace Missenden, was appointed chairman of the new National Railway Executive.

In a message to all staff of what was now Southern Region, British Railways, John Elliot as Chief Regional Officer wrote: 'I know that every one of us who was yesterday a member of Southern Railway staff, will carry into the future the long and honourable traditions of public service which our old company built up, and as a member of our new Southern Region, will strive with might and main to serve the public – not only as well as in the past, but even better.'

'We have been a happy family of railway folk and 'S.R.' has meant a lot to us, so let us keep our team spirit, working loyally together with pride in our service and for the public good.'

On 30th September, 1949, O.V.S.Bulleid retired. In a parting shot he declared: 'If new designs be developed in the light of our present greater knowledge and the servicing of the locomotive be brought up to date – in short if only we can demolish the conservatism which is destroying the steam locomotive, rather than give up any of its customary ways – then we can look forward to the revival of steam traction.' Alas, it was not to be. The future was set to be electric.

The last locomotives to be built at Ashford were all designed by the Ashford Drawing Office, in the Bulleid era, although none appeared until the new decade. The first, a 500 hp Paxman-engined 0-6-0 diesel-mechanical shunter emerged in 1950. Not until the next year did the first of three experimental diesel-electric express passenger locomotives appear, the first two from the Ashford shops, the third from Brighton. Powered by 1750 hp English Electric engines with a typically Bulleid-shaped exterior, they set the pace for future British designs. A driving compartment was provided at each end with seats for two enginemen, together with the facilities of an electric cooker, handwash basin and lavatory.

The first of the class, No.10201 was exhibited at the 1951 Festival of Britain exhibition having received special attention, giving it a 'Wembley Exhibition finish', to quote the favoured expression of the foremen. For a short period, No.10202 had the honour of hauling both the Golden Arrow and the Night Ferry.

Finally, between 1949 and 1952, Ashford constructed a class of 26 diesel-electric shunters, similar in appearance to Maunsell's 0-6-0s, again with a 350 hp English Electric power unit, but with Bulleid-Firth-Brown (Boxpok American style) driving wheels. The period also saw the emergence of carriages in their new British Railway livery of crimson lake and cream.

The Works had an interesting experience in 1951. Word was received that the Britannia class express locomotive 'William Shakespeare' had broken down at Paddock Wood, ahead of the Golden Arrow. Unbelievably, five of the six driving wheels had shifted on their axles and the coupling rods had become mangled. Fresh from its appearance at the Festival of Britain exhibition in London, it was a sorry 70004 that was towed into Ashford. An intrigued workforce claimed that it was the largest locomotive ever to be lifted in the erecting shop.

It was 1953 before Ashford finally caught up with modern practice in its locomotive shops. Instead of the old-fashioned 'gang' system, where the men completed all repairs, a production line technique known as the 'belt system' was introduced. Men specialised in their particular job and the locomotive was passed down the line to receive their individual attention.

The year also saw the first of many reorganisations when British Railways was divided up into regions, Ashford naturally becoming part of Southern Region with a welcome return to green liveried carriages.

Plenty of work was still on offer. The locomotive works was busy with the repair of engines and mobile cranes and the rebuilding of 29 'N' class and 'U' class 2-6-0s. The repair or replacement of their main frames included new front ends and cylinders. Added to this, the cherished 'Schools' class now entered the local scene. Towards the end of the war the Works had been entrusted with the general overhaul of 15 of the class. Now Ashford was to be responsible for all heavy repairs to the most illustrious of Maunsell's locomotives.

In the carriage and wagon works men were hard at work constructing standard underframes for British Rail Mark 1 carriages and bogies for both steam and electric stock at the rate of eight per week. In addition they were building 80 all-steel 16-ton mineral wagons and repairing 200 wagons every week. A prolific rate for a small works.

Haunting Nostalgia

Interestingly, despite the many upheavals, including two world wars, many parts of Ashford retained their Victorian flavour and atmosphere into the new Elizabethan age. Richard Bourne, who then lived at Chatham, recorded his memories of life during the nineteen fifties and sixties: 'As a boy I used to spend a week or so during the summer with my grandparents in

Whitfeld Road. Their link with the Works was typical of many railway families at the time. My grandfather, Alfred Coleman, was originally from the Romney Marsh. His father, a Brenzett grocer, left his business to work in the Ashford Works. Alf joined him in 1910 at the age of 15, destined to serve the railway for 51 years as a wagonmaker. Grandmother Henrietta arrived from Battersea in 1909, her father having transferred from the Longhedge Locomotive Works prior to their closure.'

'Being fascinated with railways, my visits to South Ashford brought a special magic because the railway influence pervaded everything. Every house seemed to have a clothes line strung from boiler tubes fixed to wagon headstocks. Toolsheds were made from the planks of old wagons, which still displayed their lettering and numbers.'

'Footpaths, especially in New Town, had kerbs made from old rails. Fences were constructed from old, pitch-covered sleepers and lined many of the footpaths around or through railway property, including the well-known 'Black Path' from Torrington Road to Newtown Bridge. Green enamel signs were everywhere. At night, distant whistles and sounds of wagon shunting heralded sleep, which would be broken in the early morning by the swish of bicycles and the cheery greetings of men on their way to work.'

'The domestic scene, as for working families all over the country, was driven by the job. Grandad would leave for work before I was up, but I would often go to meet him when he came home for dinner. Having walked along the brick-paved alley into Providence Street and along Torrington Road, I would see him appear from the rough road that led to the Kimberley shops, cigarette in mouth under the ever-present flat cap, trying in vain to remember the names of everyone who greeted him from amongst the flotilla of bicycles. Everyone knew Alf, especially if they belonged to Ashford Working Men's Club, where he was a long-standing committee member. During dinner there was talk of Shop 40, the Loco side and Tommy Young, the sawmill foreman. Then it was cap on top of the wireless and a few minutes doze before my Nan reminded him that it was 'five-to' and time to go back for the afternoon stint.'

'One of the last wagon building jobs in the Kimberley sheds involving an extensive use of timber, was a batch of 250 brake vans which were completed in 1962. This job was Alf's parting shot as sawmill marker-out, and I can remember him bringing drawings home during his last months at work and spreading them out on the living room table.'

'My grandparents' house was fairly unremarkable and probably similar to workers' houses everywhere. Two up, two down, plus a kitchen. Toilet on the end of the kitchen, reached via the brick-paved yard, and no bathroom. In the fifties, an Ascot gas heater provided limited hot water in the kitchen and a huge mangle with a lethal exposed gearing stood in the corner. Much of the flavour was of the pre-war era. The living-room extending-leaf table and chairs, and the sideboard with two drawers and two cupboards were identical to those found in countless other homes of the time. The mantlepiece clock had been bought with 'Ardath' cigarette coupons. Whilst carrying out the domestic chores, my grandmother would always wear a black hat with a feather on it, which suggested a lingering Victorian tradition. There was no cellar, the coal being kept in a brick out-house beyond the back alleyway. Grandfather always referred to this building as 'the lodge'.'

'Grandmother had some cork table mats, which turned out to be axle-sized cut-outs from wagon bearing-packings. In the sideboard were a pair of gilt finger plates, said to be from a door in the S E & C R Royal Saloon. As one might imagine from a wagonmaker, any home improvements involving timber were made to last. Some replacement window frames made by Grandad owed more than a little to wagon construction both in method and materials. Copies of the Southern Region staff magazine could be found amongst the newspapers, whilst on the mantlepiece in later years was the presentation clock "In appreciation of 45 years' service."'

'Grandmother was popular in the locality for her piano playing. She would often provide the music for Saturday night sing-songs in the 'Locomotive' public house (referred to as 'roun' the Loco'), pounding the keys of a battered upright with a line of drinks on top, provided by grateful friends. Being 'under aged' I sat outside the door being fed orange juice and crisps.'

'Domestic travel was very limited in those pre-car days. Weekend trips were invariably to the seaside at Folkestone, Hastings or even a Romney Marsh 'resort'. Grandfather used to get a free pass or a privilege ticket from his entitlement by filling in a little white form and presenting it at the booking office.'

Richard Bourne recalls his mounting excitement on train journeys from Chatham to Ashford. 'A sprightly run behind a tank engine, passing the golf course and the Warren, slowing down at the Ordnance Depot and Chart Road bridge, and then easing past the huge lineside sign near the 'C' signal box, which confirmed that we had arrived at the right town.'

'Leaving the station through the old down-side building we would turn southward across the road bridge, glancing up at the signals that towered above the parapet, to see if there was a fast train due. Then down Beaver Road, over Trumpet Bridge, past the sleeper-fenced railway staff's bowling green to Christ Church, left at the Locomotive, right into Upper Denmark Road, past Slingsby's Stores (with thoughts of Bing lemonade with wire-locked bottle stoppers), and into Whitfeld Road and journey's end.'

'Railwatching was my main holiday pastime and many an hour was spent at the 'country end' of the Up platform. There was also the evocative smell of the booking office – something like a mixture of cardboard tickets, serge uniforms, gas rings and oil lamps, which can still be caught today at some of the preserved railway stations. The notice at the ticket barrier which read 'Season Tickets Must Be Shewn' was in enamelled Southern green like all station signs. There were the Up starting signals on the platform, hard up against the smoke-blackened bridge brickwork, their size and distinctive red and yellow providing a pleasing contrast, and porters in waistcoats with long sleeves, pushing platform trolleys that only ever seemed to have three wheels on the ground, the fourth spinning on its castor pivot.'

'Hand barrows were used to move all manner of things being sent by the railway, still then the basic common carrier, oil-lamps were stood facing the wall to avoid giving misleading signals. Opposite each bay platform were tall, buff-painted screen fences, presumably erected in more genteel times to spare intending passengers the sight of the sidings beyond.'

'A good spot from which to watch was the flight of steps that led from the road bridge to the Up side entrance. The view was somewhat restricted, but every move by the engine crew of stopping trains – water-taking, footplate tidying, coal pulling, oiling round, could be watched as a splendid cameo. But of course the trains themselves were the centrepiece to all this detail. Local trains to Maidstone, Tonbridge, Hastings and Canterbury and main line trains to London and the coast. My father told me that in his youth, Ashford porters would announce Canterbury trains by shouting: 'Why kill 'em and Cart 'em' (Wye, Chilham and Chartham) to Cannerberry.'

'There was much variety in the accommodation offered, for coaches varied in age from vintage S E & C R vehicles with panelled sides, raised 'birdcages' over the guard's compartment, and sepia prints of south coast resorts in the compartments, to the then modern British Railways stock, still following tradition with varnished wood and string luggage racks. Stock was used apparently at random, with the newest often employed on the lesser services, and vice versa. A special favourite was the pull and push service to New Romney, propelled out of the Up side bay platform by a chirpy 'H' class tank engine.'

'There were the set pieces. Mid-morning would see the through train from the Kent coast to Birkenhead arrive in two portions, from Margate and Dover. The Margate, usually behind a 'Schools' class engine would run into the Up platform. A few minutes later the Dover coaches, hauled by an older 4-4-0 swung into the Up bay. There was then a shunting exercise to combine the train, a process which from start to finish emphasised the deliberate, disciplined nature of railway working, and gave plenty of opportunity to watch the hard, heavy work of the shunters, who had to grapple with the coupling equipment.'

'Shortly after three in the afternoon a reverent calm would descend over the station. The Down line signals would clear, following which the lovely middle C whistle of a Bulleid Pacific would be heard from the west. Beflagged and spotless, Kent's most famous train would burst through the four-arched bridge and tear through the station, a blur of brown and cream, set with golden arrows. As the vans at the rear of the train, bucking and hunting, disappeared into the distance and signals bounced back to danger, the ordinary activity resumed.'

'In contrast to all the drama and activity going on around the railway, Ashford still managed to retain its country market town identity. I recall shopping in the busy High Street, Crumps the grocers, the Saracen's Head Hotel, Rabson's Toyshop, the tank and the smart red and ivory East Kent buses. Market day was a special treat, when the two Ashfords came together. From the Market footbridge, along the footpath to Jemmett Road, one could observe the lines of cattle wagons loading and unloading, a now forgotten railway activity. Even better was the chance of seeing a boat train lean into the curve at the end of the long straight from Tonbridge, its engine rolling as it passed over the Maidstone line junction, before commencing the lengthy whistling that preceded its passage through to the station.'

'Happy days. Usually they would end with a Sunday night return journey to urban Chatham. The walk up to the station through sparsely-lit South Ashford, with the smell of coal fires and distant railway noises to accompany us. Waving goodbye from the Maidstone train through the steam rising from leaky heating pipes, peering through grubby windows at the enamelled advertisements for Wright's Coal Tar Soap, with whistles and green handlamps bringing it all to an end.'

Young Family Story

Ashford had always been a family Works. Generation upon generation followed each other into the railway industry and the grandfathers, fathers, brothers, uncles, cousins and nephews formed an intricate network, which was often strengthened by inter-marriage. Looking back, the Young family provides a typical example. Clive Young, a fourth generation Ashford Works employee, tells his story.

'Great-great-grandfather Reubin Young was born in South Derbyshire in 1780 and became the estate steward for the Darrell family at Calehill, Little Chart. His eldest son, Charles, left the family fold to join the South Eastern Railway at Tonbridge, as Carriage Examiner, moving to Ashford around 1860 as a Labourer. Grandfather Thomas Young served an apprenticeship subsequently, becoming the carriage electrical foreman and travelling with the Royal Train.'

'As a child I was told that grandfather had been on a number of Royal journeys, including one to Constantinople with Queen Victoria. I can clearly remember a photograph in the hall of my grandmother's house in South Willesborough, of the Royal Saloon at the Ashford Works, with grandfather standing in front of it. There was also my grandfather's diary with the Royal train trips described in it, but regrettably this has long since disappeared, together with the photograph. My aunt, Edith Young, married Bert Sawyer, an engine driver at Ashford running shed. Both served as Councillors on the local Council, Bert before the Second World War and Edith after the war. Their daughter, Margaret, certainly remembers seeing menu cards, printed in silver for a Royal visit, when the Kaiser was a passenger. This could have been when the Kaiser attended the funeral of Queen Victoria in 1901.'

'Grandfather must also have been a useful footballer in his time, as he was the goalkeeper for Ashford United when they won the Kent Cup in 1893. He had two brothers - Charles, who was the carriage blacksmith's foreman, and Edward who was said to be a master tinsmith. Edward was alleged to have a drink problem and would work for so long, then go on a binge and finish up being sacked. Father once told me that he remembered my grandfather walking across New Town Green with my great-uncle and secretively slipping him a ten-shilling note to keep him going until he could get his job back. Edward was beyond the pale and could not be talked about in the house at South Willesborough.'

'My father Thomas Young served his apprenticeship in the Works as a carriage body-maker and was reputed to be 'a bit of a lad'. He told me he was sent home for three days for knocking a wood-screw in with a hammer! He also related that when he was a young man his foreman would habitually walk out of his office and kick oddments of wood aside that were in his path. Father thought it might be amusing to nail a small piece of wood to the floor, retire to a safe distance, and await results. Apparently the results were quite spectacular, but history does not record what happened to the perpetrator.'

'During the depression years it was the custom to sack apprentices at the end of their time and it would be dependant upon the Company's needs whether they were subsequently taken on again. This ruling affected father at the end of his apprenticeship. However, as my grandfather had been ill with Parkinson's disease for a number of years, father was offered and accepted a job breaking up wagons to keep him in employment, so enabling him to look after his parents. Wagon breaking was carried out by hand in those days, and as a consequence he smashed his left index finger with a two-and-a-half pound hammer and became what was known as a 'Company's Liability Man'. This meant that provided you did not sue the Company for compensation, you were guaranteed a job for life.'

'A popular leisure activity at the time was fresh water fishing. Father's fishing companion was the sawmills boiler operator, Jack Chadderton, a veteran of the Jarrow hunger march. Many were the times they would sit on the bank of the Hythe Military Canal, reminiscing, whilst waiting for fish to bite.'

'For all my father's previous escapades, he must have caught the eye of management or benefited from grandfather's reputation, because he became sawmill foreman – alleged to have been the youngest foreman in the Works at the time.'

'I started in Ashford Works on 1st January, 1951, at 16 years of age, as an apprentice locomotive fitter and turner, and therefore deserted the family carriage tradition. I actually wanted to join the Navy but having had polio this was not possible.'

'My, by now exasperated, father just turned round to me and said: 'You will go inside (local vernacular for the Works) son, it was good enough for your grandfather, it was good enough for me and it's going to be good enough for you'.

'My first introduction to Ashford Works was to be taken round by father and introduced to various staff with the comment: 'This is my old boy, you'll treat him the same as everybody else'. Of course, in practice, this meant that some foremen (and others) would be very harsh with me, while other foremen would be very mild, in case I complained when I arrived home. Of course, knowing my father as I did, there could be no question of making complaints at home!'

Many were the pranks played on us – being sent to the tea house for a bucket of steam, minute holes being drilled into the bottom of our enamel mug, or a twelve inch rule quietly slipped out of the unsuspecting victim's overall pocket, coated with grease or butter or better still red lead paint, and slipped back again.'

'Discipline in those days was absolute. There was no formal disciplinary system – if you were caught out wrongdoing, the foreman could just send you home. If you were lucky the foreman would remember and send for you to come back in three days, if not you were home for a week. Of course, you were not paid for your enforced holiday. By early 1953 the erecting shop had gone onto what was called 'The Belt System', a rudimentary production line for locomotive repairs.

There were day and night shifts, which rotated on a two-week cycle. I was apprentice to Bob Wood, who thought it might be a good idea for us to have a billycan so that we could have an afternoon cup of tea. At that time there was no official afternoon tea break, you could have a cup but you were not allowed to stop work, nor must you be seen making it. So Bob despatched me across to the tinsmith's shop to have a billycan made. It was a beautiful piece of craftsmanship, all shiny, with a proper tinsmith's joint up the side, a wired and rolled top and a handle. This served us well for some weeks, but inevitably Wilfred Wright, the erecting shop foreman, noted it. So one afternoon, at about three o'clock, Wilfred decided to do his rounds.'

'Our billycan was on a rivet fire in a pit under a locomotive, just about to come to the boil. Well, we had one of the infamous Tortoise coke-fired stoves on the gang, right opposite our rivet fire, but Wilfred decided he needed a warm-up at our fire. We did not dare to touch the billycan with Wilfred there, so we just had to let it boil dry. The solder melted and it fell apart in the fire. Wilfred went: 'Ho! Ho! Ho!' and walked off, having stopped us without a word being said. A real old-fashioned show of strength, which apart from rightly not being tolerated today, it is doubtful whether a strong enough supervisor exists, to be able not just to take such a course of action, but successfully carry it through.'

'At that time I worked with fitter Charlie Payne, who taught me to play chess while on nights, in our one am break. Many years later, Charlie became my chief maintenance foreman when I was the Works plant engineer. It goes to show – do not ill-treat today's apprentice because tomorrow he may be your boss!'

'The 'Tortoise' stoves which were used as the shop heating system were in cast-iron sections about two feet square and six feet high with horizontal slots. In the cold weather we used to put a compressed air line up the chimney to act as a blower, otherwise they would only heat up the area immediately around them. The attachment of an air line could have quite spectacular results, as the stove could be made to glow to a dull red heat. During the night we would often use the stove for heating tins of food, and on one occasion an apprentice slipped his small tin of baked beans into one of the air slots, then promptly fell asleep. Some time later there was a loud boom, as the tin exploded, spraying the gang with beans. The apprentice had of course forgotten to pierce the tin to relieve the pressure build up!'

'In the 1950s there were only very basic facilities for washing one's hands, certainly no modern amenity blocks. At the end of the traverser gangway there was what was known as the 'horse trough'. This was a zinc-lined timber trough right across the fitting shop end of the traverser, which the shop labourer would fill with hot water, just before knocking-off time.'

'In the early 1950s the standard working week was still from 7.30 in the morning until 5.30 at night, and the system of collecting a brass check from the timekeeper at the gatehouse was still in operation. If you were not there at 7.30 you were shut out until 8 o'clock. After 8am you had to ask the foreman's permission to start, and this was regarded as a very serious business.'

The wages for a 16 year-old apprentice at that time were a modest 19/6d. Having given my mother ten shillings for keep, the remainder would be spent on a Saturday night dance at the Willesborough Women's Institute Hall, the Corn Exchange, or sometimes at the Odeon Ballroom. An essential was to keep back enough for tea at work.'

'On New Year's Eve there was always a dance at the Railway Bowling Club in Beaver Road, and when walking or cycling home past the running shed to my parent's home at Willesborough after the dance, it was always to a cacophony of sound, as any locomotives with steam in them would blow their whistles to bring in the New Year. Inevitably the occasional whistle stuck open and could not be silenced. A bucket of water would then be put over the offending piece of equipment to deaden the sound.'

'For those who could afford it, the Leas Cliff Hall at Folkestone was a favourite venue. The problem was that the last train home was the 11.02pm from Folkestone Central. Hanging on until the last minute always resulted in a mad rush to the station. On arrival at Ashford, the train was always held at the signals alongside Crowbridge Road, and this enabled those who lived at South Willesborough or Newtown to jump out onto the track and take a shortcut home over the stile crossing.'

Klondyke and Kimberley

Wagon work was to have an increasingly important role at Ashford. Clive Young's family connection and the completion of the last two years of his apprenticeship in the carriage and wagon toolroom gave him an intimate knowledge of life in that part of the Works.

'Sandwiched in a small triangle of land between New Town Road and the Hastings branch line was the Klondyke shop. From the early 1950s and for many years, standard Mark One carriage underframes dominated the production schedules. Some of the carriage underframes produced during that period were still on active service on Kent commuter lines and the Ashford – Hastings branch until the new century. Bert Prior (universally known as 'Tanky') was chief foreman at the time and the Klondyke shop was part of his domain. Day to day running was the responsibility of foreman Casey Smith. Chargehands were Mickey Drummond and 'Whippet' Williams. Whippet always did the piecework and there would be serious trouble if the shop clerks tried to reduce piecework value even by a halfpenny.'

'On one side of the shop was a lean-to store, haunt of the vacuum brake gang, under the wing of chargehand Arthur Hall. Arthur was of the old school, a deep voice and always the long dark coat. The real claim to fame of the vacuum gang was that when one wanted a new clothes line, a 'chitty' was obtained from the shop foreman's office for three scrap boiler tubes. In due course one would collect two short and one long tube from Arthur, all with a little pitched roof welded on, together with the necessary additions to attach the clothes and hoist lines. The difficult part was to walk home with the three poles tied together and balanced across the handlebars and saddle of one's bicycle.'

'The Kimberley workshops could be accessed by a short walk across the Klondyke yard and over the footbridge which crossed the Hastings branch line. From the footbridge to the workshops stretched long rows of sidings filled with all manner of wagons. Entering the repair shop, the territory of chief foreman Bill Dunster, were rows of wagons and covered goods vans, all in varying stages of repair, which was being achieved to the accompaniment of rivet guns and hammers. Through a doorway was the blacksmith's shop (where great-uncle Charlie Young was foreman many years earlier) with even more noise, together with smoke from the smiths' forges. Then through yet another doorway to the wagon wheelshop. This provided the same service for the wagon side of the Works as the Locomotive wheelshop did for the loco side.'

'Nearby was the sawmill which, having received a direct hit by a bomb during the war, now boasted a range of new machinery. The noise here was piercing, due mostly to two large planing machines, which could plane all four sides of a piece of timber simultaneously, but due also to the noise from the circular saws. Neat piles of timber on four-legged stillages stood all around the shop next to the machines. Through the shop was my father's office, a modest two-roomed timber affair. In the clerk's office was shop clerk, Peter Mills, who later left to manage the local branch office of the Tunbridge Wells Equitable Friendly Society in Ashford's High Street. Those were the days when there was no financial support from the state if one had the misfortune to be off work due to sickness. Despite the low wages, everyone paid into a local union, workshop sick club or a friendly society such as the 'Tunbridge Wells' or the 'Hearts of Oak' in order to survive, because when 'laid up', wages were stopped.'

'Outside the sawmill were rows of timber drying sheds and a vast store of new timber, either sawn into rough sizes or still as tree trunks, slabbed into large planks and stacked with spacing between them. This enabled air to circulate and complete the drying out and seasoning process. Incredibly, there was still some teak stored here from old South Eastern and Chatham carriage days, although now reserved for special jobs.'

'Adjacent to the sawmill stood the sawdust destructor plant. All wood chippings were collected by a huge vacuum system and deposited into a cone-shaped hopper above a Horsfall destructor furnace. Sitting with its firebox on the furnace was an old locomotive boiler, which serviced the heating system in the Kimberley shops and the canteen. A real money saver, as the fuel cost nothing. Occasionally, the wood dust in the storage hopper would ignite and explode with a huge bang, causing the Works fire brigade to turn out and prevent the whole thing developing into something serious.'

'Close by, a workshop dealt with all-steel wagon repairs and here, as in

Shop 40 in the main Works, the noise was indescribable, with the rat-a-tat-tat of pneumatic rivet hammers and the sound of men hammering new steel plates into position. Constant blue flashes issued from electric arc welding, which at close quarters sounded like sizzling bacon in a frying pan.'

'After the noise from this hive of industry, the Yard was an area of relative peace, where a shunter was often seen busily arranging, and re-arranging, wagons, to the accompaniment of metallic clattering as their buffers banged together. Repaired wagons came out of the shops in a long line, and were first shunted over the weighbridge, where the signwriter deftly painted the tare weight in tons and hundred-weights before they returned to service.'

'The Rugby Gate, alongside an old carriage used as a rifle range, exited to South Ashford. The gate keeper, one of the Barling family from Aldington Frith way, always gave a cheery wave as one headed out towards Torrington Road, although first perhaps slipping across to the Smith's Arms for a glass of Mackeson's Hythe Ale before going home. It was said that a Tommy Dutch was mine host here when he was not at work in the oxy-acetylene welding shop. True or not, Tommy certainly spent a lot of time there. This combination of jobs would not have been unusual, the host at the Black Dog at Great Chart being an Ashford Works employee when he was not 'pulling the pints'.'

End of Steam

During the fifties, the Southern had a profusion of Bulleid Pacifics available, sometimes for quite menial tasks. This, together with plans for electrification, resulted in a heavy programme of scrapping. Stirling and Wainwright locomotives went to the scrapyard but it was something of a shock for breakers to see King Arthurs and, later on, Schools class engines coming in on their last journey at least ten years before their time.

A huge row broke out when it was realised that the last Stirling F1 Class locomotive, No.1231, had been scrapped. Clearly there had been thoughts of conservation but little had been done to prevent the tragedy. It was as a direct result of this that three engines were plucked from Ashford and sent for safekeeping in the Tweedmouth Roundhouse. Wainwright 'D' class No.737, former L B & B C Terrier No.82 and LSWR No.563 escaped. Their final destination was to be the National Railway Museum at York. Another locomotive which was lost was L & S W 'T9' No.119, used in its time to haul the Royal Train. One of the cab sheets was retained and sent to the museum.

Another engine which had a miraculous escape from the breakers was Stirling 0-6-0 'C' Class No.31065, which had been built at Ashford in 1896 and achieved a final mileage of 1,388,742. It had remained on active service until 11th June 1961, when it assisted in working the last passenger train on the Hawkhurst branch line. Shortly afterwards it was despatched to Ashford, where thought had been given to its possible preservation. Meanwhile it was stored in the Ashford running shed, and later in the Works. Finally it was decided that the expense and difficulty of returning it to its original condition, having had a Wainwright re-build, was too great and an order was issued for it to be broken up. Before this could occur, a saviour appeared, in the form of Esmond Lewis Evans, a local railway enthusiast, who purchased this last surviving Stirling locomotive and returned it to working order. It is now owned and operated by the Bluebell Railway in Sussex.

The closure of the Locomotive Works cast a long shadow before the event. As early as April 1956, private discussions had taken place with local unions, confirming that while locomotive repair work would last for only another five years, wagon building would continue without change. With no further word from British Railways during the next twelve months, apprehension mounted until the local Member of Parliament, William Deedes, intervened. In a letter to the General Manager of Southern Region, challenging management, he referred to anxiety in Ashford about the future, declaring: 'Ashford Railway Works was established one hundred years ago and for a century has been the town's industrial foundation. There are families in New Town whose association with the Works covers most of this past century and from whom a new generation is looking for apprenticeships.' Deedes called for an indication as to the Works' long-term future.

A plan for a new railway works at Ashford's Chart Leacon was now revealed, which would cater for the inspection and repair of all new electric stock on the Eastern Section of the Southern Region. It was claimed there would be no displacement of men when steam work ended, many of the 1100 being transferred to the new works or other British Railway Departments. Retirements and recruitment control would also reduce the number involved, but there was also an admission that the long-term future of the Works was still undecided.

The unhappiness of the workforce was shown by an anguished letter in the Kentish Express from a leading local union official: 'No responsible citizen should close their eyes to the fact that, without the Railway Works, Ashford could easily become a ruined and bankrupt town, even though we have a fine name as an agricultural centre. Anyone but an utter fool must realise that if the Ashford Railway Works closes down, it will bring misery to hundreds of families and possible ruin to many small traders who rely on the Works for their trade.' Referring to British Railways claim that the future of rail workers was secure because of the new workshops at Chart Leacon, the official challenged: 'Before I accept this position as fact, may

I ask Mr. Hopkin (General Manager) how many men would be absorbed in these new workshops and what percentage of these would come from the men to be made redundant in Ashford Railway works? Does the Transport Commission consider it good policy to even consider closing a shop such as the present erecting shop, with its modern equipment including five overhead cranes capable of lifting between 30 and 50 tons each? …The men in the Works are worried about what the future holds for them and their families.'

Astonishingly another year passed before possible closure surfaced again and by a strange quirk it came at a public 'Any Questions?' meeting, sponsored by the Ashford Association, to discuss local affairs. Again, Deedes was to the fore. The local newspaper splashed a headline: 'British Railways "Top Secret" Attitude Over Ashford Works. MP's Criticism – What Does The Future Hold?' The MP was strongly critical of the uncertainty, saying: 'One of the things that I find most irksome is the fact that British Railways might be a top-secret organisation, having something to do with nuclear fission. I can find out more from the Prime Minister than from British Railways. Things could not be more difficult." Saying that he had seen every member of the British Transport Commission, he declared: 'I don't think they know what they are going to do.'

His criticism was echoed by another panellist, Jack Francis, editor of the Kentish Express: 'You cannot get a really reasoned reply from the railway people about the Works.' Surely they know what they are going to do in, say, five years' time?' Referring to the letter in his paper, which had appeared nine months previously, he concluded: 'There was no reply from British Railways to relieve that worry.'

These strident criticisms had an immediate effect, with British Railways issuing a statement, protesting that no secret had been made of the fact that modernisation would lead to the eventual disappearance of the steam locomotive and that this would, in all probability, lead to the Ashford Locomotive Works, with its staff of 1100, being surplus to requirements. They speculated upon the possibility of another heavy engineering company coming in to take over and employing some of the men who would otherwise be redundant.

The three local unions – Amalgamated Engineering, Boilermakers and the Union of Railwaymen, were quick off the mark in calling meetings. The latter union complained that the men were 'very sore' as they had not been consulted. The fact that the latest development had followed upon an outside 'Any Questions?' meeting only added to their indignation. Meanwhile it was announced that electrification of the Kent Coast Line was to follow in 1960 and as a consequence the Works locomotive drawing office was to be scaled down and was to concentrate solely on carriage and wagon work.

Another year passed and March 1959 found British Railways in discussion with the local Council, and announcing that the locomotive shops would close in 1965, but within three months this was changed, and the Works was dealt a new blow. The British Transport Commission, in a new statement of policy, proposed bringing forward the closure date for the Locomotive Works to September 1960. The shock wave from this announcement spread through the town, with both the unions and the local Council warning that Ashford could face five years of mounting unemployment.

Deedes raised the issue in the House of Commons and shot off a letter to Sir Brian Robertson, Transport Commission chairman, who assured him that only the locomotive side of the Works would be affected and there was no proposal to close the carriage and wagon department. Confusion clearly reigned, as the statement confirming the closure was now described as 'unofficial'.

Within three months, British Railways had another change of mind. They agreed the locomotive shops would not now close until the end of 1961, but stressed again that the carriage and wagon side was not affected. There had been strenuous negotiations by the railway unions to delay the earlier closure and in this Deedes had played his part, although he made it clear that he still did not regard the position as satisfactory.

Immediately before Christmas 1959, an already confused situation deepened. Two British Railways officials arrived in Ashford and slipped into the Works for talks with the local managers, Lt. Col. John Bell and Jim Henneker. Notices were posted stating that the final date for closure of the Locomotive Works had been set for June 1962, but this slightly better news was more than offset by the announcement that, by the same date, over 300 of the 780 men in the carriage and wagon department would be made redundant. This was a shattering blow when considered against both recent assurances and others dating back to 1956, that wagon employment would not be affected.

It was claimed by management that, with the substitution of diesel and electric traction for steam, and the greater use of high capacity steel wagons, the need for heavy repairs and maintenance would be greatly reduced. As a palliative, employment was offered at the new Chart Leacon depot, which was expected to come into operation during 1961, and redundant workers were promised priority in filling other Southern Region vacancies.

Continued feelings of uncertainty were demonstrated when local authorities, trades unions and members of parliament from fourteen railway towns held a meeting at Caxton Hall in London. It was generally held that everyone was being kept in the dark. The meeting protested at work being done outside railway workshops, which could well be left with them. There was also a complaint that a Government Act prevented workshops from producing anything unconnected with railways. Ashford was particularly concerned that they were not being told about possible surplus land that could be sold to other industrialists.

The gloom lasted until the following June, when the railway management underwent another change of mind. The Carriage and Wagon department had gained a reprieve, sweeping away the worries that had existed since the previous December. Full employment was promised for the department until the end of 1961 and hopes were entertained for more work beyond that. Of the 900 locomotive men now remaining, only 200 would be required for other work, but already men were drifting away to other jobs, even Bell had departed for Eastleigh – the last Locomotive Works Manager.

Electric train working between London and the Kent Coast arrived quite unheralded on 12th June 1961. British Rail had declined to mark the occasion in any special way, but the public had other ideas. The previous day saw the last steam-hauled Golden Arrow pass through. Crowds gathered at every available vantage point, although by far the best was surely the footbridge by the cattle market. With superb timing the famous train, hauled by West Country class 'Appledore' approached down the long straight from Tonbridge. Purring round the curve at 60 miles per hour, spotless and shining, bedecked with its golden arrows, Union Jack and French tricolour, it presented a never-to-be-forgotten sight of supreme steam majesty. To waves, applause and cheers from all the assembled admirers, the steam-hauled express passed into history.

Steam locomotives continued to come in to be scrapped. One hard-worked veteran was Ashford-built No.739. One of Wainwright's 'Coppertops', it had given 59 years of service during which time it had covered 2,002,974 miles. On 30th June 1962, steam locomotive work finally ceased, the last engine through the shop being a Maunsell 'U' class No.31807. Many of the men left for either Chart Leacon or other railway workshops. Ashford Works would in future concentrate on wagon construction and repairs.

In September, railwaymen followed the tradition of processing through the town to a meeting in Victoria Park. Perhaps because they were so obviously trying to shut the stable door after the horse had bolted, the turnout was immensely disappointing. The National Union of Railwaymen had hoped for a turnout of 2000 from all parts of South Eastern England. Instead only handfuls of men came from neighbouring towns and together with the Ashford men they totalled no more than 400.

Some carried banners such as 'What a way to ru(i)n a railway', several warned of the dangers of Dr. Beechings 'pill' and one asked Dr. Beeching to 'co-operate not operate on the railway system'. Union speakers still complained about the lack of definite plans for the future. The cause of the railways' predicament was blamed on high interest rates raising the costs of modernisation, plus the fact that contracts for new railway work were going to private industry. An official from London warned the meeting: 'If the lines that do not pay are all closed more than half of England will have no railway.'

Modernisation

As part of yet another reorganisation, Ashford Works left regional control in 1963 and became part of British Railways Workshop Division, the intention being to ensure Ashford's future as a major wagon producer. Confidence rose further when £1m was allocated for the rearrangement and modernisation of the workshops. This firstly required a clearance of unwanted buildings and so the brass foundry, forge, coppersmiths' stores, main offices and a whole range of shops such as sheetmetal, light plating welding, paint and maintenance, were all swept away.

Following their removal, the locomotive shops were cleared and the original 1847 timber roof trusses replaced with steel and re-clad, resulting in a marked improvement in daylight penetration and reduced heat loss. The long shops with their overhead cranes would prove to be highly suitable for wagon construction programmes, enabling Ashford to achieve its highest ever level of productivity.

With the changes in place, Ashford now had three construction shops which offered facilities for the construction of freight wagons on self-contained flow lines, and special jigs and turn-over manipulators to ensure a high quality output. In addition heavy, medium and light engineering shops offered a range of machines to meet the requirements of drilling, milling, grinding, shaping and pressing. One had mechanical power saws and multi-headed flame cutters installed for use in the initial preparation of steel sections and plates. Other facilities included a smiths shop for the pressing of hot and cold components, a shot-blasting shop to protect materials against rust and prepare steelwork for the paint shop, which was equipped to use an airless spray technique. Shops for sub-assembly work, wagon repair work and a metallurgical laboratory were also part of the new complex.

1965 saw the Works constructing a giant boiler-carrying wagon, the largest wagon ever constructed for British Railways. It was by any standard a truly remarkable production, consisting of four sets of six-axle bogie units with two four-wheel match trucks. The purpose of this special 165 foot long 'one-off' wagon was to transport a massive boiler to a new power station, it being cheaper to make a wagon that would only make one journey than build an 'on-site' factory for the manufacture of one boiler.

Following this achievement, the Works secured its first major contract from overseas for 250 Continental Ferry Vans. Orders for other specialised rolling stock followed. Fly Ash wagons to haul ash from Central Electricity

Generating Board power stations, articulated car transporters for the Ford Motor Company and nearly 2,000 Freightliners for British Railways fast container traffic were followed by the production of hundreds of high capacity coal wagons. These had been developed from a prototype by Ashford's Roy Donaldson in collaboration with Darlington Works and dubbed 'Merry-Go-Round' wagons because of their continuous return journeys between the mines and the power stations. During this period the Works reputation for high output was also maintained with the production of 1,200 bogie 'E' 30 ton bolster wagons.

An amusing tale is told by long-serving railwayman, Tony Addey. The year 1963 had seen the drama of the Great Train Robbery. Urgent measures were called for to give greater protection to Royal Mail vans. Thirty mail vans were sent to Ashford to be lined out with steel sheets, but what provoked the humour of the Ashford men was the decision to erect alarm speakers on the roofs of the vans, which, when triggered, broadcast the amplified message: 'Help! Call the police! We've been robbed!' over and over again.

As if previous reorganisations had not been enough, the end of the decade saw yet another when the Works became part of British Rail Engineering Ltd., along with Shildon in County Durham. An immediate advantage was receiving permission to utilise surplus capacity for private party work from whatever quarter. Strict financial rules governed these contracts as public money could not be allowed to subsidise outside work and so provoke risk of an unfair competition claim.

An early product of the new system was the construction of a 90-ton prototype bulk powder wagon, intended to carry commodities like bulk soap powder for companies such as Procter and Gamble. Orders came in from local engineering companies who had not the larger equipment or specialist expertise in their own workshops. Ashford also became involved in keeping the old train ferry dock at Dover operational. A regular job was the renovation of the shafts and provision of new bearings for the large pumps that lowered or raised the sea water level within the train ferry berth, to suit the tide.

The Battle of Newtown

The opening skirmish in what became known as 'The Battle of Newtown' took place in 1969 when British Railways sought to dispose of the village to the local Council for the lowly sum of £50,000. Incredibly, the Council declined, on the grounds that they would be buying a liability. The railway tenants' efforts to persuade them to change their minds failed, and one of their own Councillors told them that nothing more could be done.

The village was put up for sale and in due course was bought by a development company. Its intentions were soon made clear. No monies would be spent on repairs and as the houses fell into an unacceptable state, the Council would be asked to re-house the unfortunate tenants. Eventually, all the houses would be demolished and an industrial estate built on the land. Following years of neglect by British Railways, degradation proceeded at an alarming rate. Roads and footpaths continued to break up, street lighting all but vanished and the population began to diminish, as houses were declared unfit for human habitation. It would have taken a few years for the developers intentions to reach fruition; meanwhile the former railway community would be condemned to a miserable existence.

In 1973, local government reorganisation resulted in a new Council for the area being formed and residents decided to have another go. An approach was made to a new Councillor for the area and tenants poured out their hearts about their living conditions. The horrified Councillor held a meeting at the Alfred Arms, called upon the neglected tenants to form an action group and pledged that he would champion their cause. Thus, battle was joined.

Regular meetings followed under the indomitable chairmanship of Teresa Crow, whose devotion to the cause was an important factor in achieving eventual success. Demonstrations were mounted both outside and inside the Council Chamber while the Councillor gave voice to their feelings in debate. Council officers challenged the right of the Action Group to speak for Newtown. A call went out asking every tenant to contribute a 'symbolic penny' as a token of their support. The bag containing a penny piece from every tenant was presented to the Mayor at a Council meeting and the attempt to discredit the Action Group collapsed.

An early decision was to appeal for a reduction in the 'rates' on the grounds that tenants were provided with few facilities and the living conditions of many were abominable. At the appeal court, the wise old magistrates listened intently to the many tales of distress and at the end of the hearing declared: 'We must go and see this Newtown'. Within two weeks everyone was back in court. Not only did the magistrates agree to a reduction in 'rates' but from his place on the bench the Chairman declared: 'Something must be done about Newtown.'

Following hard upon this success, the tenants were advised to serve notices of disrepair upon the owners. These gave them six weeks to put matters to rights. Unsurprisingly, there was no response. Utilising a little-known clause in the Public Health Act of 1936, notices were then served upon the Council, requiring them to either pressure the owners into action or be lawfully obliged to carry out repairs themselves, making the owners meet the costs. Realising that the game was up, the owners gave in, their strategy having clearly failed. With the tenants now armed with the Public

Health Act, the houses would not be allowed to rot away and all ideas of demolition and building an industrial estate evaporated.

The developers now approached the Borough Council and the new Housing Committee, ably led by Councillor Fortescue, agreed to a purchase. The price was £450,000. A fair price, but a nice profit for the development company.

The struggle to preserve the community was not over. Month after month went by with tenants keeping up the pressure. Plans were considered, layouts scrutinised, complaints made, suggestions submitted. A particularly fierce fight was for a guarantee that tenants could stay on Newtown in alternative accommodation if their particular property had to be demolished. There was a popular demand for the houses built in 1912 to be kept and modernised. A battle was fought and won to preserve the famous Green.

A by-product of the struggle was the result of the 1976 Borough Council election. Because their Councillor had trodden on too many corns in his local campaigning, a determined effort was made to unseat him in what was the fiercest-fought election ever seen in the Ward. Newtown rallied – every house seemed to display a 'Vote for Turner' poster. In a massive turnout, which election officials said exceeded that of the General Election, the vote swung against all three political parties and Newtown's votes gave victory to 'their' man.

Finally, after years of hard work and effort, a celebration was thought to be in order. The Kentish Express commented: 'Ashford's railway village of Newtown has always known how to celebrate. It was no surprise therefore, that it's Gala Day was a real ball. The families of Newtown whooped things up to the hilt when the builders packed their bags after the reconstruction of their estate. Years of demolition, planning and re-building are at last over for the community in their modern homes and bungalows, overlooking the Green.'

Flags and bunting decorated the Green and swings, roundabouts, games and stalls were dotted around an arena. Children raced, steam engines rolled, fancy dress was paraded and babies were shown off. A highlight of the day was the unveiling of a set of locomotive wheels built in the Ashford Works in 1904 for a Wainwright class 'C' locomotive. They were a presentation from railway enthusiast Esmond Lewis Evans, and the local Councillor took them into trust as a symbol of Newtown's re-birth. He referred to the long campaign they had undertaken and said: 'The efforts of the last few years echo the spirit of the early pioneers, who were proud to live in Newtown. May that spirit of fierce determination, but also kindly consideration for one's fellow beings, live on in the years to come.' It was during this period that the community's name was officially merged into the single word 'Newtown'.

The battle at Newtown was not the only one fought out during the

Seventies. A fire in a house in South Ashford in which five children narrowly escaped with their lives set the scene later on for the tragic death of former railwayman Frederick Stokes, who was burned to death in his Council-owned bungalow at Willesborough. Paul Smith, editor of the Kentish Express, approached South Willesborough and Newtown's campaigning Councillor, and in asking him to probe into the cause of the apparent fire risk in some of the Council's properties, assured him of that newspaper's full backing. There followed two years of fierce campaigning. It was a lone battle, with plenty of abuse heaped on the Councillor's head by those who should have known better. The national press, television and government departments all became involved in what developed into a nation wide debate. The tenants from Ashford's 500 'at risk' houses, who included many active and retired railwaymen, voiced their protests, but the Council refused to face the facts, preferring to await the result of a parliamentary debate. Finally, it was poor Frederick Stokes who paid the price for their inaction. An independent report by a consultant, Mr. Parnell, blamed poor workmanship, inadequate supervision and inherent defects in the use of polyurethane and strawboard for ceilings and wall partitions. 114 eight year old houses and bungalows were demolished, and the Council's Chief Technical Officer, who had kept many facts from Councillors, was obliged to resign, ending what the Kentish Express called 'A history of protest and death'.

British Rail's most discreditable action was their part in the wilful destruction of the former Royal Train shed. One of the original Works buildings, erected in 1847, this ornate cast iron and wooden clad building had latterly served as the Works canteen. An initial attempt at demolition was prevented when a vigilant Newtown tenant raised the alarm and the Council demanded that the work be halted whilst they began procedures to get the building 'listed' as an historic monument.

Shortly afterwards, with British Rail choosing a week-end for the task, the building was brutally bulldozed. Everything was smashed up, nothing of value remained. The only subsequent action the Council could take was to issue a court summons against the contractor for carrying out demolition works without informing the local authority, the standard fine being £200. Alone in the public gallery of the court sat the local Councillor and the contractor. He being a rather quiet and timid man confided in the Councillor, not knowing his identity. 'It's not my fault,' he whispered. 'British Rail told me to get the building down that weekend. By destroying it, there was of course no profit in it for me.' 'Don't worry,' they said. 'You have had plenty of work from us in the past and we will give you plenty in the future. Just get it down.' Needless to say, British Rail, with an air of injured innocence, pleaded a mistake had been made. This untruth only added to their crime. This was a disgraceful and wicked act of vandalism, which will forever be to British Rail's shame.

Wagons Roll

The 1970s were an 'Indian Summer' for Ashford Works. Massive orders poured in, new staff were recruited, the future seemed assured. By 1974 a Yugoslav contract for 800 covered vans had been satisfactorily completed. The vans left Ashford at night on special working to Dover Docks. Being larger than British Rail standard gauge, temporary bogies were used to offset the body and obtain the necessary clearance. Upon arrival at Dover, the bogies were changed for the correct ones, enabling the vans to then travel via the ferry, across Europe, to Yugoslavia. Investment in railways by the government now resulted in an increased demand for freight vehicles – British Rail calling for 100 Freightliners and 557 bogie steel-carrying wagons, orders that would take two years to complete. British Steel followed through with orders for 50 lime-carrying bogie hopper wagons.

Adding to Ashford's success, a further £2m export order was secured from the Aquaba Railway Corporation for 140 bogie hopper wagons to convey phosphate from the mines at El Hassa to the port of Aquaba over a section of the Hedjaz – Jordan railway. Alongside this order was one from Israeli Railways for 31 wagons of the same type. As they too did not conform to British Rail standard gauge, they were sent to Swansea Docks in two sections, underframe and body, and then assembled and welded at the dockside by Ashford staff prior to despatch. Careful arrangements were made in order to isolate the two contracts because of the tension between Israel and the Arab states. Production lines at Ashford were kept strictly apart and British Rail even indulged in the fiction by using two quite separate addresses when corresponding on the two orders. Ashford had become BREL's major export builder.

Although at this time the works provided employment for over 1,000, the orders that were pouring in from home and abroad together with the constant stream of repair and maintenance work resulted in a staff shortage. A centre-spread advertisement in the Kentish Express extolled the wonderful prospects facing prospective employees. Continuous work was promised through to 1978 with repeat orders for freightliners, bogie steel carriers and covered vans for British Rail, together with long-term prospects for more orders up to 1985. To meet a projected continuous demand for the repair and maintenance of existing rolling stock, a heavy investment programme was planned for refurbishing workshop facilities and bringing in new machinery. It was claimed existing and new contracts would ensure a full order book for the next seven or eight years.

A new pay structure offered top grade shopmen the chance of earning £60 per week compared with the existing minimum for craft grades such as fitters, turners and welders of £42.40.

At this time the possibility of a Channel Tunnel was under discussion at national level. From British Rail's advertising it is evident that they regarded the prospect of Ashford playing a major role in the building and maintenance of Tunnel rolling stock as a foregone conclusion.

In anticipation of securing the contract for building Tunnel vehicles, a full sized cross sectional model of a double deck car carrier was built. The Works was also ready to construct special vehicles to carry single deck buses fitted with air-conditioning and lorries loaded with standard containers. Emphasising its closeness to the Tunnel environs and the possibility of extending Continental gauge to the town, British Rail claimed: 'With the exception of some alterations to one or two workshops, we have the technical and engineering ability here, on the spot, now. Feasibility studies have shown that Ashford is in the best position for the maintenance of these vehicles.'

In a spirit of optimism, British Rail announced the need for 200 more workers and in a note of urgency said: '130 must be found by the end of the year.'

In 1978, Ashford's golden age of wagon building was clearly continuing unabated. 'Wagons roll!' 'Order books are bulging!' proclaimed the local newspaper. The previous March, BRE-Metro Ltd., the joint export sales company of British Rail had won the company's biggest-ever export order. A multi-million pound contract was secured for 1,240 wagons from Kenya Railways. Needed to replace existing 40-year old stock, the wagons would haul ballast and general cargo, and the vans would haul sawn timber, cotton, sisal, coffee, maize and wheat for the African railway.

When the wagons left Ashford, they were in kit form and taken by rail to Dagenham Docks to be shipped the 5,000 miles through the Suez Canal and the Red Sea to Mombasa. Taken on to the 1896 British-built Nairobi workshops, local men were responsible for their assembly. Four different types of wagon had been required and so a completed wagon of each type was shipped as a guide. An assembly flow line was set up by Ashford staff and two men remained to assist until the contract was completed.

BREL's Commercial Director expressed his confidence that they could look forward to more export orders in the future with a large part of the business coming to Ashford. With the rosy prospect of a steady work flow, 100 new jobs were created and the number of apprenticeships doubled. A delighted Mike Cockburn, Works Manager, claimed: 'With this work we have the opportunity to put Ashford right in the forefront of BR engineering workshops.' He declared that a further confirmation of Ashford's positive role in the future was the recent authority to spend over £600,000 to provide modern cranes, office improvements, new canteen arrangements and covered storage.

The existing overhead Craven and Vaughan cranes dated back to 1898 and apart from their conversion to electrical working in 1911, they had remained in service with virtually no other alteration. Five new 30-ton ac machines were now installed at a cost of £300,000 and the works also gained a Hepworth computer-controlled lathe at a cost of £80,000.

During the mid-seventies, private work poured into the shops. 250 British Leyland ferry vans, eight 90-ton bogie wagons for British Petroleum, thirty-six 80-ton bogie 'Shell Star' fertiliser pallet wagons and 100 Blue Circle tankers were ordered. Because Ashford's bulging order book also included the refurbishing and modernisation of 200 bogie steel-carriers, 50 covered vans and 500 open wagons, together with the building of sub-assemblies for the class 56 locomotives of British Rail, a £1m Continental truck order had to be transferred to Shildon.

With the successful conclusion of the Kenyan order in 1979, Ashford was made responsible for a major order from the Tanzanian Railway Corporation. The contract was for 200 open wagons and 300 covered vans in kit form together with ten completed crew vans. The crew vans were despatched from Newcastle, but the remainder were all taken to Felixstowe, from where they were shipped to Dar-es-Salaam. Here the final assembly was carried out at the old steam locomotive works, which had been built by the Germans when it had been part of their colony of Tanganyika. Taken over by the British during the First World War, they were run under British guidance until Independence in 1962.

Four Ashford men went to Tanzania to assist in erecting the first batch of wagons and, as proof of their confidence, took a 60 mph ride in one of them, over a stretch of track where a train of tank wagons supplied by another country had been derailed only days earlier! Figures show that in the construction of the Tanzanian low-sided wagons some 105,600 holes were drilled in the underframes, and 154,000 nuts, 121,500 bolts, 233,500 washers, 212,500 rivets and 76,500 split pins were used.

Following hard upon the heels of this order came one from Bangladesh Railways. This was an unusual one, inasmuch as there are two different rail gauges in Bangladesh: broad gauge for the western side of the country and narrow gauge in the east. This posed immediate transport problems in England, which were solved by using road trailers for the 419 broad gauge for their journey to London's Royal Albert Docks. When unloaded at Millwall, some were left to stand on the quayside while others were temporarily loaded onto barges until there were enough for a shipment. The journey to Bangladesh was a long one – vessels taking 24 days to cover the 7,700 miles to Chittagong. By contrast, the 406 narrow-gauge wagons were mounted on accommodation bogies for their journey to Dagenham Docks.

An unusual feature of the contract resulted from the extreme weather conditions found in Bangladesh. There is a salty atmosphere of high humidity with temperatures varying from a maximum of 11°F (44°C) to a minimum of 42°F (5°C). For much of the year, the conditions are dry and dusty, but for four months prolonged and intensive rainfall is experienced, averaging 120 inches. There was, therefore, a requirement that the wagon design and construction should be 'proved' in a monsoon test to the satisfaction of the Crown Agents Inspector.

By the time the last Bangladesh wagon had passed through the Ashford workshops, arrangements for this contract had proved their worth. Three production lines had been in operation in the new construction shop and all were double shifted, resulting in maximum output.

1980 saw the Ashford men hard at work with orders for the home market. They were contracted to build 500 45-tonne open wagons and refurbish and modernise 200 bogie steel wagons and 50 covered wagons. They were also entrusted with a specialised order from British Rail Civil Engineering, for 40-tonne 'Sea Lion' ballast wagons with air and vacuum braking.

Final Closure

In August of 1980, reminiscent of the occasion in 1959 when two railway officials came to the Works to announce the closure of the Locomotive Works, two senior men from British Rail Engineering Headquarters at Derby arrived in Ashford. At their meeting with local managers they delivered a bombshell. Nearly half of the 1,000 workers were put under threat of the sack. A mass meeting of staff was called immediately.

The shock of the announcement was likened to a train hitting the buffers. Workers were told that 350 of them could be redundant by March and a further 80 by the following October unless new orders came in. Given the industrial recession and a cut-back by British Rail, the capacity for the manufacture and repair of rolling stock had been re-assessed. Because of Ashford's concentration upon freight orders from overseas markets, they would suffer more than other depots.

After the buoyant years, the news seemed unbelievable. Money had been poured into modernising the Works and in accordance with Ashford tradition, high quality work had gone hand-in-hand with a record of superb productivity. Expectations for the future had been high, not least because of the optimism of management and the fact that the Works profits for the past year had been £1m. The railwaymen and the town were stunned.

It was claimed that cutbacks would be softened because quite a number of men had joined the Works when the War had ended and were now coming up for retirement. If redundancies came they would be right across the floor and include salaried staff but in any event, the Company was not at that stage contemplating total closure.

Matters came to a head in May, 1981, following the completion of the Bangladesh contract but with no overseas order to replace it. Some railwaymen accepted voluntary redundancy but the unions were in fighting mood. BREL were clearly set on major sackings by September and complete closure by January 31st, 1982. Sir Peter Parker, British Rail chief, held out little hope for the Works. 'We have to make economies to meet the external financial limits imposed by the government. One way is to cut down on our investment in the construction and repair of rolling stock.' Sir Peter expressed his awareness of Ashford's tradition as a railway town but warned 'BREL is in serious financial trouble.' In order to ease the situation, a four-day working week was being considered.

Ashford's trade unionists responded by calling on the National Union of Railwaymen to reject the closure proposals and to mobilise the full industrial strength of the union for strike action. At a weekend conference of NUR shopmen's delegates there was a unanimous vote calling upon their national executive to oppose the closure of Ashford Works. 'Failure by the British Rail Board to withdraw their threat of closure should result in the declaration of a national rail strike by the NUR.' Unionists complained that the number of railway employees nationally had reduced from 68,000 in 1962 to 34,000, while the former 32 workshops had reduced to 13.

In July they received the support of a delegation of civic leaders led by local Member of Parliament, Keith Speed, who put a forceful case to Sir Peter Parker. Little came from this meeting, probably little was expected.

Grim reality forced itself upon the scene the following month, when local railwaymen expressed feelings of betrayal. Newly elected Works convenor, Bill O'Sullivan, and Works Committee chairman, Jimmy Fleming, told the local newspaper they were disgusted at the way their national union officials had abandoned the workforce. It was no doubt evident to those officials that with the country suffering from an industrial recession and with a government that had cut off the railways' money supply, no action on their part could help. The union leaders claimed there was enough work available to keep the Works busy for up to four years, but without the investment of money, the need was not going to be met.

A partial lifeline was thrown to the Works when the British Rail Board offered to keep the wheel shop open and give Ashford an order for the dismantling of 10,000 wagons. More jobs were saved when a last minute contract was signed at the end of September for the manufacture of nine giant carriers for atomic waste flasks. Dogged resistance by the workers at the stricken Rail Works earned a reprieve for yet another 119 men. Union officials had been told that wagon work already begun at Ashford would have to go elsewhere. The Ashford men refused to release materials, jigs or paperwork for the job. Outside railwaymen were instructed to 'black' movement of materials while storemen refused to handle the loading. Management gave way and agreed to leave the work at Ashford.

Speaking of the workers' victory, the Works convenor declared: 'This work was assigned to Ashford originally. We started the job and we are going to finish it.' The celebrations were short-lived. In October BREL announced redundancies for 280 men although an immediate closure had been postponed. That month saw the departure of Works manager, Mike Cockburn, who warned that Channel Tunnel work would not save them.

During the following twelve months there was a continual run-down in the workforce. Some transferred to railway jobs in other parts of the country, some joined private industry, some took retirement. The unions, grasping at straws, put forward a suggestion that the Works be mothballed, in the belief that better times were around the corner. The idea was dismissed by the director of a company which had just completed a study for British Rail into problems associated with rail works closures. He said: 'I don't believe anyone seriously believes the Works will open again in a few years' time. It is a silver lining that unions are trying to sell to their members.'

In August, 1982, BREL confirmed that crane repairs would continue at Ashford and that the wheel shop would remain, but that was little consolation to men who had built some 11,000 wagons during the previous twenty years. Fewer than 200 men now remained, completing contracts, but without further orders, they too would have to go. The Kentish Express lamented: 'The Rail Works, once Ashford's biggest employer, has been run down, almost to the point of closure, since June last year.'

And so, on 31st May 1984, after nearly 130 years, Ashford Railway Works finally closed. As the clock in the tower by the main entrance clanged five o'clock, where once hundreds poured out, the last fifty men walked through. For the last two years they had been breaking rail wagons for scrap. Now, although offered alternative employment in the railway workshops at Ashford's Chart Leacon, all had opted for redundancy. Most had records of long service and some were nearing retirement.

Ashford railwayman, Ron Hover, summed up the feeling of sadness felt by Ashfordians: 'Many families' lives revolved around the Works; nearly all the older families in Ashford had some connection. It was a heavy industry which gave many school leavers apprenticeships in so many varied trades. No more will the lads have this opportunity, Many, redundant or retired, mourn the loss of the Railway Works. So many spent their lifetime working there...'

And so the Works lay abandoned. Walking through the echoing workshops, memories are stirred. Thoughts of early pioneers and their hardships, of engineers whose locomotives were a source of such pride, of carriage makers and wagon builders with their talent and dedication, of men who had come as boys, learned skills, married and had families, whose whole lives revolved around the Works, of the good times and the bad.

No more the clang of metal on metal, no more the heavy thud of the steam hammer, no more drilling and welding or the noise of belts and pulleys, no more the whirring of overhead cranes, no more the heat and glare of the furnace.

All machinery now stilled, odd timbers left unused, the last wagon gone. No more shunting trucks or friendly whistles of locomotives, no more clanking pistons or hissing steam, no more voices of men about their daily work. Everywhere a silence.

A silence almost making itself heard, the very walls of the idle shops crying out against their abandonment, the atmosphere seemingly charged with a despair. And everywhere a strange emptiness, a loneliness that knows no explanation.

The weeds already sprouting from nooks and crannies, the cries of wheeling gulls adding a piquant mournfulness. The achievements of years past all gone. The Works are closed. It's all over.

APPENDIX 1

Air attack on Ashford

Revelations since the end of the war permit a better understanding of the events of 24th March 1943. For years it was believed that the spotters on the Railway Company's Bath House at Newtown sounded the alarm which alerted both the Works and the Beaver Road School to the coming danger. Certainly the spotters' action prevented a huge loss of life inside the Works, but there were other crucial factors which affected the outcome of the raid.

From the point at Mersham at which the attacking bombers were first seen by the spotters, the flying time to the Works was 22 seconds. The school would have been reached within a further 10 seconds. Clearly this would have given insufficient time to get all the children to shelter. It was the genius of local townsmen, William Richardson and Herbert Wilson, in devising an early warning system that was an important element in ensuring the children's survival. Richardson, a Marconi trained engineer given to unconventional ideas, conceived the idea of warning bell alarms in places of importance such as schools, hospitals and Civil Defence Posts, which would sound slow rings for a general alert, and short, sharp rings for immediate danger. Wilson, the Urban Council's electrical engineer, had the brainwave of using the disused street lighting network to carry the signal and thence by overhead cabling to the appropriate buildings.

On that fateful morning the first alarm bell was received little more than two minutes before the raid. It was followed within 60 seconds by the immediate danger signal. This warning originated at County Civil Defence Headquarters at Maidstone and was routed through the Ashford HQ, who also received a verbal warning: 'Heading Ashford! Heading Ashford!' It is curious that, although everyone was familiar with the bell warning system, its importance appears to have been overlooked on this occasion. Instead, a wave of emotion and overwhelming thankfulness was directed towards the actions of the Railway Works spotters. Living so close to enemy occupied France, the public were certainly well attuned to the possibility of surprise attacks. Perhaps this was the reason the lack of warning was not questioned by the general public.

Two weeks before the raid, the authorities were aware of a high flying German reconnaissance aircraft taking photographs over the town. Shortly afterwards, Ashford, already bristling with anti-aircraft guns, saw the defences at the Railway Works and along the main line heavily reinforced with Vickers guns, double Bren guns and Oerlikon cannon, armaments particularly suitable for defence against attacks by low-flying raiders.

Questions that arise are – were the authorities aware of the German reconnaissance planes' purpose? What caused the military to reinforce the Works anti-aircraft defences? How could the authorities know with sufficient confidence the bombers' target, thus enabling a verbal warning to be given to Ashford? Why was the story of the Works' spotters 'saving' the school left undenied?

Throughout the war, British Intelligence was heavily engaged in keeping a close watch on the Luftwaffe. German reconnaissance aircraft communicated with their base by wireless telegraphy, using hand-operated Morse in code, and this was easily intercepted by the chief intercept station, RAF Cheadle. The Luftwaffe communication code had been cracked early on but, unaware of this, German aircrew and controllers freely used their transmissions, little realising they were being constantly monitored by the British.

In addition, the breaking of cipher messages sent by the Enigma machine gave strategists a huge insight into the German administrative command and provided Britain with enormous advantages. In this way, Intelligence could have learned of the German reconnaissance planes' mission and interpreted messages concerning a coming attack. Although not necessarily detailed as regards date and time, there was a sufficient sureness that an attack upon Ashford was intended. Undoubtedly this resulted in the decision to rapidly expand the Railway Works anti-aircraft defences.

The other missing piece of the jigsaw involved another of the war's heavily guarded secrets. Radar. The system had gained prominence during the Battle of Britain, enabling the plotters to receive scans, which penetrated across the Channel and into the airspace of occupied France. Enemy planes were located as they rose into the air and assembled over their bases in the Pas-de-Calais. A drawback to the system was that it could only locate planes flying at medium height and above. This now changed. By 24th March 1943, the day of the attack on Ashford, a new type of radar dish had been erected on the tower at Capel-le-Ferne, 550 feet above sea level. Britain now had a capability for detecting low-flying enemy aircraft. In use for the first time, this new radar Type 277(T) picked up the incoming raiders flying at wave top height when still 20 miles out. The plot was flashed to No.11 Group HQ at RAF Stanmore and, there being no friendly aircraft in the area, the sighting was identified as hostile. Coastal air raid sirens were sounding within 70 seconds of the first plot – 2.2 minutes before the raiders crossed the English coast.

In Ashford, the school's alarm bell sounded at much the same time as an early 'look-out' warning was given to the railway spotters via their field telephone, putting them on full alert. The Beaver Road school head teachers, and in particular Miss Adams, demonstrated admirable caution in shepherding their pupils to safety. But an enormous tribute is due to William Richardson and Herbert Wilson, who devised Ashford's ingenious bell alarm system. This was rung before the public air raid sirens sounded, giving the children sufficient extra time to reach their shelters before the bomb hit the school, avoiding what would otherwise have been a scene of indescribable horror.

Hugely admirable though the actions of the Works' spotters were in saving the lives of their fellow railwaymen, they were separate from the circumstances surrounding the school.

Clearly the authorities were going to be highly sensitive to any discussion about this country's defence system. It was of over-riding importance that at no time should the Germans suspect either the extent of our radar or our ability at code-breaking, advantages which, if revealed, would have widespread ramifications damaging to the war effort. The praise heaped upon the Works spotters helped to provide a useful cover story, effectively diverting attention away from this country's defensive arrangements.

A final question remains unanswered. Why did Ashford's air raid sirens remain silent even when the alarm bells were sounding? The coastal areas received just over two minutes' warning, yet in Ashford the bombers were almost upon the town before the public alert was given. It was so late that, for the first and only time during the war, the 'alert' changed to 'immediate danger' in mid-warning. While the bombs were dropping and the Works and the town were being shot up with cannon and machine-gun fire, the warning blasts were still sounding their late warning and this was a direct cause of the heavy death toll and the large number of casualties. It was something which must have been a cause of some embarrassment to the authorities.

Following every raid upon this country, a local inquest was held the following day, which involved the police and Civil Defence services. Unfortunately, police records of the period have not been preserved, and the conclusions of the inquest can only be the subject of speculation.

That there was the most tragic blunder in failing to activate the town's air-raid sirens cannot be in doubt. It was a cruel irony that this negligence happened directly following the introduction of a new Radar system specifically designed to give early warning of any such high-speed attack.

APPENDIX 2

Historic Railway Names at Ashford

Newtown

Cubitt House[1]	Sir William Cubitt – Engineer in Chief, South Eastern Railway, 1836-1844. Responsible for construction of London – Dover line.
Baxendale Court	Joseph Baxendale – Chairman, South Eastern Railway, 1836-1846
Beazley Court	Samuel Beazley of Tonbridge Castle. Architect of original New Town. 1847
Stirling Road	James Stirling – Locomotive Superintendent, South Eastern Railway, 1878-1899. Resided at Ashford.
Wainwright Place	Harry S. Wainwright – Locomotive, Carriage and Wagon Superintendent, South Eastern & Chatham Railway, 1899-1913. Resided at Ashford.
Maunsell Place	R. E. L. Maunsell – Chief Mechanical Engineer, S.E.&C.R. and Southern Railway, 1913-1937. Resided at Ashford.
Bulleid Place	O. V. S. Bulleid – Chief Mechanical Engineer, Southern Railway, 1937-1947
Alfred Road	'Alfred Town' - original Company name for New Town

South Willesborough

Cudworth Road	James L'Anson Cudworth – first South Eastern Railway Locomotive Superintendent, 1845-1876. Resided at Ashford.
Surtees Close	Robert Surtees – Chief Draftsman, South Eastern & Chatham Railway, 1899 –1914. Resided at Ashford

South Ashford

Torrington Road	Viscount Torrington – Chairman South Eastern Railway

---

[1] Formerly the Bath House on Newtown Green

BIBLIOGRAPHY

Official Guide to the South Eastern Railway : George Measom 1853
Pigots Directory of Kent : 1840 – 1845
Cantium Journal : Editor, John Whyman 1970
Minute Book of the Mechanics Institute : S. E. Railway
Ashford Fire Brigade History : H. Wood, Capt. F. S. Hart
History of the S. E. & C. R. : D. L. Bradbury
Carriage Stock of the S. E. & C. R. : David Gould
Ashford Works Centenary : Southern Railway 1947
South Eastern & Chatham Railway : R. W. Kidner
Boat Train & Channel Packets : Rixon Bucknall
The Railwaymen : Philip S. Bagwall
Wainwright : K. Marx
Ashford Works order book : 1916
Locomotives of R. C. Maunsell : O. S. Nock
Maunsell's Moguls : J. Rowledge
Locomotive History of the Southern Railway : D. L. Bradbury
Bulleid : Sean Day-Lewis
Bulleid's S. R. Steam Passenger Stock : David Gould
Front Line County : Andrew Roots
Hell's Corner : H. R. Pratt Boorman
Battle of Britain : Richard Hough, Denis Richards
Kentish Express
Kentish Gazette
Tuesday Express
Military Railways in Kent : R. M. Lyne